MW01232260

Vets Helping Vets Anderson:

In Their Own Words

Compiled by Angela Mason Lowe
Anderson, South Carolina
2022

Angl. Mason Lowe

VHVA Press
Anderson, SC

ISBN: 9798831527155

FOREWORD

In October of 2021, my husband, Tommy Lowe, came to me with a request that we find a way to help veterans document their stories. Vets Helping Vets of Anderson is a group of veterans who served their country with valor. They represent all branches of the United States Military and have served during war and peace time. These veterans continue to serve within their communities by reaching out firm hands to help lift those veterans who may have stumbled. They lend a listening ear and an arm of support to keep going.

These stories represent a part of history that will be lost to the generations to come if not preserved. Important declarations are repeated throughout the pages of these veterans' stories: freedom is not free; lives were sacrificed, and lives were changed. These facts deserve to be told. Many expressed the hope that their own families understand with compassion their journey. Words of wisdom from lessons taught to them through experience are found within each veteran's story.

I may have paraphrased some of the statements, but I tried to repeat the stories as they were written or told in hopes the veterans' own voices can be heard as they tell their story *In Their Own Words*.

Angela Mason Lowe

ACKNOWLEDGEMENTS

This book would not have been possible without the veterans who served, lived the stories, and agreed to be interviewed. We commend the spouses, families, and friends whose love and support encouraged them.

A special thanks to Todd Carpenter who volunteered to help interview the combat veterans' support group. His outreach brought a well-rounded view of the lives of our veterans.

The generosity of Joe Walters and Tommy Lowe insured every veteran interviewed received a copy of *Vets Helping Vets Anderson: In Their Own Words.*

Thanks to Dr. Rebecca Hopkins who proofread the stories with heartfelt admiration. She succeeded, with dedication, in keeping the veterans' voices intact.

To the Foothills Writers Guild: With your guidance and encouragement, words turned into pages and completed this book.

TABLE OF CONTENTS

TABLE OF CONTENTS

INTRODUCTION

I retired in 2009 and shortly after that, my wife had a friend that was going to a group for combat veterans in Greenville, South Carolina and she thought I should go. So, I did, and it was the first time that I had ever experienced anything like that. I soon realized that I was not the only veteran who had issues with anger, frustration, etc. I went to their Monday night meetings for approximately four months when I heard through the grapevine, that the Anderson VA Clinic had a similar program. That program was meeting on Wednesdays at 10 am.

I went to the Anderson program and was introduced to a lady by the name of Ellen Russell. Ellen was the first person within the VA that I encountered, who actually listened to what a combat veteran had to say. She was exactly what most of the vets needed. She was a person that could get you to open up and talk about your anger issues. I continued to attend these meetings with Ellen for three or four years.

One day she told the group that the VA was considering banning the groups and that there was no explanation. The only reason for this action that we were given was that the VA had made the decision to pursue more one on one sessions versus group sessions. I'll be honest with you; the group setting was the best thing that I ever experienced in my life. I was just comfortable in the group setting with other veterans who could share their experiences. I was starting to finally feel pretty good about myself.

Ultimately, the VA terminated the groups sessions. About two weeks later, I made an appointment with Ms. Russell to come in and talk with her. I had been thinking about doing something on my own, but I needed to talk with someone about getting started. I had questions of where to start and how to do it. I followed up that meeting with her with another one the following week. I wanted to set some goals and a path forward. I even asked her if she could join us at one of those meetings, however, she was just a few months from retirement herself and couldn't get away. I wanted to set our program up to be like the program we had with her.

I obtained a copy of the group contact sheet, listing the names, addresses, etc. of all the men in the group. I went home that evening and began to reach out to those men. I believe there were 16 names on the list. Fourteen of those men were interested. Two never returned my calls.

When we started out, we met at the library. I couldn't find a place, because many of the places I did reach out to, including the VFW and the American Legion were simply unwilling to take on the additional liability of having another group use their facilities.

I went back to see Ms. Russell. I was starting to get pissed, and rejection was something that I had experienced all my life. Ms. Russell was the one who recommended the library. So, I went there, and they were very accommodating. The only condition we had there was that we had to renew our commitment with them every ninety days as a measure of scheduling for them. I told the guys in the group that this was just temporary, that we would eventually find a home. As with starting any new organization or even business, you just don't know if its gonna work out. I wanted to see just how this group was going to progress before we made the commitment to a more permanent facility.

So, on October 14th, 2014, we started meeting. We stated considering things we wanted to do as well as things we didn't want to do. We decided that we wanted to try and preserved the original format for meetings that we had had with Ms. Russell and that we would meet on Wednesday's at 10 am. We got together the following week, getting into more detail of how we would operate. From my own business experience, I knew that I could not do it all on my own. I needed help.

With that, I nominated Don Saxon to be our XO and Randy Crawford, the biggest man in our group, to handle our money. Curtis

Thomas would serve as our Chaplain. Years later we added Chuck Watts as our secretary.

We met there in the library for about four months. One of our members had a family member that was associated with the Elks Club here in Anderson. This gentleman from our group began sharing with his family member what we were doing as a group. He set up an appointment for me and Don to come over and talk with the leadership of the Elks Lodge. During that meeting, we came to an agreement whereby we would pay them $125 a month for the use of the facility and kick in a little extra to help with maintenance and other expenses. At that point in time, I would have done whatever it took to get us a more permanent place that would allow for growth. I had a lot of ambitions and things I wanted to see us accomplish.

One of the first things we needed to do was to come up with a name for ourselves. We decided upon Vets Helping Vets because that was our primary goal…to help one another. I wasn't interested at the time with cutting anyone's grass, I was more concerned that our men had a place to come together to talk, get help if needed. I wanted the PTSD group from the clinic to carry on. After about three years of operation, I came to my attention that we needed to change our name because there were other organizations across the country using that same name.

We decided upon Vets Helping Vets – Anderson. We followed that by filing for a 501c3 Non-profit status. It was then that our group really started to get recognition. We had media outlets and personalities visit with us to get our story out. Gordon Dill spent three weeks with us and did several personal interviews with members. That event alone really put us on the map in a national way. As a result of that, we have become a resource for numerous other veteran organizations.

After less than a year at the Elks Lodge, we began to see signs of growth, maybe two or three guys a month would come in.

We finally got up to around thirty guys. Strictly then, we were still mainly Combat Veterans, infantrymen, combat medics, engineers, and the like. But basically, it was still PTSD (Post Traumatic Syndrome Disorder) related.

I used to drag race boats as an amateur, but I loved it. I knew with that experience, if you want to be the best you can, it takes money. So, I threw out to the group, that if we are going to grow, we must open our doors to all veterans, including the Army National Guard and Reserves. Everyone in the group agreed.

I had some business cards made for the first time. We put our logo and name along with contact information on the front side and put lines on the back for our members to place their name and contact into on it. These were used to recruit and invite new members to the group. I told our members that while they were out, if they came across anyone with a t-shirt, hat, bumper stickers, or anything indicating they were a veteran, they were to "card" them…give them one of the business cards as an invite to join us.

That was a huge success for us. I even had a few members that would hang around over at Sam's Club in Anderson, just passing out cards. This resulted in us getting more people in the door. We soon found ourselves at 50 – 60 guys in less than a year's time and we maintained that for quite a while. Keep in mind, this was all pre-Covid. The card is the main tool we used. That was a huge success for us. I even had a few members that would hang around over at Sam's Club in Anderson, just passing out cards. This resulted in us getting more people in the door. We soon found ourselves at 50 – 60 guys in less than a year's time and we maintained that for quite a while. Keep in mind, this was all pre-Covid. The card is the main tool we used. Soon we had guys coming in from Greenwood, Greenville, Belton…we even had one guy coming all the way from Hartwell, Ga., to attend. Walhalla, Seneca, Central…they started coming in from everywhere. Just prior to the Covid epidemic, we were hitting one-hundred vets every week.

Just prior to the Covid outbreak we had a member, Billy Conrad, who had been travelling back and forth to the Duke Hospital in North Carolina. It had been determined that his liver was bad, and he was going to need a liver transplant. This took place in the summer, and I came up with the idea that we could help Billy out by going over to his place and help with maintaining his property because he was in no condition to do so. Sometimes Billy would be at Duke for up to two weeks. That's how we got into the yard working business.

From that, it grew into staying in contact with the widows of other members of our group that passed away. We'd do the same thing. We would go out and take care of the property for them and we still do to this day with the exception of one widow. She eventually moved out of the area. To this day, we have about twenty-five properties that we take care of each week. In addition to that, we build wheelchair ramps, and we even purchased a Conex container to hold property donated to us, that we refurbish and pass along to others in need.

Over the years, we have made some good decisions and things were booming for us. That is in large part due to the caliber of people we have here. We all have the same mindset of wanting to help other veterans. We have folks from all walks of life and all walks of military backgrounds…doctors, lawyers, construction workers, nurses, retail workers and fully retired military veterans. We have a vast knowledge base within Vets Helping Vets – Anderson and that has served us well in reaching out to those in need.

Our recognition and affiliation with other like-minded organizations has opened many doors for us. Our partnership with Patriots Last Patrol has given us the opportunity to provide Thanksgiving meals for those families dealing with Hospice Care and the care of loved ones. It's just little things like that, that let the families and veterans know that they're not forgotten.

Vets Helping Vets – Anderson is a class act. I've got veterans that are motivated, veterans that have goals. We keep attracting key people that want to carry this organization forward. We have several that have that burning desire to help other veterans. We don't just talk the talk…we walk the walk. We simply make things happen and get things done. We do everything within our power to assist other veterans, be it helping around their homes, providing a place to meet other veterans, or just doing whatever we can to make their lives a little more comfortable.

I don't know exactly, but I'd say the average age of this group is sixty-nine years of age, and they still get out and work and participate. I've had wives call me up and thank me for getting their husbands out of the house and off the couch, doing something constructive once again. That makes me happy because we are genuinely helping and receiving the recognition, even from the Governor's Office in Columbia. I am amazed every day at where we are compared to where we were at our humble beginnings seven years ago.

Looking forward, I have already begun thinking about the day that will come when I need to either step away from leadership of the group, or the Lord calls me home. I've begun compiling a list of whom I would desire to see take the reins of this organization. I've started this process because I know you need someone who has that fire in their belly and the intestinal fortitude to drive on when things get tough. I want to see this organization moving on. I've already begun those plans. I have them in the back of my mind, and I have written them down.

I'm kind of like a proud papa. I see this group continuing to move forward, continuing to break new ground and do great things. I tell people all the time, when you get a group of folks like we have, that is made up of mostly Alpha males and there hasn't been a killing yet…you must be doing something right. I just see this group going on and on. I really do. The foundation has been laid and it is strong. You must identify someone who has the genuine desire to help vets carry it forward. I know from my retail and business experience that you can have a group of twenty people and one will stand out as the star. You don't have to get on their case or babysit. They have the natural desire to be the best they can be. That is your star.

As for this book and its intentions, I would encourage everyone at Vets Helping Vets to share their story. Here's an example of why that is so important. If you read my personal contribution to this book, you will learn that my father served in the Army Air Corps in WWII. My sister asked me recently, "What was the name of daddy's airplane in WWII? What was the nose art that was painted on the plane?" I said, "You know, I don't know. I never heard him say and I never asked him." It's a little thing like that, that you wished you knew today or others following you knew.

I want my children, my grandchildren and even their grandchildren, to know me and know what I did on their behalf. What I did on their behalf hoping they would never be called upon to do the same.

I want all vets from Vets Helping Vets to relay and tell their stories. It's in those stories that you will live forever in the minds of your friends and families. Having your story in print allows you to share that with the world. I want veterans to be recognized and I want their stories to be told.

Jesse Wade Taylor

In Memory of
Gary Phillip Acker

Known by Vets Helping Vets as "Corner Man," Gary Acker welcomed the veterans as they walked through the door for the weekly Wednesday meeting. He proudly wore his 82nd Airbourne cap and shared many paratrooper stories of honor and bravery.

Gary Phillip Acker enlisted in the US Army on March 22, 1962. His Basic and Advanced Individual Training (AIT) was at Fort Gordon, Georgia. He successfully completed eight-weeks of airborne training at Fort Benning, Georgia and then assigned to the 82nd ABN 505/8th Infantry Division in Germany.

Decorations include the Parachutist's Badge, Expert M-14 EIB (Expert Infantry Badge), and Expert M-60. He also drove an Armored Personnel Carrier. The 505th rotated back to Fort Bragg, North Carolina. While assigned to the 509th, Gary got to see Europe.

Gary often said he would take nothing for his experience with his famed 82nd Airborne. The Army honorably discharged him on March 22, 1965, as a specialist E-4. Gary said he was an acting Jack E-5. His best friend while serving was Joe Gagnon.

Elizabeth (Lib), his hometown sweetheart, married Gary while he was home on a fourteen-day leave. She patiently waited for his return to civilian life. He and Lib joined the Riverside Baptist Church in their hometown of Anderson, South Carolina, in 1966 and continued to serve the Lord and their community. They have twin sons and two grandsons.

Gary's love of adventure and patriotism shone through his many decades of volunteering. His passion was sharing his wisdom and time with youth at church and Boy Scout Troop 356. Gary's life reflected Troop 356's Bible verse: "Trust in the Lord with all your heart; and lean not on your own understanding. In all your ways, acknowledge Him and He shall direct your paths." Proverbs 3:5-6 KJV

He was the owner and operator of Acker Automotive. The number "7" brought Gary lots of luck. Number "7" painted on his helmet in an old military photo and on stock cars he drove on dirt tracks at the Anderson Speedway, Toccoa Raceway, Lavonia Speedway, and others throughout the south. Gary raced to win, and he did, often! His competitive skills got him elected to the Anderson S.C. Men's Bolling Hall of Fame.

Gary Acker lived a full life and enjoyed camping in the mountains and at the beach with his family. With his big smile and firm handshake, Gary never met a stranger and was always willing to lend a helping hand. He stated that joining Vets Helping Vets gave him a new breath of life and he look forward to each meeting.

The 82nd Airborne soldiers wear an "AA" arm patch and nicknamed "All American." Gary carried out that title throughout his life with his reputation as a husband, father, business owner, church worker and as a proud veteran.

Michael J. Alewine

My name is Michael Johnny Alewine, better known as Michael J. I enlisted with my best friend Bobby Whitfield on the buddy plan which meant we would go to basic together. We were both born and raised in Anderson County, South Carolina.

We were both sworn in the Air Force February 1971. We chose to join because many of our friends and family members were serving, and we wanted to do our part. We joined the Air Force because we thought our training would help us land a job with the Air Lines after our service.

Basic Training was a mind game and once I realized that, do what you're told when and how you were told, it was really fun. Raised in the country doing farm work made basic training's physical part a breeze. One funny moment in basic that stands out was when the Drill Sergeant was chewing out Bobby for screwing up. I started laughing (could not control it) then he was on my ass with both feet!

Adapting to military life was not hard for me. I was raised in a family where Mom and Dad had complete control and respect, and discipline was taught. I am thankful for that.

I completed basic training at Lackland Air Force Base in San Antonio Texas. I received my weapon mechanic training on F-100's, F-105's and F-4's at Lowry AFB, Denver Colorado from February 1971 through September 1971.

From September 1971 through March 1973, I served in Okinawa, Korea, Thailand, and Taiwan. Serving in these four countries made me realize that I was blessed to be an American and surely "God shed His grace on thee."

I served at Homestead Air Force Base, Florida from March 1973 until I was discharged from active duty February 1975. I served in the Air Force Reserves from February 1975 until February 1977.

Serving in the Army Reserves from September 1977 through September 2000, I was deployed to Saudi Arabia during Desert Storm in 1991. During all my service, I was never in a fire fight "Thank God!" I was there, as were all my comrades, willing and ready to defend our freedom.

I was First Sergeant during my second deployment and being in a combat zone, what I feared the most was not being killed myself. As a born again Christian, I would be going to my heavenly home. My fear was of one of our troops being killed because I didn't do my job.

I vividly remember as myself and the commander gave the order to load the buses from Fort Jackson, South Carolina to our flight to Saudi Arabia. A grandmother of a young eighteen year old who had just graduated from high school four month earlier, tugging on my arm and saying, "Bring him back alive." I told her I would and realized I had made a promise that I might not be able to keep. Thanks to the grace of God, I left with fifty-four, as I remember, and returned with fifty-four. All alive and well.

Coming home the first deployment, no big deal to anyone other than family and friends. The second deployment, there was a parade of people who you didn't know, and they did not know you. It was a feeling of pride that I had never felt and have not since!

The military taught me many things just to name a few disciplines, how to work as a team, being on time, and integrity, which have all helped me throughout my life. I am very proud to have served my country and would not trade the experience for anything.

Kim Alsip

My full name is Kimberly Susan Alsip. I am called Kim. I enlisted while living in Rock Creek, Ohio. During my senior year in high school, I was working as a nurse's aide, working with handicapped kids. The place I was working was sold to become a drug and alcohol rehab facility. This made me mad because the families were given only thirty days to find a place to live. I said, "I'll join the Army where I can do some good."

When I got ready to go, my brother-in-law, a former paratrooper with the 82nd Airbourne Division gave me some words of advice: "Anything they offer you, you do. If they offer you to jump, do it and if they offer you a class, take it. Anything you do puts you apart from anybody else that you serve with."

I had to get a medical clearance before I could go in the Army because for years I would just pass out for no clear reason. I had to pass all these tests to prove I was medically safe, and I did. Within seventy-two hours of getting to the reception station, I passed out. It turned out it had something to do with going from heat to air conditioning. The First Sergeant told me the next time I feel I'm about to out to fall, to fall backwards so I wouldn't be seen. I completed basic training at Fort Jackson, South Carolina in 1981.

My mother's favorite story about me was that I grew up with four brothers and five sisters and how I always said I couldn't wait to get out of there to have a room to myself. She wrote me a letter that said, "Where did you go but to barracks with fifty women in bunk beds. How do you like that room to yourself?" Mom's sense of humor followed me to AIT (Advance Infantry Training). I asked her why she didn't write me a note once in a while. Remember I still had five younger siblings at home. Her solution was to get a piece of paper and write a musical note on it, then send it to me. I got a big laugh out of her antic, and I still have it today.

While serving down at Fort Sam Houston, Texas, I took my brother-in-law, Rodger's advice. The Drill Sergeant came and asked for ten volunteers. My hand went up before I heard the job I volunteered for. I ended up serving with an audiovisual crew at a surgeon's convention in downtown San Antonio. Keep in mind I was eighteen, I had three days with no bed check, and was paid an extra two-hundred dollars. Someone up on stage flipped off and someone called out, "Is there a doctor in the house?" at a surgeon's convention. We thought that was hilarious.

In Germany, I went to a Nuclear Biological Chemical Course to be a NBC Non-Commissioned Officer in our field hospital. It's something I may never use but yes, Roger, it put me apart. I've done some crazy stuff. You may say I have re-invented myself, often. When it comes down to it the Army helped me fulfil my dream of being a nurse and a teacher.

Fort Campbell, Kentucky, Walter Reed, Fort Gordan, Georgia, Fort Bragg, North Carolina, and Fort Bliss, Texas are a few of the other places I have served. I got out of the Army after sixteen years and so close to retirement. Having children and being divorced made it harder to leave them. I got out to be a full-time mom.

I was an E-7 at my Expiration Term of Service in 1997. Seven years later and after 9/11, I went to the recruiter to sign back up. It took months for them to give me the rank of E-6, and the next year I made rank again. In 2004, I joined a reserve unit in Ohio, and I was deployed to Iraq in 2006-2007. It offered me an opportunity to remain on Active Duty under the Sanctuary Program until retirement.

I barely qualified at the rifle range my entire career and I liked to use my upbringing to the Drill Sergeant as an excuse. Growing up, my mother hated guns and never let us play cops and robbers. Fortunately, as a medic, I didn't have to use my weapon. Unfortunately, as a medic, I was surrounded by the sound and the results of enemy and sometimes friendly fire.

While deployed, the hospital where I worked was located at Mosul in northern Iraq. It was right beside an airfield and close to another base. Not only did we have American casualties, but we also had Sunnis and Shi'ites casualties. These two religions refused to be near each other in the beds. Let's just say there were wars inside of wars. The Code of Conduct means treating soldiers or civilians as good as they would be treated in their own country.

Translators from both sides chose sides and could not always be trusted. If we asked a simple question to a patient and the translator relayed a three-minute speech, we could figure the translator did not ask them our question. So much with red tape, nothing appeared cut and dry.

A fun duty that they assigned me was to open the mail addressed to the unit or any soldier; I'd separate and disperse the packages. They called me the Queen of the "Crippity Crap." Everyone appreciated the Americans who sent packages to support our troops more than they knew. Soldiers come from all walks of life and so did the packages. I got pretty good at matching lifestyles and regions the wounded soldiers were from with the individual gifts and cards.

The Wounded Warrior Project touched everyone's heart. The president of the project stayed in communication with me and sent numerous care packages. Every time someone or a group sent a package, we sat down and wrote a thank you. If a soldier received a blanket or something personal, we would gather around and take pictures and send them by emails to the group responsible for the gift. A documentary about the wounds of war, filmed by NBC at our hospital, portrayed the ways we tried to lift the morale of staff and wounded soldiers.

Even if you never put on a uniform but you wrote a letter, sent a card, or packed a box for a soldier, you helped serve our country. We could never have done it without the support of family, friends, and even strangers who took the time to write or send a card.

Once I got the privilege to meet a CEO of the American Greetings Corporation in Ohio. She gave me three baskets and told me to fill them. I filled them with cards that would be suitable for both male and female soldiers to send home to loved ones. I had found cards appropriate for female combat soldiers hard to come by. As a kind gesture, she shipped them directly back to the hospital.

A lawyer in Pennsylvania sent us a commercial size snow cone machine and all the fixings. We had the ice, so every Sunday we went around the hospital giving out free snow cones to the patients and staff, free of charge. That was a gesture that brought out the smiles. It became snow cone Sunday!

After tending to traumatic injuries of all kinds, I know how fortunate I am. The only physical injury I obtained was a twisted ankle while running from a mortar back to the bunker. Coming home is an overwhelming feeling when you reach American airspace and the wheels come down and hit the tarmac. The family, friends, and soldiers you served with become a part of you. Like my friend, Sharon, who was hoping my son would be born on her birthday the 22nd. She calls him still today on his birthday, the 21st and it's been thirty-five years so far.

Things I took for granted became eye-openers when I got out of the service the first time. For example: What do I wear to work? I had worn a uniform to work for so long. Transitioning to civilian life came with more decisions to make. What insurance plan to choose for the family. I was working at the University of Arkansas in the employer's health department when I was handed a book with two hundred plans to choose from. I called Mom for help.

As a Veteran and a mom of five, I have learned I can overcome about anything. I remarried right before I retired to another retired soldier, Jim Alsip. We have fostered thirty children and adopted three in four years. My grandparents came to Anderson and bought property before Lake Hartwell was built in the 'sixties. While I was at Ft. Bragg and Ft. Gordan, we'd visit my dad and grandparents. We decided Anderson would be a nice place to retire.

My advice to anyone getting out of the service, go to a Veteran's Affairs Office and file. I hear others complaining how hard it is to get in the system after they waited years to file. File as soon as possible when you leave the service. Don't give up if you waited and are trying to file.

I think every high school student should experience volunteering in a VA setting or serve a minimum of two years in the military. Those who don't know what they want to do with their life, like go to college or work, may find the answers for which they are searching. Regardless, they would learn what we are fighting for. Military service can offer them structure to obtain what they want from life.

Although, female veterans have come a long way since I enlisted, there are positions females are restricted from. They are increasing positions, but personally I would not want to do something just because it is a male position.

I miss the camaraderie of other soldiers. When you meet another veteran, the conversation starts. It doesn't matter what branch you served in, you're my brother and you're my sister. When I worked at a local cardiology office, veterans would come in and hand me a Vets Helping Vets card and invite me to a meeting. Unfortunately, while working, I could not attend. Since retiring, my husband and I are thankful we found Vets Helping Vets. Vets Helping Vets of Anderson is a very impressive group.

Edward S. Barnett

I am Colonel Edward Scott Barnett, recently retired US Army Chaplain. My nickname is "Happy Chap" because of the strong positive attitude I illustrated as an Army Chaplain. I enlisted in 1997 in Hampton Virginia for I had many of my family who served in the military.

Climbing high towers on the Confidence Course along with long road marches and field exercises made Basic Training physically challenging. The academic testing of officer class work challenged us mentally. I give God and the teamwork of other basic officer course members the credit of helping me get through all the training.

Humorous events during basic training lightened the load sometimes at the expense of others. On a field exercise, a male soldier put a rubber snake inside a female soldier's tent. She jumped a mile high and began to scream.

Adaptation to military life began in the eighth grade at a high school military academy. At an early age, I was shining shoes and brass, acquiring skills at the rifle range, learning facing movements and the Manual of Arms. The military life seemed to be in my blood.

The places I was deployed to included Mosul, Tel Afar, and the Syrian border of Iraq. The Army assigned me as a Brigade and Battalion Chaplain. I served as an International Zone Chaplain in Baghdad, Iraq.

My last duty assignment was the Pentagon. My department monitored America's adversaries. I was the Chaplain response for chaplain movement in computer wargaming of our nation's potential wars with hostile countries.

God and friendship helped me through my deployments. I prayed regularly and socialized around campfires, played softball and basketball. Soldiers learn they can count on each other in ways civilians do not. Stress forces us to learn truth about ourselves. We learned God, Country, family, and friends are important.

During my two deployments to Iraq in the Iraq war, I experienced three roadside bomb attacks (IED) while convoying throughout Iraq. My vehicle was blown up. Also, I was present at the Mosul insurgent suicidal bombing on 21 December 2004 of a dining facility, which at the time was the largest attack on US forces in Iraq. If you google Chaplain Eddie Barnett, you will see news reports and pictures of my actions that day.

There were casualties in my unit: two soldiers killed in action and over sixty wounded. The number of Post Traumatic Syndrome Disorder (PTSD) casualties are sometime not accounted for. Some wounds aren't visible. I learned not to take life for granted; family and friends are more important. One thing for sure, America's courage and selfless sacrifice is greater than Iraq's.

I returned home with no visible injury, yet I felt like an alien in my own country. I had to deal with the nightmares. My thanks go out to the Vietnam Veterans that helped me cope back in the states. I found experiencing death and combat is something hard to express to family and friends.

Lieutenant Colonel Richard Morgan was my battalion commander. He was very religious, and I convoyed with him regularly. We convoyed regularly outside Forward Operating Base (FOB) to be with battalion soldiers. We experienced IED attacks together while on convoy. General Patton had a famous relationship with his chaplain in WWII, Chaplain O'Neill. I often joked with LTC Morgan that General Patton and Chaplain O'Neil had nothing over LTC Morgan and Chaplain Barnett. He remains in regular contact with me today.

I received a Bronze Star, Distinguished Service medal, Meritorious Service Medal (2), Iraqi Campaign and Global War on Terrorism, Combat Action badge, Meritorious Unit Citation, and the Valorous Unit Citation at unit formations. Americans have little to no knowledge of the sacrifices made by military service members for the freedoms they enjoy.

I retired from the Army with twenty years of service. I planned to continue more years of service, but I developed unexpected bone marrow cancer and was forced to retire. The doctors gave me a thirty percent chance of survival and nine months to live. I fought that personal war in 2018 and as of now I am cancer free.

There are opportunities to serve after the military. My advice is to join a group such as Vets Helping Vets and the American Legion. Develop a strong relationship to God. Don't take these opportunities lightly. I want to be more active and serve as an American Legion Honor Guard for veteran's funerals, police and in the VHVA chaplaincy when the doctor allows me. The bone marrow cancer and stem cell transplant left me with a weak immune system.

A phrase that stands out in my memory is "It don't matter, man." There are important things that do matter. Americans need to know the journeys of the veterans who provide their freedom. They need to learn military history and the meaning of "duty, honor, country, and sacrifice."

David Bauman

I am David Lee Bowman, United States Air Force. Growing up, and while in the military, I never picked up a nickname. People simply called me Dave, or David. I grew up in St. Joseph, Missouri, one of four boys. Each of us attended the local Catholic school. I and my brothers all graduated from the Catholic High School and have attended college. I have two older brothers and one younger brother. In addition to myself, I have a brother that served in Korea in the Army, on the DMZ. My brother Bob served in the National Guard. Of the four brothers, three ended up serving in the military.

Mom was mom. Mom was an alcoholic. She kept a paper bag in the pantry with a bottle of whatever she drank in it. At times during the day, you could tell that she had been tasting the bottle. I guess she thought that nobody knew she was drinking. Dad worked for Western Tablet. They made "Big Chief" writing tablets. He handled the loading of railroad cars with these packaged tablets. That's how they shipped them, and he was responsible for determining how many they could load on each rail car.

Mom and Dad stayed married, yet I do not know how they originally met. I don't think any of us boys know that. For that matter, I don't think that any of us ever thought about it. My dad never served because he had four young boys at the time. During WWII, he was exempt because of us. Instead, he served with the fire auxiliary…much like todays volunteer fire departments. I did have two uncles that served during WWII, one in the Pacific and one in Europe. I am not sure what they did because they never talked about it.

I thought about serving in the military when I was young. I have often wished that I could have attended a public school, because they had ROTC programs. We didn't have ROTC at the Catholic school. I wish that I could have had that experience, looking back.

During my childhood years, we spent a good deal of time

building model airplanes, flying airplanes, and going out to the airport looking at planes. I had a childhood fascination with airplanes. Prior to the Air Force, I had served in the Air National Guard. When I ultimately joined the Air Force, they selected my job for me, I had no say in the matter. When I enlisted, I enlisted to go to basic training. During that time, they tested everyone and decided where you would best fit according to what their needs were at the time.

I ended up in the military police, or at least, the Air Force's version of military police. I worked with sentry dogs. Boot camp wasn't really all that bad for me. Remember, I had attended Catholic school. How hard could Air Force basic training be? At the Catholic school, you didn't do a lot of backtalking and such. You just did what you were told to do, or you paid the price. Being around Drill Instructors didn't bother me that much either. I had those in Catholic school. The thing I had the most difficulty with in basic was all the marching. I had trouble keeping in step. One time the DI came over and kicked me in the foot because of this and I ended up the hospital with a badly bruised foot. I just had a hard time keeping in step.

For fun in basic, we'd pull pranks on one another by short sheeting their beds or doing something else to their beds to aggravate them. We had one Drill Sergeant that stands out in my mind. I can't recall his name, but I do remember his face. He was just "gruff." He never let up on us. I don't think he even smiled. He never gave anyone any positive reactions.

I had little issue with adapting to military life. I had already been trained at the Catholic school. You simply did what you were told, when you were told, and things went well for you. If you didn't, things did not go well. The Catholic schooling taught me how to listen and follow orders.

My time in the Air Force encompassed 1958 to 1962. I served primarily during the Cold War, prior to heavy engagement in Vietnam. Our primary concern at that specific point in history, was the possibility of Russia launching missiles at the United States. We knew that if that occurred, we had fifteen minutes before they would start impacting targets in the U.S.

Within the canine service, we patrolled the runways as our main focus. The purpose of the canines was to help us find people that may attempt to sabotage runways and to alert aircraft on the ground. The dogs were trained to "grab and hold" anyone we were pursuing. During my time in the Air Force, we never had any issues, nor did I see any combat.

I gave all my medals to my son once he reached an appropriate age. Mainly, they were what all airmen received during
that time. Nothing of any special note. I doubt that he still has them. We don't talk anymore.

I left the Air Force in 1962, came back home and went to school. When I first came back home, I felt like people didn't care whether you had served or not. When I was ready to go to school, the only benefit I received was the cost of one book. That was just society at the time. That was the military at the time. The GI Bill had not yet been restructured, so little assistance was available. My general feeling about society at the time was that they just didn't care about the military. Being on the heels of WWII and Korea, I guess people were just tired of war.

I remember my section chief fondly. Smith was his last name. He was a squad leader/flight chief. He was our boss. We didn't see officers. He was the senior enlisted man in the group, and we got all instructions and guidance from him. He lived off base, as did I, so we would ride to and from the base together. We became more than just a leader and a subordinate. We became friends. When I got out in 1962, he went to Vietnam. When he came back from Vietnam, people who knew him said that he had really changed. He wasn't the same guy anymore. I haven't seen or talked with him since I left the Air Force.

When we had some downtime, we would play with the dogs. There was no bar hopping or that sort of thing. I had been married and my wife died two weeks later. I lived off base and we just didn't do a lot of socializing back then. I didn't have much money to do a great deal of socializing. I only made $113 a month then. I figured it out one time and it came to eleven cents an hour. For pranks, we would hide a man's gear from him, or, in the barracks, we would do things to his bed and other items he had.

I decided to leave the Air Force in 1962. When I had told the Air Force that I was unlikely to reenlist, that was it. I was basically dead meat to them. I didn't get any promotions or anything in my last two years. That did not sit well with me, but that's just the way they did it. They did what they wanted to. To this day, it still makes me feel crappy. It makes me feel like they wasted two years of my life. You didn't get any training; you couldn't move up the ladder. I left as an Airman Second Class after four years. I think that if the Air Force had approached this whole matter, by promoting me or giving me more responsibility, it may have changed my view of the Air Force, and I might have even stayed in. I could have lied to them and said that I was going to reenlist. Plenty of people did that, but I was taught that you do not lie to people.

When I left the Air Force, I was single again because my wife had tragically passed. For a while, I just lived with my parents and went to school. My parents didn't seem to mind this. We were a close family. During my first few months out of the military, I worked in the local hospital emergency room. I held the role of Admitting Clerk. I enjoyed that job. You were able to help people.

I started my college work at St. Joseph Junior College. It is there that I got all the basic courses taken care of. From there, I went to Northwest Missouri State. I studied education and became a teacher for forty-two years. I taught virtually every subject from kindergarten to college. I taught at Coastal Carolina here in South Carolina for a time. I earned my master's degree and Doctorate during my career. All four of us boys in my family have college degrees. Each of us has at least a bachelor's degree.

The military affected me in that it sure taught me discipline and how to go about getting what you wanted out of life. I was always happy with the time I spent in the service. I always enjoyed the people that I worked with. One other thing that I learned about myself in the military was that I wanted to be a teacher. I wanted to do this because I was appalled and just how little people knew about history of the United States. I just couldn't believe how educationally deficient people were.

If I were talking to someone interested in the military today, I would tell them to go to college first. Become an officer and not an enlisted person. That would afford them more prestige and position, not to mention better pay.

Looking forward, I get tired of the bickering among nations, but we can't change that. People need to learn to be content in life. You cannot please everyone. No President or other leader is ever going to be entirely what you want of them.

I think the attitude about the military has changed dramatically since my time in the Air Force. When I got out, you didn't wear your uniform or attend veterans' clubs. I think people are more aware today of what veterans have accomplished and what they have sacrificed. When I got out of the service, you didn't even talk to people about it. They didn't want to listen. You felt like you were a second-class citizen if you were in the service. That's not happening now and that's a good thing. In my day, people thought you were dumb for being in the service. Most felt that the military was not a good pursuit for someone trying to better themselves. Many women who served in the military at that time were even looked down upon more harshly than men.

I miss the order, the discipline, and the ceremony of the military. Regarding my time in the military, I am most glad that I don't have to pull KP anymore!

I would want my son to know this about my military service and why I served. I did what I thought was necessary for my country and I was happy to do it. I grew up during WWII and Korea. It was a patriotic time. It was the right thing to do, and I'm glad I served. I would hope he understands that. Whether he does or not, I don't know.

As for Vets Helping Vets, we get a lot of benefit out of that group. The meetings, the camaraderie, meeting with other people, I enjoy greatly. My wife finds them to be very caring people. Very uplifting. The men and women in that group have done so much for me. They cut my lawn and so much more. When around that group, you always feel like someone cares. I carry the Vets Helping Vets cards and pass them out to folks regularly. If I could tell Jesse Taylor one thing. It would be this…I am thankful that you started this group.

Cathy Bowler

My name is Catherine Ilana Bowler, and Anderson, South Carolina is my hometown. Family and friends call me Cathy. I picked up the nickname Kitty Cat in the military. Once during one of my first field exercises in a combat zone, I heard some prankster I worked with outside the tents calling "Here kitty, kitty," and I knew it wasn't a cat they were calling.

I joined the US Air Force while in the eleventh grade of high school. My guidance counselor basically told me that I wouldn't be able to afford college, so I joined to get college money. The Air Force had a six-week Basic Training Course that was two weeks less than the others. Dad, also, helped me make the decision. He had served in the Army and wasn't going to sign the papers when I first enlisted, but he did. I told him I would join anyway when I turned eighteen.

The first couple of weeks of basic training at Lackland Air Force Base in Texas was rough because I couldn't talk to Mom and Dad. The first time I talked to them, I broke down in tears and told them to come get me. It was homesickness for sure.

I learned to find humor in the situation. Our group's drill Instructors kept changing each week due to emergency leave. They called us the orphans. I went to Keesler AFB, Mississippi for training after basic. My first duty station was at Edwards AFB, California, serving as an Avionics Specialist and Navigation System Specialist.

I served a total of twenty-four years. When I re-enlisted after leaving California, I cross-trained in the Cyber Security Specialist field that was specific to Colorado Springs AFB. I worked at an offsite test facility at the Cheyenne Mountain Complex. From there is where I went on my first stent overseas to Korea.

Serving a year in Korea, I came into contact with a piece of transportable Army equipment, Tri-Service Tactical communication van (AN/TTC-39) set up inside like an office. E-4 and below had do security training to be ready troops if North Korea decided to take South Korea, we would be part of the first speed bump system of defense.

While training, Security Police took us through the woods, jumping off one thing and then another. When I jumped off of one, something popped. The security guy said, "Please tell me that was your knee popping." As soon as I put my foot down, I knew it was my ankle. At the hospital I found I had a left ring fracture with a dislocation.

They used four screws and three pins to hold it together. Months later they did a surgery to take the hardware out. I had a podiatrist tell me later that I must have had a good orthopedic surgeon. I was the first person he had met that had that surgery and was still in the service five years later.

From Warner Robbins AFB, Georgia, when I left for Korea. From there, deployed to Al Jaber AFB, Kuwait. I didn't actually see combat until the last couple of years of my career. Our group got divided into different duties and all anyone could do was make the best of a bad situation. I worked the 39 van and I've never seen so much sand.

The last duty location of my deployment was in Afghanistan. I was in the Air Force unit at an Army Base for six months. Some where there for twelve to eighteen months. I know there are some in all walks of life that fake injuries of this and that. Those make it hard on anyone with the real injury.

The Army has always ribbed the Air force, but after seeing some of the treatment the Army soldiers received when they served, I am proud to say I served in the US Air Force. A group of Army soldiers let me join their group for counseling in Ft. Hood, Texas. I fit right in with them. Right before I retired, the Air Force started changes, some extreme. It was like they didn't care about the soldier as a person. It became a power struggle. Soldiers booted out because someone didn't like them. Through the years of my service, it was my job to protect my airmen.

The ones I served with in the Combat Command became part of my family. We deployed together, went on field exercises together. When reunions for the 5th command are planned in Warner Robbins, I try to attend. The faces change as others transition out of the military. We all have something in common, the same mentality. I miss the friendships we shared.

As I transitioned out of the military, I took terminal leave from the unused accumulated leave during active service. Other retirees gave me advice. They said the first year can be pretty tough, so I made sure I had enough money to sustain me. Unlike what some people think, you don't come out of the military rich. This gave me time to make plans and get use to civilian life.

Good advice: make sure you communicate with family and friends' things that might trigger reactions even if you don't share the reason. They deserve an explanation for your good and theirs. I am set in my ways and found adapting to change hard. I am trying to be more flexible. I like order instead of chaos. If someone says they are coming at a certain time, I still don't like to wait. After twenty-four years of wearing a uniform, buying regular clothes was hard for me.

Old habits are hard to break. If I go into a restaurant, I scan everything and everything around me until I find the seat I prefer. I don't like crowds and I won't go to a movie on opening day. You can adjust to situations if you prep yourself first. Go to the movie when less people are there and don't sit in the middle.

My advice to those in military service: make sure you get copies of your medical records and start filing with the VA. This makes it easier when you transition out. When you get out, make copies of your DD214. Don't hide them in your house. Put them in a place where you know they are.

Join an organization like Vets Helping Vets. It's like having another military family. Vets who know what you are talking about when you need to talk. Like talking about losing a counterpart on another shift in Afghanistan that committed suicide, not even a month into his deployment. Pulling his shift for eighteen to twenty hours for a month until they could get his replacement. I was in charge of the office and dealt with any problem.

An IED went off outside our office in Kabul. It was supposed to go off down the road at the Embassy, not our base. It went off at our gate and fifty yards from my sleeping quarters. I had just gone to bed when the IED blew me out of bed. Then the percussion blast ripped through our living facilities. Our quarters were like shipping containers with added windows and air. I don't remember much but I was standing with my weapon on in shorts, tank top, flipflops, and a gash on the back of my leg, I didn't know I had.

Others said I was walking around like a hundred-year-old, more like shell shock. Watching a Macedonia woman care for another Macedonia woman, I was concerned about the whereabouts of my airmen. Medics wanted to put me on a helicopter and send me for x-rays. I refused because I knew they were shooting at anything coming and going. I didn't tell my mom what happened because I knew she would worry.

Other veterans understand between the lines; they understand the language. They accept each other regardless of rank. As part of my retirement, I chose to be a care worker continuing to serve others. My first client was a veteran. Satisfaction comes from knowing other veterans ask for me to care for them. Knowing and being told I am an asset to the company because I am a veteran.

Military service in any branch is a good choice for young people who may be floundering around in career choices. It would help the younger generation to serve in the military. They would learn to discipline themselves in money matters and educate themselves in what it takes to survive in this day and age. Not be led like sheep to slaughter because they have no goals or plans for their own life.

My dad raised a house full of girls. He gave us good advice: Do not depend on a man for your livelihood because it can get you in a situation that you think you can't get out of. The military allowed me the opportunity to show that I could succeed as a female in a male dominated career. Remember to remind family and friends that females serve too. Sometimes people forget. Once, I pulled into a parking space reserved for veterans at Lowe's. A fellow came up and told me that no parking allowed without my veteran husband. Well, I told him I didn't have a husband and I was the veteran. One day, I hope to see equal treatment for all across the board.

Charles Burnside

People called me Earl when I was growing up because daddy's first name was the same. Daddy gave me his first name, and my second brother, his middle name. He didn't want a Junior. I was born in September 1940. I was raised in Walhalla, South Carolina. I went to Walhalla High School where I graduated in 1959. Up until this mess with COVID, we had been having class reunions, but that has stopped.

I have four brother's total. There were five of us boys and no girls in the family. I am the oldest. I was in the Navy, my first brother was in the Navy, my second brother was also in the Navy and my third brother was in the Air Force. The final brother was in the National Guard. He served and retired from the South Carolina Army National Guard.

Sometimes my brothers and I got along, sometimes we didn't. You know how that goes. My second brother went into the Navy, and he took a liking to drinking and carrying on. He'd come home, and if he was drunk, he'd look at me and say, "Don't you say a word." He knew that I didn't like what he was doing. I let him know about it. I told him there was no sense in him getting drunk and coming in here and showing out. That's the way I felt about it. He was this way most of his life but thankfully, towards the end before he died, he changed.

Mama was raised in Salem, South Carolina. Daddy was raised there in Walhalla. They were farmers, they both came from farming families. My grandfather had a thrashing machine, and he would go around to different people's farms and do thrashing work for them. My daddy would always go with him. My daddy also had several brothers and sisters, but he was the baby of the family. My parents and I got along well. We had a very close family. Mama had five brothers and six sisters. Back in those days, people had big families because you needed people to work the farm.

Regarding my school years, I didn't want to go to school. Mama and daddy made me go, but I didn't like it. I just didn't like it.

I did like math and the woodworking classes, and I took agriculture because we raised hogs and what not. However, school just wasn't my thing. I eventually graduated from Walhalla and the woman who was over the Draft Board at the time, kept telling everyone that "she was going to get them Burnside boys in the Army." I said, "She ain't gonna get me in no Army." Shortly thereafter, I received a letter, telling me to report to Columbia, SC. I decided then that I was going to do something. When I got to Columbia, I joined the Navy Reserve here in Anderson in 1961.

I went on active duty from 1963 – 1965. When I went on active duty, I was supposed to report in at Columbia, right before Thanksgiving. That was at the time right after John Kennedy had been killed. When I got to Columbia, everything was closed. So, I turned around and came back home. I went back down to Columbia after Kennedy's burial, when everything calmed down and signed in.

While I was still in high school, I worked at a hardware store and continued to work there after I graduated. Then, I later moved over to a job in Seneca, SC, at a service station. I worked there for about four years.

My Navy Boot Camp took place at Great Lakes, Illinois. When I got there, it was 48 degrees below zero. Great Lakes was alright, but it was cold! We had an E-6 who was over our training class. We didn't have enough men to make a large battalion for training because there was only thirty-eight of us at the time. Most of the other classes had around one-hundred men in them. Snow was on the ground, and we had to march over to the mess hall, but we could walk back by ourselves. Our commander didn't make us walk back together in formation. He told us to go back on our own and what time to be there. Our Commander gave us a degree of leeway, but other Commanders were strict on their sailors. What we did learn about our Commander, was that when he told us to do something, that's exactly what he wanted us to do. We should not try to get out of doing it.

Our class received all the awards and accolades because we were such as small group. We were better able to function and perform all the tasks, than were the larger classes. Our Commander seemed to be able to get more out of us as a small group than the larger units.

Basic training wasn't all that bad for me. The physical aspect was pretty easy, but at times, the mental side of it was tough, it would get to you if you let it. I remember the gas chamber. We had to go in and take our masks off, but we had one in the class who wouldn't do it. We got ahold of him and took it off for him. He fought us like crazy. We'd already had ours off for some time and were ready to get out of there. Only when everyone had their mask off, could we come out. We got that man's mask off, and the Commander let us out, but made the reluctant one stay in the chamber a little while longer.

One of the funny things about basic training occurred when we'd go out marching. Someone would inevitably fall down because the ground was covered in ice. You couldn't help but laugh. You weren't supposed to laugh, but you couldn't help it.

Since I was in the reserves, I came back to Anderson after boot camp. I had to go to drill for two weeks every year. I'd put in for the location where I wanted to do my drill time and sometimes, I'd get, sometimes I wouldn't. My job in the Navy was to work in the engine room. I was a Machinists Mate 3rd Class. We ran the evaporators that turned salt water into drinking water.

While I was on active duty, I was on a ship that carried food. We carried enough food to feed the entire city of New York for one whole day. We carried what amounted to 500 head of beef on that ship. We had enough coffee to make 5 million cups of coffee. We didn't eat any powdered stuff. Very seldom did that happen. Most of it was fresh eggs and such. The only part of the ship that wasn't frozen was the super-structure. Everyone had their personal areas in the super-structure portion of the ship. The rest of the ship was deep freeze. There were big openings on the main deck, and some of these freezer sections would extend four levels down. We used a winch to go into the freezer and pull things out.

This ship was built as a commercial ship. It had a ninety-foot bowline on it. It was ninety feet from the bow to the waterline. They called it a hurricane bow. Once again, it was a commercial ship, but the Navy adopted it for service among the fleets. Back in the very aft end of the ship, at the time, they were experimenting with lettuce. In that container, we carried lettuce that was three months old and still good. They took the oxygen out of that portion of the storage area and to go into it, you had to wear a respirator. It was all quite interesting. I was on that ship, out of Norfolk, Virginia my entire time on active duty.

From that ship, we would feed troops on both land and sea. We'd be out anywhere from six – ten weeks, resupplying ships, and troops, then we'd come back to Norfolk and resupply ourselves, then go back out and do it all over again. The other fleet ships protected us. We had minimal firepower on our ship, so we fell under their protection while we were out at sea. We frequently replenished the Enterprise, the Bainbridge, and the Long Beach, out at sea, before they headed out for round the world cruises. As an example of just how much food we'd carry, before the Enterprise would head out for their long cruises, we would give them nine-hundred tons of food. The Enterprise was an aircraft carrier…only one ship in the fleet that we resupplied at the same time.

I didn't have a hard time adapting to military life. I'd had good discipline at home, but I also had good officers and leaders over me. In the Engineering Department, of which I was a part, we had an officer that was a Mustang…he had worked his way through the enlisted ranks to become an officer. He did a great job with us. That is one thing I can say, "I had good people over me all the time."

The closest I ever came to actual combat was during the flare up in Santo Domingo. We went there to bring food and were fired upon. We didn't fire anything because the other ships had it under control. They were taking care of us.

Sometimes when we were replenishing, especially in the Mediterranean, we'd have Russian ships or submarines that would try to come between our ships. The other ships in our fleet would deter that. We almost always had Russian ships trailing us wherever we sailed.

One thing that sticks out to me the most about life on a ship is that it was awful close quarters. In our bunk area, there were bunks, five high. It was just a thin mattress with canvas and rope holding them all in place, suspended from the ceiling. On each bunk, there was just about enough room to turn over and that was it. Everything we had aboard ship was stored in a small wall locker near our bunks. We also had a guy on the ship who would cut hair, free of charge. The ship was manned by about 200 – 250 men. The Officers had their own Quarters area.

In our resupply operations, we'd sometimes use helicopters to transfer food from one ship to another. We could also transfer personnel from one ship to another, along with other supplies, mail, etc. On the helicopters, the crew chief always had a chalk board where he would write on it the amount of weight they could carry. Supplies we were transferring always had the weight written on the pallet being lifted. The ship crew would use another chalk board to signal this back to the crew chief. That's how we communicated with the choppers during resupply operations. As their fuel level dropped, they could pick up more weight, so we constantly needed to know this information.

We didn't have a helicopter on our ship all the time. Most of the time, them came off the Enterprise. I recall one time we picked up two Spitfire airplanes and brought them onboard to transport them. We put them on the helo (helicopter) deck and strapped them down.

Well, later, we ran into a bad storm. The captain of the ship was worried to death that we were going to lose those planes.

The Navy brought me a greater level of respect for people. Much of that came from the leaders I had. Some sailors would try to get you down, some would try to get you to do things you knew you shouldn't do. I learned to respect people more while I as in the Navy. I gained a deeper respect for people and the way they should be treated. I was awarded a medal for our time in Santo Domingo. My other awards were pretty much what every other service member at the time received.

When I finally left the Navy in 1974. After all my active-duty time, I rejoined the reserves and we drilled once a week, and we got a day's pay for it. The folks got to bellyaching about the way we were meeting. We started going to Greenville, one weekend a month. They kept changing things and we eventually had to go to Charleston, SC for drill. It was at that point that I began to think that it wasn't worth it anymore. I'd get off work on Friday evening, drill on Saturday, then drive all the way back home, just to be at work again first thing Monday morning.

That's when I decided to leave the Navy for good and it wasn't a hard decision at all. Especially with the way they kept changing things on us. I wanted to stay and finish my career, but the Navy kept changing things so much that it was no longer worth it.

After leaving the Navy, for the first few months, I just felt lost. I no longer had meetings to attend. Doing what the Navy had done, had pushed me away. I didn't have any real problems with the transition because I was working at the time. However, having all that time invested in the Navy did make it tough. I had wanted to stay. I just couldn't.

I remember a guy named Butcher, who was on one of the ships I served on. He was just a little ol' small guy, but he would always pick on me. He was bad to drink. We were out on a beach overseas, at a bar there and he was drunk. One of the barmaids grabbed me and told me that I didn't need to be in there and that I should get out...the MPs were coming. She was trying to protect me. My buddy was trying to get something started. Well, the MPs came and left, so I went back to try to carry my buddy back to the ship. He didn't want to go back. He started fighting me and pulling on me. I then turned around and punched him right in the nose. His nose stayed red for about two weeks after that. Needless to say, he remembered that from that day forward.

On the ship, we played a lot of cards or went up on the deck and played around for fun. On our ship, it wasn't like other ships. We had a protective wall that went around the entire deck so there wasn't much chance of one of us falling overboard. Another reason the wall around the ship was important came when we were resupplying other ships. This wall prevented anything from going over the side. During this type of resupply, we had what was referred to as a bowling ball that we would throw over and the other ship would reel it in, pulling a cable across with it. They'd anchor it off and we'd send supplies over on the cable.

We did horse around on the ship, but we tried to keep it away from the Officers. I learned in the Navy that I had to respect and do what I was told to do. That's just how the Navy operates. The only exception came with issues of safety. If you brought up something that you felt was unsafe, the Officers would gladly listen to you.

Looking back now at eighty-one years of age, my hopes for the future of this country are easy. I want everything to go well. I'd like to regain my health so I could help Vets Helping Vets cut grass and help others. I'd like to see this country in a place where everyone is not fighting with one another all the time. I'd like to see this country stop trying to destroy our history. I don't like that at all. What will the young people learn if we do away with our history?

In the past, I don't think the military has been treated as it should be. Many people and the different administrations have shown vastly different levels of support for our military and our veterans...to include the way, they were treated when they came home.

Things I miss about life in the Navy include the travel. On active duty, I was able to go to a lot of places that I would never have seen otherwise. In two years of active duty, I went to Spain. At the same time, one of my brothers was in Spain, serving in aviation. He was on aircraft carriers most of the time. I've been to Holland, England, and Sicily. There are many others as well. When we were over there replenishing ships, would always spend a few days in one of the nearby ports. That was always a nice experience.

My family has asked me on occasion about my military experience, but remember, I have three daughters and that's not always an interesting topic for them. I have no sons. I do have one grandson in the Navy. He and I have always talked about the Navy. I would want my children to know that I felt I needed to serve our country. We need to respect our country. Respect our flag. People burning our flag is not right. We should try to be a better country.

Vets Helping Vets has helped me. It gives me something to focus on, something to do. It helps me to get out and get around people. Just being around that bunch of folks helps me feel better physically. That group makes me feel that I still have a purpose in being here. Vets Helping Vets lifts my hopes every week.

Dee R. Cannaday

My name is Dee R. Cannaday, and also known as Sugar Bear. I got that nickname while in the Navy. Once I had reached Vietnam, before a flight, I would always go to the Galley beforehand and put a few small boxes of Post Sugar Crisp in the pockets of my flight suit to eat while on the plane.

I enlisted in the Navy in 1969. It was actually my father's idea. He wanted me to join the Navy Sea Bee's as an electrician. He had sat next to a Navy Sea Bee on a commercial flight and had had a good conversation with the sailor sitting next to him. However, Hurricane Camille came ashore in Mississippi and destroyed the Sea Bee bootcamp facility. My Navy recruiter, therefore, asked me, "What else would you prefer?" I said, "Electronics school and I would like to fly…"

At the time I enlisted, I was living in Orange City, in Orange County, California. I loved it there because I loved to surf. I chose the Navy because my father wanted to make sure that I had good training, in a skilled field, so I could get a good job on the outside when my enlistment was over.

I attended Navy bootcamp in San Diego, California. It was a bit tough, but I got through it. We had a Navy Chief as our Company Commander who had been brought up on "Unnecessary Meanness Charges" three times. I liked most of the training even though our training class had learned how to cheat on the testing. This seemed to make Chief, who was commanding us, a bit nicer. I'm not sure if he became nicer because we had found a way to cheat, or that he was happy that we were all passing the tests. One of the funny moments that I remember during bootcamp was that we had three really smart guys in our class that figured out some signals for us to use, so that the slower guys could actually pass the tests and keep the Company Chief happy. We had a good laugh in the barracks once the slower guys could return all the secret signals correctly.

Adapting to the military wasn't all that bad for me. My mother was killed in a car accident. Most of my growing up was guided by TV shows about families; Father Knows Best, etc. The judge handling the case made sure that the insurance company involved, set aside money for all three of us brothers. However, within a year, my father had wasted all the money on his schemes. I guess it was my early experiences in life that prepared me for life in the military.

I served in a couple of different areas during my time in the Navy. My first assignment was in Atsugi, Japan. We also had U2 planes located at this base. The first flight for all of us newbies was around Mt. Fuji. Mt. Fuji always had unstable winds in the area, which made for rough flights. Of the thirteen newbies, eleven ended up with their faces in a barf bag we had given them. Upon landing, they all chose not to be on flight status.

My first mission as an Aviation Electronic Warfare Aircrewmen was in the Sea of Japan. Within an hour of us arriving on station, the North Koreans sent out three MIG 21's to shoot us down. Four F4 Phantoms flew over us while we were kissing the waves. When we landed, we noticed that we had seaweed on the tail of the plane. Three years earlier, the North Koreans did shoot down one of our planes with 34 crew members on board.

My next assignment was Vietnam. Upon arriving in country, I was tasked with searching for electronic radar signals, both air and ground. I caught on fast and within seven months I was moved to Radar Operator. That radar had an output of 4 million watts, which was good for about four-hundred miles.

The second day we were in Da Nang, we were told to get on a bus for a weapons orientation class. This was a war zone. The Gunnery Sergeant met us at the base of Freedom Hill with two tables loaded with weapons. It's interesting, Bob Hope and the USO also held performances there. The Gunnery Sergeant had everyone grab an M16 rifle and a magazine of ammo. Everyone fired as the Gunny instructed us. We then took turns using all the weapons available, when suddenly, someone is shooting back at us. The Gunny waits for the second shot then tells every one of us to make the single bush on the hill above us disappear. We did, and there was no further gunfire.

That was my first taste of combat. More would come later when I was to report to Marble Mountain, to see if I qualified for their missions. I did. The requirements were quite simple…you had to be single, good with all weapons they used, stable, but somewhat crazy as well.

I saw multiple deployments during my time. Flying as an aircrewman, we were often bounced all over the Pacific Ocean: Black Ops flights over both Cambodia and Laos, Thailand, Taiwan, and Midway Island. Other flights included Hawaii/Barbers Point Naval Air Station, Sangley Point in the Philippines; Subic Bay; Attu, Alaska; Misawa, Japan, and Kwajelin Atoll.

I received awards for my service in the Navy. They include: Aircrew Wings, 6 Air Medals, Republic of Vietnam Air Gallantry Cross with Palm Leaves, RVN Service Medal, Navy Campaign Medal, Armed Forces Expeditionary Medal, 3 Meritorious Unit Commendations, RVN Meritorious Unit Commendation with Palm Leaf, Humanitarian Service Medal x 2, Two Good Conduct Medals and the National Defense Medal. Some of these awards were presented to me in front of the squadron, Fleet Airborne Reconnaissance Squadron One. Most were simply handed to me at my next duty station, the Airborne Electronic Warfare School at Corry Field in Pensacola, Fl.

While in Vietnam, I did suffer some wounds due to combat operations. In Da Nang, we often received rocket attacks. The EP-3B aircraft were parked in tall revetments. Since the Air Force had lost an aircraft while it was in a revetment, our Squadron, VQ-1, had the policy of getting the planes out of Rocket City, a term given to Da Nang, as soon as possible. Since I was a radar operator, I had to go with the aircraft every time it went somewhere. I was also armed with my personal sidearm for safety reasons. When this attack began, I was running with my ditty bag toward the aircraft, when a rocket exploded right behind me. I literally did a forward somersault and landed on my butt. I had burning in both legs and reached down to pull the shrapnel out of my legs that was burning me. I then grabbed my handkerchief and tied it around the leg that was bleeding the most and took off for the plane. Once we were airborne, the plane's captain was nice enough to disinfect both legs and bandage them.

I was later offered the Purple Heart for these wounds, but I told them, that the Purple Heart was for people that really get hurt. When my time in Vietnam came to an end, I was glad to be going home. That is, until we departed the plane, where we were pelted with rotten eggs, vegetables and nasty jeers and comments.

I do have fond memories of those I served with. One in particular is Dave D'Amor. Dave was a funny guy, and terrified of going bald. Everywhere we went, even to foreign countries, Dave would run as fast as he could to see what they were selling to prevent baldness. He had a large shoe box that was stuffed with so many bottles of hair tonic and pills. It was hilarious! Some of my other friends and I played tennis, traveled around the local areas, drank, and surfed the waves of China Beach. For good luck, I prayed and helped everyone that I could.

I do remember the pranks we played on one another. One sticks out. Some of us were over at China Beach and had just come out of the water. Some nurses showed up, spread out a big blanket, and headed for the water themselves. One in our group asked that we help bury him in the sand, under their blanket. He laid down with his arms stretched wide and we put the blanket over him. When the nurses came back, he just laid there until he suddenly roared and grabbed the two nurses through the blanket. Everyone got a good laugh out of that one.

My career didn't immediately end when I left Vietnam. I reenlisted off the coast of Poverotnyy, Russia during a mission there, and I was sent to Advanced Aviation Electronics "B" School outside of Memphis, Tennessee. I then got called back to VQ-1, but by this time I was married. After my second stint with VQ-1, I was sent to Pensacola, Fl., to start up the Advanced Naval Aviation Electronic Warfare School that both officers and enlisted would attend. Since I was only a 1st Class Sailor, and everyone else was either a Chief or Officer, I got to write and research all the curriculum for each class. I had a lot of long days while on that assignment.

After leaving the military, we somehow ended up in Orlando, Florida. I couldn't find a decent job there. I finally applied at 84 Lumber and worked harder than anything. One day, this bum of a man came in with a big order for lumber. We went out to get him loaded and I mentioned that the thing on his old hat looked like a Hellfire Missile. He said it was and I told him how I had written all the information for a class at Corry Field on that missile and others like it. He asked me if I was Navy and I responded, "Yes." He then asked how soon he could hire me. Come to find out, he oversaw the entire Test Department at Martin Marietta on the other side of town. I was hired two months later…I retired from that job after twenty-seven years, having worked on aligning the Targeting Dayside System on Apache Helicopters.

My advice for those transitioning out of the military. When you enlist into the military, be sure to get the training that will lead you to a good job when you leave the military. My time in the military matured me. Not only did it teach me about electronics and troubleshooting, but it also taught me much about personal hygiene and medical care.

What I have learned about myself is that most people don't care that you are a veteran and have a lot of valuable training in certain fields. My hopes for the future are that those young men and women going into the military today, will sign up for something they can continue to do once they leave the military.

There are two phrases that have a special place in my heart. 1 – Freedom is not Free. 2 – Sincerely thank a veteran. There is something that I wish civilians understood about the military and it is this: Without the veterans protecting them, they could be living in a third-world country, speaking a different language. Lessons I learned in the military: Brush my teeth twice a day, shower daily, plan ahead, and conduct preventative maintenance on my vehicles.

I close with these final thoughts…I miss the comradery and brotherhood of the military, where everyone is trusted. I miss having a Diplomat Passport. I have found it difficult to communicate to others why the military must do what it does better than anyone else in the world. I want my children to know the things that the military does, allows us to keep our freedoms and keep enjoying this great country.

To Vets Helping Vets – Anderson, I say this…I am amazed and relieved to finally find a place where I feel safe enough to not sit at a corner table. I'm proud to be a member of a group and enjoy the comradery of an intelligent and natural born leader that knows how to perpetuate the good within veterans.

Todd Carpenter

My full name is Darryl Todd Carpenter, but family and friends call me Todd. My mom chose to use my middle name versus my first name. I enlisted in the United States Army on April 17th, 1981. I was attending Travelers Rest High School and living in Travelers Rest as well.

At the time that I joined the military, my family was not able to pay college tuition even though I had been accepted at Clemson University. I have three brothers and three stepbrothers, so in the early '80's, money was tight in our household. I chose the Army because I had an interest in Civil Engineering at the time and becoming a Combat Engineer (MOS 12B) seemed like a logical choice for me. Besides that, my mom was a vital part of the process, and she grilled every recruiter that came to our house. If she didn't like the individual or his responses, she crossed them off the list. She fell in love with my Army recruiter who took extra measures to spend as much time with her as possible to answer her questions.

The one that has always stood out the most was an event that happened between our Basic Training and Advanced Individual Training (AIT). We had been given a four-day pass for Ft. Leonard Wood and the immediate areas right outside the gates of the base. We were to report back, in formation, no later than 12 midnight on Sunday evening. We had a rather odd character in our basic class, who thought he was Captain America. He was a great artist and spent all his free time drawing instead of studying and trying to correct errors the Drill Instructors had pointed out to him. As it turns out, he had stayed in the barracks the entire pass period working on his comic drawings.

As we all began arriving for the accountability formation, we had a Drill Sergeant that we had nicknamed, "Richard Pryor." He looked and even acted like Richard and was hilarious. The Drill Instructor is standing at the front of the formation when suddenly, one of the drunk privates in our ranks, hollers out, "Drill Sergeant, Captain

America is on top of the barracks!" The Drill Sergeant then turns and looks toward the night sky and asks Private Rose, what the hell he was doing on top of his building. Rose replied, "I am here to save the world and I'm going to jump from this building if you don't let me do that." In his best Richard Pryor style, the Drill Sergeant looks up at Private Rose and says, "Well then, if you're going to jump, then hurry the hell up. It's cold out here and we don't have all night!" Needless to say, Private Rose came down from the roof and was quickly subdued by several within our ranks. The very next day, he was headed to the psych ward, then on a bus back home.

Adapting to military life for me was not all that difficult. As I stated above, I came from a large family of all boys and most of my uncles on both sides of the family had served in the military. My grandfather's both served in WWII, two uncles served during Vietnam, but never in Vietnam. A third uncle was a Recon Marine in Vietnam and earned a Bronze Star and two Purple Hearts. My dad and his twin brother served just after Korea. All my brothers and stepbrothers have served in the military as well. The only exception was our oldest brother. Adapting to military life was almost like it was in my blood, something that was part of what a young man should do.

During my time in the military, most of the conflicts the United States faced were small and short-lived. These include Grenada in 1983 when I was assigned to the 58th Combat Engineer Company, 11th Armored Cavalry Regiment in Fulda, Germany. While assigned there, we did have the real-world mission of guarding the East-West German border in Fulda, Germany. We regularly observed East German military activity along the border and sadly, watched unable to assist, as several times, East German citizens tried to escape across the heavily mined, fenced, and guarded border areas. These citizens were summarily shot by East German troops. We could only assist them if they made it over the last fence
which led to our border outpost. From the 11th Cavalry Regiment, I

was assigned to the 1st Cavalry Division at Ft. Hood, Texas. Training there was unremarkable, except for constantly being in the field and the dust. The dust was as fine as talcum powder and even reached into homes and businesses off base. It was the dustiest place I've ever seen.

My initial job assignment was as a 12 Bravo, Combat Engineer. I served in that field until I volunteered for Special Forces training in 1985. Prior to Special Forces Training, I attended Basic Airborne Training at Ft. Benning, Georgia. Upon completion of Jump School, I was assigned the 1st Special Warfare Training Battalion at Ft. Bragg, North Carolina, where I would undergo training to become a Green Beret. My chosen Specialty (MOS) with Special Forces was initially 18 Echo, Communications Specialist. I served in this role while assigned to 10th Special Forces Group at Ft. Devens, MA and then as a Communications Sergeant within the 1st Special Operations Command at Ft. Bragg. While with Special Operations Command, I attended further training to become an 18 Foxtrot, Intelligence Sergeant. At that point, I was reassigned to the 3rd Special Forces Group at Ft. Bragg to be part of the reactivation leadership to stand up the 2nd Battalion.

During my time in conventional units, and the peacetime army, deployments were not usually conducted. It was not until I reached the ranks of Special Forces that deployments became a regular part of our mission. In these deployments with 10th Special Forces Group, we had responsibility for Europe. A great majority of our training and deployments were conducted into various European Nations to train, assist and advise host nation armies. 3rd Special Forces Group held more of the same except for the area of responsibility. While in the 3rd Special Forces Group, we were tasked with the Caribbean and Africa.

I did not see combat in the traditional sense as most people understand combat. Remember, during my time in the service, we were mainly a peacetime force. However, while in Special Forces, the tide changed. We often worked with numerous government interdiction with the Border Patrol and DEA were commonplace. While I cannot comment on specifics of these operations, enemy fire was always a factor when dealing with personnel seeking to enter illegally into our country with drugs and other undesirable activities.

In training with a combat arms unit, casualties often occur. Some of these men were friends. Some were men from other Special Forces teams. Yet, we were all brothers fighting for the same cause. Some lost their lives in training accidents, while others lost their lives while on deployments.

During my time in the military, especially Special Forces, deployments were a common part of our mission. These deployments took me all over the world. Some were conducted as training missions in which we trained host nation forces, and some were conducted as real-world missions gathering intelligence and observing forces hostile to US interests. Each deployment was different, even if we found ourselves returning to a nation, we had previously served in. Each deployment held its own level of difficulty and hazards.

These deployments changed me in several ways. I changed in the way I trained and lead people. I changed in the way that I felt about our Nation. After observing and serving in many of these foreign countries, you cannot help but see the vast difference between the two. I learned first-hand the importance of the freedoms we have in this country. I learned that we were a truly blessed nation.

During my career, I was presented with the following awards:
o   Army Lapel Button
o   Army Commendation Medal (x3)
o   Army Achievement Medal (x3)
o   Army Good Conduct Medal (x4)
o   Noncommissioned   Officer's   Professional   Development Ribbon with Numeral 2
o   Army Service Ribbon
o   Overseas Service Ribbon
o   Expert Marksmanship Badge with Automatic Rifle Bar

- Expert Marksmanship Qualification Badge with Grenade Bar
- Expert Infantryman Badge
- Master Parachutist Badge
- Special Forces Tab
- Belgian Armed Forces Parachutist Badge
- Ecuadorean Parachutist Badge
- Spanish Armed Forces Parachutist Badge
- Military Freefall Parachutist Badge

For the most part, injuries in training were commonplace. However, the most severe injury that I suffered while serving in the Army came from a Military Freefall incident. While serving as an instructor at the USAJFKSWCS, Operations and Intelligence Sergeant Course, we were tasked with making a HALO jump into a drop zone that the students had established. Admittedly, the jump parameters were dangerously close, but we chose to make the jump. High winds pushed 11 of the 12 jumpers off the drop zone. I, being one of them. This is typically not all that uncommon, but on this night, the wind made it difficult to find a suitable place to land.

I ended up in the trees as most of the other jumpers did as well. In a situation such as this, you can generally find a small open spot in the trees in which to land. I found such a spot and maneuvered my way towards it. Upon entering the opening in the forest, your parachute will typically get caught in the trees. When that happens, you can then climb down and safely reach the ground.

On this night, my parachute totally collapsed about fifty feet from the ground, and I fell straight through the trees. I hit the ground moving slightly forward and landed firmly on my backside. The result was a rupture of several discs in my lower back. This injury plagued me for the remainder of my career and ultimately led to my medical retirement from the United States Army.

As I mentioned earlier, my career was somewhat different than most combat veterans. While my career did not involve combat in the traditional sense, the missions we undertook were no less dangerous. Most of these missions were conducted under covert protocols. In other words, we were never there in the eyes of our government. However, I was always grateful to arrive home after these missions. To this day, my wife and family know little about these operations and based upon security restraints, they likely never will.

During my career, especially in Special Forces, there are a number of men that I remember fondly and still have a special form of relationship with them. Within Special Forces, unlike the conventional Army, relationships and trust are a key factor in the overall success of the missions you are assigned. While there are often differences in opinion and tactics, at the end of the day, you are all brothers with the same goal in mind – coming back home safely.

One such man is a former teammate, Carl Lee. Carl was an Engineer Sergeant on my team while serving with the 3rd Special Forces Group (A) at Ft. Bragg. Carl and I really hit it off and became, and to this day, remain close friends. We just seemed to mesh so well together. It was almost as if we could read each other's mind at times. A funny note about Carl that kind of freaked me out was seeing him sleep with his eyes open. I first experienced this on a training mission to Puerto Rico and it still remains a point of humor between us.

While preparing for and conducting our assigned missions, it was all business. However, we always had time to unwind. After the mission or during breaks in the training cycle, we took it upon ourselves to generate some humor to break the tension. These antics came in many forms. Some of them are not safe for the general population to hear. Others were in the form of duct taping a guy to his bed and standing the bunk outside in the freezing rain. If a guy said or did something stupid, he had simply opened himself up to an endless cycle of good-hearted remembrance of his mistake.

Another fun thing we attempted to do as much as time and circumstance allowed was to immerse ourselves into the local culture with the troops, we were training. This often led to some hairy situations where we had to eat or drink an unknown substance only to later find out that it was nothing we would have ever put in our mouths, had we been given a choice. At other times, it led to us being in a place that put us all on high alert.

I have never believed in "good luck" as we commonly refer to it. For me, "luck" was the result of meticulous planning and solid training. We relied heavily on our training and training methods. Luck was simply not in the equation for us. I do know guys that did follow this path though. Some of the things they did ritually were praying, carrying a picture of a loved one, wearing a certain piece of clothing on all missions or carrying some other item that had significant meaning to them.

This is one area that was generally "not safe for family environments." This one in particular: While assigned to the 10th Special Forces Group at Ft. Devens, Massachusetts. We had a guy on our team that was in a bad habit of stealing other teammates food from the team refrigerator. He did it to aggravate us more than anything else. If it was put in the fridge, he felt that it was open game. One morning after physical training, most of us went to the dining facility for breakfast. We always brought back yogurt or some other items to have later in the day. On this morning, one of our Engineers brought back several containers of yogurt. He told us what he was going to do with one of them and we all joined in the fun. He was intent on breaking the culprit of his nasty habit of taking things that did not belong to him. Upon arriving back at the team room, he proceeded to enter the toilet, with the yogurt in hand. He took a dump and then proceeded to remove some of the yogurt so he could place feces into the container. Once he accomplished that, he covered the feces up with the remaining yogurt and placed the container in the fridge.

He then began warning the guilty party not to touch his yogurt or else there would be consequences. He kept up these warnings for several hours, knowing that he was merely prompting our teammate to do exactly what we wanted him to do...take the bait and eat the yogurt. Well, as time would soon tell, he moved in on the fridge. He took out the yogurt, grabbed a spoon and proceeded to take a big bite. To his surprise, he noticed the treat left in the yogurt. His reaction was priceless. He began running around the team room like a man with his hair on fire. He cussed us all as we rolled on the floor laughing at him. Needless to say, we never had a further problem with missing food from the fridge.

I left the military in December of 1995 because of my back injury mentioned above. My condition had gotten to the point where the Army would no longer allow me to conduct parachute operations. This is a mandatory requirement as a member of Special Forces. If you cannot jump, you cannot remain in a Special Forces assignment. With the Clinton drawdown also in effect, I had no other choice than to accept the early retirement.

This was a hard pill for me to swallow. At the time, I was serving at the Special Forces training center and jumping was not necessary to fulfill my job requirements. I wanted to finish my last tour there at the school, but the powers that be gave me no options. Admittedly, I was bitter about this for a long time. Why would they not let a seasoned Special Forces veteran remain in a teaching capacity where he was productive and had received many high remarks about his performance?

My first few months out of the Army were filled with anger, a sense of loss and not much direction. My departure from the Army was swift and felt like I had simply been tossed on a trash heap as a result of my injuries. I felt as if the Army, and consequently the Veterans Affairs, had used me for all they could get then simply tossed me aside.

My advice today to those serving is to take care of yourselves. By this I mean, documenting fully any injuries you sustain, no matter

how slight. Make sure your personnel records are accurate and current. I also encourage men and women serving
currently to plan for the day they leave the military. Get as much education as you can while on active duty. Don't leave your entire future in the hands of the military. Once you leave their ranks, their care for you is lost.

Overall, my time in the military had a great effect on me. It helped to shape me into the husband and father I am today. The Army taught me many lessons about myself, leadership, honor, loyalty, and integrity.

In the Army, I learned that I am stronger than I ever thought possible. Hardships are just a fact of life that can be overcome with the proper mindset. I came to understand that simply holding a certain position did not make you a leader. It's what you do while in the position that determines whether you will be remembered as a leader.

Right now, one of my biggest hopes for the future is that our country will be more careful in determining who will lead us into the future. This holds true for both civilian and military leadership. Our military has become too politicized. Let the military do its job without the pandering of politicians and civilians, many of whom have never served a day in uniform. A phrase that will never be the same for me since I served is, "Be All That You Can Be." It would more accurately be stated as "Be All the Army Wants You to Be."

I wish the civilian world understood the brotherhood of the military. The civilian world simply does not understand what you build with your mates in the military…the relationships, the trust, the loyalty, the family bonds you make while serving this great country.

The importance of time is a key lesson I learned from the Army. Not only being on time, but what you do with your time is crucial. Too many people in the civilian world spend too much time lamenting things that they could easily affect in a positive manner if they would only redirect their time in the proper direction.

The things I miss the most about the Army are the relationships that I was blessed to have. While I still remain in contact with many of my former teammates, the daily interaction
with them is no longer there. I miss the comradery we shared. That sort of relationship is hard to find outside the military today. People are so self-absorbed. They think about only themselves and their own self gain.

The most difficult area for me to explain about my time in the military, is my time downrange as we call it. Those times when real world missions received little to no public mention or acknowledgement. Times when we were operating in areas, we were not openly supposed to be in.

I would want my children to know that I served for them. I served in the hopes that they would never be forced to, nor serve against their will or desire. I served that they may have a brighter and more prosperous future and world to live in.

Wow! What can be said about Vets Helping Vets – Anderson that has not already been stated? This organization has been such a blessing to me. For years, I stayed away from Veterans organizations. I didn't want to be part of just one more drinking and bitching club. I wanted nothing to do with grumpy old men who did
nothing to implement change in our society. Vets Helping Vets is not that type of organization.

From the first day I accepted an invitation to join a friend at their meetings, I knew I had found a home. The leadership and membership at VHV have been more than welcoming and supportive of every vet that has walked in the door. Jesse Taylor has done an outstanding job in setting the tempo, direction, and example for what this organization should be. It's a no-nonsense organization. Vets truly come first!

Roger Dale Cater

I enlisted in the military after I graduated high school in 1962. It was the last year that Anderson had the Boys' High School, which was not far from where I am living currently. Growing up, I had two older brothers, born in 1930 and 1932. I have an older sister that was born two years ahead of me, in 1942. I was born in 1944.

My older brothers rode motorcycles with my dad, all the time. My dad was 6'4" and rode a Big Chief. My second oldest brother taught me how to ride. He took me over to where the Wal-Mart is now and pushed me off the top of the hill there, behind what is now Lowes. I rode it down the hill, through the holler, and up the hill toward where Wal-Mart now stands. I turned around and headed back up the hill to where he was. He told me that I had done pretty good. That's where I learned to ride a motorcycle.

After that, he went over to the Harley shop, got a Sportster with a suicide shift on it, and gave it to me. I told him that I did not like the suicide shift. He didn't buy the bike; he was just borrowing it to teach me. When he went back and got one with a hand clutch and foot shift, I loved that. I rode it all over those hills back there. I was fourteen at the time.

With my brothers being so much older than me, they were out of the house, so there wasn't really a lot of interaction between us on a personal level. I really grew up with my sister since we were so close in age. She was my babysitter and took care of me as the baby of the family. My relationship with my sister was very close. Sadly, my two brothers and my sister have now passed on.

My relationship with my parents was good. My dad was in textiles over at Orr Mills. The mill originally started out in Easley, but he ended up transferring over here to Anderson and moved the family down here. My dad traveled a good bit to other textile mills. He'd leave out on Monday and often would not return home until Friday or Saturday. Mother was the disciplinarian and took care of everything...she was the boss of the house. Even when my dad would come home on the weekend, mother was still the ramrod that kept everything running. She ran the house and Dad knew that, despite him being 6'4", two-hundred fifty pounds.

Mother would cook us just about anything we wanted. She let us grow up and do just about anything, within reason. I remember that I made a racetrack for my 165 Harley, in the front and back yards. I spent hours racing around the yard, jumping off the terrace in the back and sliding around the trees in the front. I bought that first motorcycle myself. If I recall correctly, it cost me about $800 - $900. Brand new. Mine had the big cow horn handlebars on it. Other bikes in the day had just a flat, racing style handlebar. I was fourteen years old when I bought it, and fourteen years old when I got my license. To pay for the motorcycle, I collected money for the city paper routes. Other guys would deliver papers in the morning and evenings; all I did was go around and collect payments for the service. Our boss would give each of us a tablet with the amount owed by address and we'd just pick it up. On the weekends, he would take us all down to Broadway Lake, where we would swim and hang out for a while. He was a good guy. We'd have fun making money and having good times.

I wanted a motorcycle before a car. Back in that day, my mother had a car, and my sister would drive me around to all the places I needed to go like school and such. I knew I had a car that I could drive, but I wanted a motorcycle. So, I bought mine, knowing that if needed, I could drive mom's car. Back in that day, the age for driving and the requirements were very different. I can only imagine what that 1958 Harley would be worth today if I still had it.

My second oldest brother, being in the Army, is what initially got me interested in the military. My oldest brother worked at Monsanto as a tester. He tested the fibers and fabrics Monsanto produced. He had also worked at a bomb plant and Cape Canaveral in the late 1950's. My dad's younger brother was in World War II. He was a cook in the Third Army under Patton. We had some pictures of him in the service. I talked with him a good bit about his service. He's the one that gave me more information about the military than anyone. He told me about his experiences and his pride in having served and that further sparked my interest.

Between graduation from high school and my enlistment, I worked for about a year at Foundry and Steel in the machine shop here in Anderson. I also worked on lawn mower engines and other small engines. I liked the mechanical work, but I couldn't see any future in it. I could see it getting "old" quick. I got tired of the jobs pretty quick because the bosses weren't very good; they'd stab you in the back every chance they could. I determined that this was not for me.

I got with a buddy of mine, Gary Carnes, and asked him if he ever thought about going into the service. Come to find out, Gary and one of his best friends were talking about going in. There were two other guys we graduated with that were also thinking the same thing. There were five of us in total that were contemplating joining the military. We all went in on the buddy plan.

We all traveled to Charlotte to get our physical. We were told that we had all passed our physicals and we would all be packed up and sent to Lackland Air Force Base together to undergo training. Me and four others from high school joined the Air Force and started our training together. That took place in August 1963.

We had all joined with the intention and promise that we would at least start out together. It got interesting from there. They came back and told us that they may not be able to do that. We had all entered to join in as mechanics. They told us that they had more mechanics than they could handle in tech school. They needed one of us to transfer to the electronic field. They needed them right away, and whoever chose to transfer could be sent right away together.

We got together as a group and discussed it, and no one wanted to change. I told them that if I had to go back home, I may not come back. I said, if nobody's going to change, then I'll change. I don't want to go back home. I've already said "goodbye" once and I don't want to do that again. I'm ready to go. I want to go ahead, get in and get settled.

I made the change to electronics, and they sent the remining four off to Lackland. My specific job title was "Ground Support Equipment." Everything they used to work on the airplane, support the plane, shine lights on the plane…anything on the flight line that was used to work on or check out the plane while it was on the ground, I worked with. I maintained all this support equipment. I received this training at Chanute Air Force base in Illinois after basic training at Lackland.

I thought basic training was fun. I enjoyed it. For me, it was always something new, a challenge. I enjoyed all the physical aspects of basic training. I was in tech school in Illinois when Kennedy was killed. We had been in class that morning and were marching back to the barracks area. The First Sergeant came out and told us what had taken place. Kennedy had been killed and we were now on lockdown. You cannot go downtown; you can't do anything. We could go to our dormitory, but we could not leave the base. There was an increase in the security presence, but the next day, training picked up as usual.

For fun, we held a couple of blanket parties for members of our training class. They were guys who constantly complained about how they hated the place and just generally caused issues for the rest of us. So, we took it upon ourselves and took care of them.

Several of the guys that joined with me are still alive and we talk on a regular basis. Just about all of them ended up as jet engine mechanics. I was the only one from the group that made a full career of the Air Force. After basic training, we all sort of went in different directions.

As for adapting to the military lifestyle, I can't think of a thing that proved to be overly difficult for me. One guy from a neighboring flight in basic hung himself in the barracks while we were at breakfast. Some of the guys afterwards commented that he was always complaining, wanted to go home ; he couldn't adapt, he just couldn't stand it. No amount of talking from anyone registered with him. That was one of the worst things I had to deal with in basic training.

When I finished technical school, I was sent to Myrtle Beach, South Carolina. My preference was Donaldson Air Base in Greenville, South Carolina. I thought that I could sign into Donaldson and live at home here in Anderson. That would be great! I got word while at basic that they had chosen to close Donaldson. However, Myrtle Beach ended up being a blast. I was gone TDY all the time, flying all over the country. After Labor Day at Myrtle Beach, everything was shut down. We used to say that they rolled up the sidewalks after the summer was over. I've been back a few times. As a matter of fact, my old shop is still there on the base.

While at Myrtle beach, I was sent to Italy and Turkey all the time. Ataturk, Turkey's leader at the time, took all the poor people and moved them into the area around Incirlik Air Base. They used horse drawn carriages as taxis and lived under some of the most archaic rules you've ever heard of in your life. They lived a very primitive life. The odor was terrible. One of the things that I remembered was that if you were a passenger in a horse drawn taxi, and the horse fell on the cobblestone streets and needed to be put down, you as a taxi rider, were responsible for paying the owner recompense for whatever the taxi driver thought the horse would make him. If you were in the taxi, the fall was considered your fault, because had it not been for your need to be transported, the horse would still be alive. Needless to say, I didn't take many taxi rides.

On the other hand, if you ran over someone in a military vehicle, and hurt them, you would pay to support all the people that he had been supporting. If you ran over a person, you were to back over him to ensure that you killed him. Then you would only have to pay for the funeral. If you found yourself in jail as a service member, then the US military was held responsible to feed you. Over there, you could not expect a speedy trial as one does in the States. Back then, the military did not have the "Status of Forces Agreements" they do now.

I left Myrtle Beach and went to Vietnam. I had returned from an eighteen-month rotation in Turkey and the Air Force was looking for volunteers to go to Vietnam. They were sending a Squadron of 100's to Vietnam and needed support personnel. I decided then that I was not going back to Turkey, so I volunteered for Vietnam. I was stationed at Phan Rang, just south of Cam Ran Bay. We had 100's and F-4's; the Australians had Canberra bombers.

When our Squadron arrived in Vietnam, we started living in tents. We built tent cities there on the airbase. There were six to eight people per tent. We each had our own bunks and mosquito nets all over the place. There was a little beer bar across the way. Fifty-five-gallon drums, cut in half, served as toilet facilities. Someone had to complete the nasty task of burning them every day. Again, as in the States, my job was to take care of any problems the maintenance crews had with equipment. We had to repair it and get it back on the line to be used.

My first impression there was almost like recalling Boy Scouts; living off the land and making do with what we had. The base did, however, change while I was there. They built dormitories and such. It took about six months, or half my time there, to see these changes materialize. We'd often travel to a bar off base and run into the Korean Marines. This was new to me, because typically, each one of them would have three or four ears of enemy soldiers pinned to their shirts. We were advised not to mess with the Korean ROC's, they are crazy! We had a beer with them quite often, but you could always sense when it was time to close the door and get out.

While I never saw direct combat as some did, we did have to maintain security on the base as the security force. Dogs were used to assist us in the matter. Most of my time there in Vietnam was spent on the relative safety of the airbase, working, and repairing equipment.

I was nearing the end of my tour, when I received a letter from the woman who would soon be my ex-wife. While I was in Vietnam, she had gotten pregnant, and had the child. I left in August, and she had the baby the next July. I didn't even know she had filed for divorce until I received the papers in the mail. She had remained in Myrtle Beach when I left for Vietnam. We had a nice mobile home, and a 1966 Chevy 2 Nova hot rod. When I got back to Myrtle Beach, my only words to her were, "Where's the car?" Everything that she left me was put into one small dresser drawer. She told me that she had sold the car. That was the only thing that I wanted. If I had stood there much longer, it would have gotten very ugly for her and the man she had run around with.

I left Vietnam with a final divorce decree, delivered by mail. My thought was there's no use in me going home. I had planned to get out, I was being discharged. There wasn't anything for me to go home to now.

I did come home to visit and met up with a good friend who was in the Army. He was a tunnel rat. I invited him over to my place and we cooked out and partied pretty hard that night. There was nothing for me at home so I stayed in and put in for whatever the Air Force would give me. They sent me to Luke Air Force Base in Arizona. I stayed there for two years. I met a friend there and we were going back to Vietnam together. He was hit by a car and killed before we left.

When I arrived back in Vietnam at Tan Son Nhut, the first night there, the motor pool was attacked and destroyed. We were only a few blocks from it, but I slept through it. It wasn't until the next morning that I realized something had happened.

I met my future wife during my second tour in Vietnam. I met her the first day in country of my second tour. She was working as a cook/housekeeper for one of the ARVN officers. What she was really doing was basically being a nannie for an ARVN officer and his family. I met her and she came down to the base where I was stationed, and we rented a house. We lived there together until I took my thirty-day leave. I came home and talked with my family. I said, "I don't know how you're going to take this?" I showed them some pictures of her and told them that I was going to marry her and bring her home with me. I want to know right now whether you are going to accept her or not. If you're not going to accept her as my wife, know this, I'm not going to give her up for anybody. If you will not accept her and treat her as any other daughter-in-law or sister-in-law that you may have, I will not be coming back.

My dad and my mother looked at each other. My mother eventually took my father's hand and brought him over to where I sat. She said the only problem you are going to have is if you take her as your wife and you do not come home. They made it clear that she was welcome. I was twenty-four and my new wife to be, was twenty. I was seventy-six and she was seventy-one when she passed.

One of the memories of the war that my wife shared with me was of her mother laying over the top of her in the rice fields when planes flew over dropping bombs. At that time, those would have been French warplanes. Her thoughts about the American presence were ones of gladness. She was glad we were there. She supported the American military and what they were trying to accomplish. She felt her country would not be worth anything without the American military.

Before we became fully engaged in Vietnam, she had had her fill of the North Vietnamese. An and I were married a total of forty-eight years. We have no children. She simply could not carry them. She told me later, after we lost a couple of babies, that the little boy in some of her pictures was hers. When she told me that, I told her, please don't misunderstand me when I say this, but if I had known that you were coming with me and leaving your child behind, I would have been as mad as hell. Her thoughts were that I would not bring him. He was two or three years old when we left.

She let a doctor there in Vung Tao adopt him. One of the things that we always wanted to do was to go back to Vietnam to see what became of her family. She had a large family, but she became deathly afraid of flying. She felt that we would crash if we attempted to take a flight over there. An had an odd way about her. She would frequently say only what she thought I wanted to hear. The differences in our cultures often came through. The wars that she had been through as a child and young adult took their toll on her as well.

She always asked me early on, why I loved her so much? Why do you care so much for me? I told her about my former wife, and she knew that was my opinion about American women. They don't do what they're supposed to do. Most of our friends' wives cared about them. Yet I got one that didn't. I said to her, "You are leaving your mother, father and all your brothers and sisters, your whole way of life, everything you've ever known, just for me. I can't love you any more than that."

We had our share of problems. She was totally jealous of me. If I ever ran across an old female friend and hugged them…well, don't hold on too long or she would come over and tell me, "That's enough."

I finally left the Air Force after twenty-two years. I left in 1985. I was going to retire at twenty years, but the Cruise Missile program had just gotten started. I wanted to learn about these new, high tech, electronic weapons we were now fielding. I just wanted to get in and be a part of that program.

I went to Tucson, Arizona for a school and from there to Fort Huachuca, to learn how to properly set up the command and launch areas for these missiles. These launch teams were responsible for their own security, so we had to learn how to properly select sites, conceal ourselves and launch the weapons. We were to be able to remain undetected until the short window for launch was determined. The Cold War started to wind down because the Russians realized that they could not shoot these things down.

I was somewhat disappointed when I left the Air Force because it had changed so much. I was disappointed that I had to leave the military. The attitudes of many people in the military were different from when I first went in. During most of my time, even if it wasn't my job, I did everything I could to make the jobs of others better. The younger guys I saw coming in, didn't have that approach.

Times had changed and the work ethics found in my generation were fading away. Guys my age wanted to do the right things all the time; younger guys sought shortcuts.

After my service, I went to work for Darby Electric Company, rewinding electric motors. From there I went to Glen Raven Mills in Anderson. I worked on putting in spinning machines and other equipment. It's sort of funny that I went into the military to get away from textile mills and here I was after retirement, working in a textile mill. I retired ultimately from the very place I sought as a young man, to avoid…textile mills.

I've been involved with Vets Helping Vets – Anderson for about six months. I lost An, one year ago. I didn't do anything except stay at home. My nieces and nephews tried to keep me busy, but it was hard. Things started to get bad. I was over at the Nutty Sweet Shop one day, and a current member of the group started talking with me. He asked if I had heard about Vets Helping Vets. He shared a bit about the group and what they do. He gave me a card. I didn't go, but I kept the card for a good long while.

Again, it was getting pretty bad for me. I was going downhill pretty quick. I was here at home, isolated and all by myself. A lot of the guys that came into Vets Helping Vets since I did, have done a great job of expressing how I feel about the organization. If I had known that this group was here, I would have been here a lot sooner.

The change it has had on me has been good. I've learned to accept that my wife is gone. I didn't know that I was going to lose her until about ten days before she went into Hospice. She had had her share of physical ailments over the years to include multiple surgeries. She also battled diabetes and we had a couple of instances where we had to call for emergency support.

When I go into Vets Helping Vets, it's as if I am back in my old outfit. The conversations I have and the friends I sit down close to…I'm at home. I'm at home with it.

Buddy Compton

My name is Buddy Compton and I served in the US Army National Guard during the Vietnam War. I was in high school at the time and knew that it was just a matter of time before the draft numbers would come calling. To be honest, I did not want to go to Vietnam. But I knew that was a distinct possibility. So, I chose to take matters into my own hands. I chose the National Guard. I knew at the time that if I were drafted, it would only be a matter of weeks until I found myself in some line unit in Vietnam. At the time, as a young man, that's not something I looked forward to. I didn't feel like it would end well for me.

Yet, looking back today, I would go. If I, had it to do all over again, I would have chosen to go to Vietnam. I see things differently now, compared to how I saw them back then.

Growing up, I had a pretty normal childhood. My dad was a supervisor at the local mill, and my mom worked in the labs there at the mill. With my dad being a supervisor, we were allowed to live in one of the nicer homes on the mill village. Me and my friends did what most boys do…we hung out together, ran the neighborhood and got into our fair share of mischief. Nothing serious, just boy stuff. We all became friends, and it turned out, many of us joined the military at the same time. Some chose other paths than me.

Basic training was not all that bad for me. I mean, there was the usual level of harassment from the drill sergeants, but the bottom line is this; do what you're told when you're told to do it and things will work out ok for you. Be a problem and problems will follow you.

I do recall my arrival at basic training. It was hectic the first couple of days. Unfortunately, a group of us arrived late. We were taken to the area where we were supposed to report to and dropped off. Men were lining up in front of the buildings with all their baggage and what not. I'm looking around, trying to figure out where I'm supposed to be. Then off in the distance, I hear my name being called. I hear "Compton, Compton" about three companies away. So, I proceeded to move to that area. I finally get there. The drill sergeants were not happy to say the least, but I was there. Unlike the others lining up with me, I didn't even have a haircut yet. So, there I was, standing in formation with my bags in front of me, long haired and still confused about what the hell was going on.

One day during basic training we were placed on a detail to stack mattresses. This other guy in the group started bossing us around and telling us what to do. In fact, he was giving us a real hard time. The next morning when we fell out into formation, we saw this same guy. Turns out, he was a recycle. Recycle meant that he had failed or gotten hurt in the previous basic training class and was held over to try again. This soldier eventually went AWOL, and we never saw him again.

Once I arrived at my permanent unit after basic training, I began to settle into the military life. There was nothing really, that stands out as hard to adapt to. Again, it's all a matter of following the instructions you are given. I served a total of eight years in the National Guard when it was all said and done. We did conduct training missions and war games at other military bases in the US while I was a member of the National Guard, but none of these stands out a significant in my career. I was simply doing my job. The war in Vietnam was winding down and the chances of me going there were decreasing by the day.

My first few months outside the military were pretty normal for the times we were in. I was living next door to a guy that was a manager at a jewelry store. He approached me and asked if I would like to learn to make jewelry. So, I told him that I'd give it a shot. I learned how to repair jewelry, make chains and other jewelry related things. I did that for a few years before moving on to something else. Woodworking has always been a big thing for me. It has always been my "go to" when I needed something to do.

Shortly after my jewelry job we moved to North Georgia where we built a business. We had some success there, but ultimately, we were forced to shut it down. Too much government red tape and other issues lead into that decision. Then we moved to Ellijay, Ga. Ellijay was a little town about thirty miles from any other town. The people there kept to themselves, but it was a poor town. Bootleg liquor was the product of the town. In fact, you could drive by most houses and see cases of liquor stacked on the front porches. Nobody messed with it. It was their way of life. It was how they fed and kept their families.

The military impacted my life in a few ways. The most important area I feel was in the area of compassion. I saw guys struggling in areas within the military and I felt sorry for them. You want to help them, but you cannot always do that. Sometimes a man must accomplish things on his own, yet while he is struggling, you want to reach out and give him a hand.

Another thing for me while I served in the National Guard was that my time was spent stateside. Unlike many veterans of my day, I didn't have to see and experience all the things they did. Yet, later in life, I realized some of the things that I did miss. It's those things that have had the greatest impact on my life in regard to my military service. About ten years ago, I found myself in Hawaii, working on an Army base. I learned a great deal more about the military and military life while there. I learned about the comradery and relationships people build with one another. When troops were in the field or deployed somewhere, our neighbors came together. When one of them needed something done or repaired around the house, we just took care of it. We looked after one another. That's the military way.

I miss that level of comradery that exists in the military. That is something that is almost impossible to find in the civilian world. You may have friends and neighbors, but the level of trust and compassion for each other is not the same. I really miss that. Civilians just don't understand the military. They don't get it.

Kids today do not have the discipline needed to accomplish what previous generations have accomplished. They want, and even expect, that everything they need or desire, should be handed over to them. They don't want to work for the things we worked for. They feel they are entitled to things simply because they want them, with no consideration of who's going to foot the bill. Socialism and communism are on the rise in this country. The sad part is that many of our younger people have no idea what the real motives are behind those forms of government. All they're concerned with is the possibility of getting things handed to them for free. They don't realize that nothing is actually free. Someone down the line is going to have to pay the price for all this.

Vets Helping Vets – Anderson has been a great organization for me personally. It has helped me to understand better the things men experienced in Vietnam and other battlefields across this world. My heart goes out to those men and women. I am proud to be a member of Vets Helping Vets – Anderson. They are doing an incredible job and are making an impact on the lives of many veterans and their families.

William Crawford

My full name is William Quinton Crawford IV Wild Bill is my nickname. When I enlisted in the US Navy in 1959, I was living with my mother and my stepfather in Valley Stream, Long Island, New York. I needed to get away from my mother. I went to the recruiters at school in the 11th grade. Every recruiters was represented there. First, I went to the Army recruiter and said, "I want to be a pilot." then I went to the Marine recruiter and said, "I want to be a pilot." The Navy recruiter offered me that chance and explained how I could be a pilot."

I quit school after the 11th grade and got my GED for second year college. and that's how I qualified. The reason I left high school is that the principal said, "All we're going to do is repeat the 11th grade in the 12th grade." I said, "I'm wasting my time."

I told my father what I wanted, and then he pulled his strings with his boss, George C Texter, the chairman of the board of the Marine Midland Bank. In the background, things were happening that I didn't know about. In fact, my father's girlfriend in Washington DC was Margaret Adams. Margaret Adam's father was the commander of the Eleventh Naval District the Pacific fleet.

Naval Air Station Pensacola is where I attended basic OCS training. The drill instructors were pretty tough with officer candidates which served me well later on. I adapted well to the military because it was a daring adventure. There was always something new. Being sent to one school after the other for a few years, the training always gave me a good challenge mentally and physically.

I served with VF-121 Fighter Squadron in Miramar, San Diego, California. Introduced to the F4H Phantom, I flew the fourth production airplane delivered to the Navy which was later destroyed. At the time, it was a rocket sled and the best fighter in the world. Yet it needed many modifications that we did while testing its operational limits. I was first deployed TAD on the USS Lexington. Then I was deployed on the USS Bonhomme Richard Shard which was later called the Bonnie Dick. All our deployments were TAD, Temporary Additional Duty. The squadron's main objective was fighter training or converting old equipment to the new F4H Phantomand training pilots in new tactics used against the Mig 21's.

I was deployed TAD to Vietnam, 1962 and 1963. VF-121 (Fighter Squadron), specialized in Broken Arrow operations. Broken Arrow is when the fire bases were calling for ordinance directly down on their position because they were being overrun. A battle ship throwing one ton of explosive right down on their position causing a lot of friendly casualties. The solution was napalm. With napalm, the only casualties were from collapse lungs. When napalm goes off it creates a huge vacuum, and if you were unconscious and your mouth was open it would suck the air out and collapse your lungs. If no one was there to reinflate your lungs, you were DOA.

The Army or the Marines all had their tarps to cover themselves and lay on the ground. The napalm would hit the tarp and it would fly up in the air so they would be OK. Now, anybody running around, standing up like the VC, became fried chickens.

Officially the war was not declared until 1964. I left there in 1963 and deployed back to San Diego. Funny thing happened to all those records which mysteriously got lost. Interesting, but that was the way of the politics. I served until 1969. The executive orders from the higher ups said I needed to come home.

One of the funny things that went on was when we left Yokosuka, Japan. Our 750 centerline fuel tank just happened to be filled with sake. Thank goodness for our mechanics who disconnected the tank from the rest of the fuel system. When we came back to San Diego, we would take off from the carrier with our cargo of sake on board. At Miramar, those tanks were used for baseball parties and many other events. We were happy sailors for a long time.

At a game, the mechanics would turn the tank over, put a spigot on it. The whole baseball field would be cordoned off. The whole squadron would get drunk on the baseball field. If you were outside the perimeter of the baseball field, you were taken to the Brig. Even if your buddies decided it would be fun to throw you over the line.

We did a lot of a lot of things we shouldn't have done. For example, we rented a house on La Jolla, the California campus of the Scripps Institute. This was directly west of Miramar and the town of La Jolla. A very posh community. Several of us officers got together and rented a house the fourth house, south of Scripps Institute pier. We put a sign right on the beach that read "Beach girls wanted" with an arrow. Well, the city posted a police officer there so our girls supply dried up at once.

Pay back… we located through intelligence, the mayor's house. During VF-121 morning training operations, we took off at 0600 in the morning, flew over his house at the minimum 800 feet, for we did not break the law. Then we went ballistic or straight up using our afterburners. The impact actually broke some of his windows. Results…all of a sudden that police officer disappeared for good.

I left the military in 1969 and was employed at Marine Midland Bank, New York, with their computer system. My father's boss George C. Textor was the chairman. This was my first job after the military, and it became really interesting. The computer system used was, Remington Rand round hole punch cards. Marine Midland being the state bank, made it mandatory that if the Rockefeller Foundation was trading in a particular stock, I had to check whether they met their regulatory requirements before I allowed them to make the trade. Receiving the information that there was 250,000 shares in this stock in this trade. I was about to authorize the trade. Before I called them to give them the authorization, I called my broker. I said buy this stock. When 250,000 shares are traded, which would drive up the price because of the volume, then sell. We were doing insider trading. We would take that money and go up to Watkins Glen in a limousine for the Formula 1 Races and have a big party with the money. We were not greedy and had a good time flying under the

FCC's radar.

The military helped me learn to never give up and you will get it done. There is always a way to go in the back door of any project. I would tell a young person transitioning out of the military to select what they like to do from ten to fifteen hours a day and not get tired of it. So, if it is your choice and you love what you're doing, you will succeed. Learn to say no to other people's opinions on what they think is right for you. Stick to your guns and mean it. Don't let anyone influence you with their advice. So, here is my advice: Don't take my advice, learn for yourself. Because the sum total of your life is completely different from mine. Use your contacts, I did. That's my philosophy. However, if you can use, some of what I tell you in your life. I am proud that I have paid my knowledge forward through you.

The military had a positive effect on me. It made me think I was invincible because I could do anything I put my mind to. I learned to focus. My hope for the future of today's youth and military is we will get a strong leader back in office. Trump got things done. He did not walk softly but he carries a big stick. If you fail to do the job "Your Fired."

I have eliminated the word "WHY" from my vocabulary. Why is a weapon everyone uses. When I was a kid, my mother constantly asked, "Why did you do this or why didn't you do that?" I had to immediately defend or justify myself, if not in speech, in my mind. If you're going to remove why from your vocabulary, you need to replace it with something. "What is the reason?" is softer. It gives the other person, especially me, time to explain the circumstance. People use why on themselves a lot, and that's not good for anyone's life's journey. Isn't it interesting that what you sat to and about yourself, is what becomes true. Think about it.

This is the part that really stuck with me for a long time when I came home. When I left the military, it seemed everyone was against the service like the flower power groups, and the Hare Krishna group. At the LA airport headed to San Diego, I got off the plane in my dress whites. We took a commercial flight from Hawaii for some reason. We were walking through the airport and this guy comes up and he spit on me. Automatically my elbow crushed his nose, and he was on the ground screaming like a pig. We just kept on walking away. The police came over and looked at us then waved me on by.

My father was friends with William Childs Westmoreland through close association between Westmoreland and the Marine Midland Bank. I met him through my father. I sent him a letter on July 17, 1974. Thru my father he responded back. The letter is dated 26 July 1974. One of my biggest disappointments in life is not taking up his offer of going fishing at that time. This I realized after recently finding the letter in my papers by accident. I share this letter, for it is a part of history. History should not be erased.

> *Dear William, Many thanks for your warm and thoughtful letter of July 17th. Although disappointed in the outcome of the military campaign, I hold no animosity and have no regret at getting involved in the action in Vietnam. I understand from your father that your contribution, of giving close air support to our forward fire bases with low to no visibility was a most interesting and educational experience for you. One of the rewarding experiences of the of the campaign is to renew old friendships and to make new ones. The renewal of your father's friendship, I would put at the top*
> *of the list. I like your analogy to fishing and hope that someday we can take rod in hand, side-by-side, test our luck in that arena. Kitsy joins me with our warmest best wishes. Sincerely, Childs (W. C. Westmoreland)*

A business venture brought me to make Anderson, South Carolina now my home. I used to vacation in Anderson. A partner Harris A Coller and I bought the Anderson Cotton Mill downtown. We made cotton buff cloth for a company called Jackson Buff. During the Clinton administration, 1985-1993, the country entered a recession. Textile mills started shutting down in 1991. Most manufacturing and textile equipment was sent to Mexico. In 1993, due to Clinton signing NAFTA. Clinton's last act as president was to sign the banking bill which drove our interest rate from 5.6% to 22%. The decline of the textile industry continued throughout the years, as cheaper labor drew jobs overseas and DHEC Regulations drove the textile industry out of business.

I've live for a long time with a nightmare since I had to kill a VC face to face. That haunted me for a long time until I died for 3.5 hours in 2010 while having open heart surgery. I was having heart problems, chest pains, and pains in my jaw. I drove myself to the emergency room at 0200 in the morning. They gave me Nitro and then my blood pressure dropped from 110 to 60 and then to 30. I was essentially dead. I saw this halo of green light and the light faded to a dot. The light started growing not in brightness but in strength and it enveloped me. The stronger it got the better I felt.

They put me on the heart-lung machine. During open heart surgery, the surgeon was working with my heart and zaps me to check for leaks. I woke up, and said, "What's up, Guys?" I had pipes in my throat and just gurgled, they said. What amazed me was when I woke up, they jumped back with fear in their eyes and the anesthesiologist put me back under. I guess my heart was pumping. What is interesting is that my life's viewpoint has changed. The nightmare I use to have about killing somebody and seeing life drain from their eyes, made me realize dying isn't as bad for them as I felt
about it back then. In fact, I feel death is pure pleasure.

All my family has passed on. I'll get to talk to them when I take that trip. With that said, talk to your family and friends now. The Vets Helping Vets is a band of brothers that understand without judgement. Come join us.

Bob Fellers

My name is Robert Glenn Fellers. Friends called me Bob in the Navy, but my family back home called me Glenn. I was born and raised in in Greene County, Tennessee with four brothers and one sister. Drafted into the military in January of 1971, I joined the US Navy at the military induction center in Knoxville, Tennessee.

There was not much work around home except farming. People grew tobacco to make a living. My dad was a contractor, doing house painting, carpentry, and floors whatever he could do to work. He grew tobacco, also. I lived with my mother's parents until I was about six or seven because Daddy was traveling around to find work. We lived in a place back in the mountains, in a little house or a shack. Even then, we were about twenty years behind the rest of the world as far as technology.

We had no electricity. I remember it being a big deal when they ran the wire up the road so we could get electricity. It was a big deal because we cooked on a wood stove. We drew water from the well and heated it to take a bath in the front yard in a tin tub. I was cutting up and splitting wood for the wood stove when I was five years old. It had to be a certain size and type of wood. I cannot remember ever not working as a young boy. Granddaddy plowed with mules and raised tobacco, corn, laying chickens and cows. Life was hard but he was self-sufficient and didn't need to work a job. Everything he needed was right there.

Growing up dealing with wood is something I enjoyed. Now I take a chainsaw, a chunk of wood, and a lathe to turn wood into bowls and other items. In Grandma's time they were a necessity of life. Everything was mixed up in them to feed the family. I enjoy the satisfying work, and my wife and son are proud of what I make with my hands.

Both of my grandparents were farmers and never held a public job. One of my grandfathers served in the US Army in France during WWI. His sons, my uncles served in WWII. I remember listening to their stories.

Boot camp was a little rough for a hillbilly from the mountains, but I made it through without any major problems. I served from April 24, 1971, to December 17, 1974, on board the USS Saratoga CVA/CV 60. It was a new experience for a boy from the mountains to see the ocean for the first time and especially when you can't see land around you. Seems like you can adapt to anything you need and want to do. I really never had a problem with sea sickness. Even learned to walk with the ship moving while keeping my balance.

I don't miss any of the bad habits I picked up in the military. Sometimes when I watch a program on TV of the places and countries I visited, I feel a little wanderlust. Makes you think it would be nice to go back.

Assigned to the B Division #2 Main Machinery Room, our mission was to operate and maintain the 1200PSI steam system. Our two boilers were oil fired conventional boilers which supplied the steam power to propel the ship as well as operate systems, including launching and recovering aircraft. Our working hours were long, eight-hour shifts, plus two four-hour watches per day, seven days a week. This amounted to 16 to 20 hours out of every 24 hours while at sea. The working conditions were very hot and dirty. The hours were a bit shorter when we were at port. The ship homeported at Mayport, Florida, although I never spent much time there during my time on board.

In 1971, we spent several weeks at sea in the Caribbean area conducting carrier qualifications. We continued to make North Atlantic and Mediterranean deployment. When we returned from the Mediterranean deployment in early 1972, I was granted a ten-day shore leave to go home to Tennessee. Our ship was ordered to leave the Mayport Naval Station in Florida to relieve another ship, while I was home in Tennessee. A ship was damaged by a fire while off the coast of Vietnam. This was an unscheduled operating emergency deployment, and all shore leave was cancelled. The ship was given 12-hours to prepare and leave Mayport Naval Station.

I was unable to get back to the ship before it left. When I got back to Mayport, I was assigned to the transit barracks along with some other sailors who had missed the ship as well. We stayed there for about a week waiting for information about returning to ship.

When I went on shore leave, I only took civilian clothes and my ID card since I was going home for only a few days. All my military attire stayed on the ship. I didn't know how much of a problem this would be until I returned to Mayport. I had no pay records, so I could not get paid. I had no uniforms for muster, or work and I had no shot records to show I had the required immunizations for traveling. I only had a few dollars in my pocket.

After about a week, we were put on an airplane to Treasure Island Naval Station in San Francisco, California. While there, I was able to get twenty-five dollars from the navy relief fund to buy personal items like toothpaste, razor, shaving cream, etc. I was also able to get a set of dress whites from the lost and found, which was necessary for traveling on military aircraft leaving the country. Since I had no shot records, I had to get all required shots again before leaving country!

After about a week at Treasure Island Naval Station, they put us on a bus to Travis Airforce Base for travel to Clark Airforce Base in the Philippines. We waited in the Airport terminal for 24 to 30 hours, sleeping whenever we could. Finally, we left Travis for Anchorage, Alaska where we stopped for a couple of hours for refueling. We left Anchorage for another Air Force Base in Japan where we stopped again for a couple of hours. We flew to Clark AFB in the Philippines. It's hard to remember now but the entire trip was 26 to 28 hours.

Next, we were put on a Navy bus with the window covered in chicken wire. The country was in the middle of a revolution which made the trip from Clark AFB to Subic Bay Naval Station very dangerous. Hence, the chicken wire covering the windows of the bus. They told us the bus would not stop for any reason until we reached the Subic Bay Naval Station about 2-hours away.

When we arrived at the Naval Base, we went to the transit barracks where we were told they were full. They assigned us to a decommissioned WW2 ship on the pier. I don't remember the name of the ship. This is where we waited for the USS Saratoga to arrive. I was due to arrive in a couple of days. I was never so glad to see that ship! After a couple of days taking on supplies, we departed for the coast of Viet Nam.

April of 1972, the ship's port changed to Subic Bay Naval Station, Philippine Islands, from which we operated in the Tonkin Gulf off the coast of Viet Nam. We conducted air operations in North and South Viet Nam from May 1972 until mid-January 1973. During our time in the Tonkin Gulf, we lost four aircraft and three pilots to enemy fire. One pilot was rescued by our helicopters from behind enemy lines the following day.

We had a fire in our main machinery room in October, while anchored in Singapore Harbor during a stand down period. We lost three crew members to the fire. The ship returned to the states in 1973 and spent the rest of 1973 in the shipyards at Portsmouth and Norfolk, Virginia for repairs.

In early 1974, we were back to the Caribbean Sea (Guantanamo, Cuba) for carrier qualifications lasting several weeks, then another deployment to the Mediterranean Sea. I left the ship, December 17, 1974, in Naples, Italy to return to the States for the last time. It took me a couple of weeks to get home.

My rank at the time I left the Navy was BT3 (E-4). I made (E-5) a couple of months before my enlistment was up but had to extend my enlistment to be advanced, so I declined. I left active duty in January 1975 and returned to Tennessee. In 1979, a few years after the Navy, I moved to my wife Jo's hometown, Anderson, South Carolina. We still live here after forty-two years.

I received five awards while serving in the Navy: National Defense, Good Conduct, Sea Service, Viet Nam Service and Viet Nam Campaign. Two awards left off my DD214 by mistake were the Good Conduct and Sea Service. I didn't notice until years later and it is a hassle to get things like that straightened out. They listed my home of record as South Carolina instead of Tennessee. I recommend anyone transitioning out check the info on your DD214 for mistakes.

I had done a little welding in the Navy. We had to do all the maintenance and operation of the equipment and repair when it broke down. I decided I'd better stick to a trade instead of just bouncing around. Using the GI bill, I enrolled in the welding program at Tri County Technical College, and I graduated. It never crossed my mind to teach, but my welding instructor saw something in me, and he said he thought I'd make a good instructor. I've instructed many students at different schools, and I have operated my own metal fabricating business.

I share the work ethics I learned from the military that helped make me successful in life: it required hard work and long hours. You've got to show up to work every day and on time. I tell students even if you are the best in what you do, if you are not dependable and honest, you are the worst. If young people don't have a plan already in place, the military is a good place to start. The military can help you decide what you'd like to do and help with your education.

A friend of mine, Bob Humphrey, invited me to a Vets Helping Vets meeting. He was a fellow welding instructor. I met him while I was in welding school. As we got to talking and got to know each other, I realize that he was in the Marines the same time I was in the Navy. He was stationed on a ship homeported in the same homeport as mine. They were actually tied up close to each other on the pier. We didn't know each other at the time but it is a small world. Ended up working together as instructors and as welders back and forth over the years from then on until he passed away with cancer.

He was right, Vets helping Vets is a good place to go. Everybody is interested in helping everybody. They all speak the same language and don't put you on the spot to talk about what you've been through.

Maurice Hastings

I was born in Roscoe, Texas. My parents named me, Maurice Hansen Hastings. Growing up on the farm gave me my work ethics. I farmed for my dad and hired out to others for tractor and farm work on their farms. Growing up with 50's, rock and roll, WWII and the Korean War, the United States and Texas Flag. The Boys Club of America had a great influence on this small town boy.

At the age of thirteen through sixteen, I was a member of Sweetwater Civil Air Patrol which was an auxiliary of the Air Force. I went to summer camp at Goodfellow Air Force Base in San Angelo, Texas. At age seventeen and a half, I talked my parents into signing for me to join the US Navy Reserves.

After graduating from high school, I went to San Diego, California for basic training. My duty station after basic was Norfolk, Virginia. I was stationed on board the U.S.S. Cadmus AR-14, an auxiliary repair ship, for 21 months. While on orders at Norfolk, Virginia, the first 3 days, three of us new guys stayed at the ship's Master of Arms area (the ship's police). One Master of Arms (the ship's police) ask if any of us three newbies could type. I was the only one. He said come with me; you are now working in the office. I was supposed to be working in a machine shop. Everything worked out though. I worked in the repair department's main office as a Yeoman (Clerical). I worked for Lieutenant Commander Fred Ewing and a Chief Scully in the Repair Department. We had a complement of 350 men. The department was divided into four divisions. There were 300 other men that ran our ship separate from repair, a total of 650 men on board. Beside my duties in the office, Commander Ewing also assigned me to the diving crew as a helper. I help suit up our divers, handle the lines, and watch the gauges on our dive boat's compressor. I was also on the ships pistol team. That was lots of fun and memories.

I went through hurricane "Gracie" September 30, 1959, in Norfolk, VA, tied up to the pier. Our ships boiler was out, and we were probably the only ship left in Norfolk.

Every three months we would go out to war games for a couple of weeks. We left Norfolk on a Monday thru Thursday, pull into a port on Friday thru Sunday. Pull out on Monday for more war games until Friday. On Friday we pulled back into Norfolk for another three months of working on other ships. Our Ports were exotic places like Puerto Rico, New York, Baltimore, Boston, and New London, Connecticut. We were at Newport, Rhode Island, for six-weeks in the dead of winter. It was snow and ice that whole 6 weeks we were there. I liked to have frozen to death while we were there.

I nearly went to Salvage Diving School. I went to the diving school on the base. They put me in one of the deep sea suits with the big metal helmets, a canvas suit, weighted shoes and belt, and helped me into the water. I walked to a designated point and back with no trouble. Back at our ship a little later, they wanted me to sign up for another year so that I could go to diving school. I declined. Later, I had second thoughts.

Our sleeping quarters in R2 division was with 125 other guys. My job was to take care of paperwork for the repair department and its personnel. I was keeping up with the liberty cards and passes and other requests that had to be signed off in our office. We were a repair ship between yard periods. Every two to three weeks we took two to three ships to work on. Our ships repair department crew would remove broken parts on their ship, bring it to our repair department shops. Our repair department crew would reinstall the repaired or new parts on their ship. One of my jobs was to go to the shops and check the status of the jobs being repaired.

When completing active duty, I went back to Roscoe, Texas, and went to work at Acme Cotton Gin as a pressman during cotton season.

In the Naval Reserves I was on a six year plan, two years active and four years active reserves. After active duty, I went back to Active Naval Reserves at Abilene, El Paso, and Dallas, Texas. I was honorably discharged in 1963.

I landed a job at the First National Bank, Sweetwater, Texas, in bookkeeping. I then moved to two other banks in El Paso, Texas. I decided to apply for a job in Dallas, Texas. I got a job at Texas Instruments in Dallas. I started going to night school on the G.I Bill. I retired from Rockwell International as a draftsman, with a pension. I also was employed at Northrop Grumman making Night Vision for the military.

I was a drafting checker at that point in my career. At age 70, I was laid off. After the layoff, I found out that I also would get a pension from Northrop Grumman. Our facility at Garland, Texas was closed and was moved to New Hampshire. There were around 400 people that lost jobs. I was going to retire at 70 and ½.

I enjoyed shooting sports, shooting competitively, scuba diving, hunting, and golfing, boating, motorcycles, snow skiing, playing slow pitch softball, and attending church. The friends I made along the way added to the enjoyment. I also had a Federal Firearms License (FFL) and sold guns as a side job for 25 years.

At the American Legion Post 369 in Richardson, Texas. I served as Service officer, Adjutant, Executive Board, and Chaplain. We moved to Anderson, South Carolina in 2011. I served as Chaplain for the American Legion Chapter Post 121 in Williamston, South Carolina. I feel that I am a Patriot. I tear up when I see a flag draped coffin and hear taps played. The Vietnam Wall in Washington, DC is a special place for me. Many who were my age gave their lives, at such a young age, including my close friend, HM3 Philip Converse, US Navy who died in Quang Tri, Vietnam. I have had two other very close friends that I grew up with die from agent orange.

In 2018, I put together a booklet with my words and pictures to present to my family and friends, entitled "Why I Am Me." It is filled with advice that has worked well for me throughout my life. I remain active in church and belong to the group of Vets Helping Vets. VHV are friends who served and gave of their time to our country. Getting to know them and listening to their stories gives me the opportunity to pray for the homeless or wounded vets and the ones with personal or mental wounds (PTSD). I have a very soft place in my heart for all our veterans and active duty military. I am proud to have had the opportunity to serve. <u>Freedom is not free.</u>

This information has been taken out of a book I have put together for my family.

C. W. Hicks

My name is Charles William Hicks Jr. I had an uncle by the name of Charles, so my family called me, C.W. I've been called Chuck, too. Especially when I was in police work. I don't know why.

I enlisted in the US Air Force in August 1966 while I was living with my parents at 2005 Woodside Avenue, Anderson, South Carolina. My girlfriend's (Sue Ellen) dad was in the Air Force. Thank you, Howard Norris.

Basic Training was scary and fun. Once you got settled into what you were to do and knowing you were going to be hollered at on a regular basis. Basic was, OK. I was lonely at times, missing my girlfriend at home and my brothers.

My Training Instructor was from Greenville, South Carolina. He picked on me about my Southern accent compared to the Yankee's accent. He had lost his southern drawl. Basic Training consisted of getting up early, making beds right away, getting a shower (no bathtub), writing letters, and looking forward to mail call. Being told what to do every minute of the day was a big challenge.

I served on an Island named Kume Jima off the coast of Okinawa. I was an Air Traffic Controller. One year on this rock was very long!

Though I didn't see combat, the locals in the village were not friendly. I was not a prisoner of war but a prisoner of isolation! I received no physical injuries but the mental injuries of the isolation on the island. I was healed as soon as I got to leave the rock (hill).

With different assignments stateside, military service was more like a job. I had things to do and did them. I grew up to be a man in the service to my country. I learned no one else is going to do it for you. You learn to take care of yourself.

Like most soldiers, I drink beer and played cards; and as all soldiers, fought each other. I didn't have a good luck charm just hicks from the sticks! We played pranks like putting shaving cream on the hand and tickling the nose resulted in a face full of cream for the sleeping soldier. Placing the sleeping soldier's hand in water. They either get wet themselves or up and run to the bathroom. We would short sheet the bed for the one who thought they knew everything.

I received the normal medals for training by letter, so I could put them on my dress blues. I was honorably discharged in June of 1970. I interviewed for a job as a police officer and was hired. I started work four days after I got home.

I was involved in a shootout at McDonalds in Belvedere Shopping Center. One guy got away, and later caught in Georgia. One was shot, trying to run away, by one of the many police officers who responded to the call. He was shot in the butt. I can remember standing guard at the hospital while he recovered. That set the stage for an exciting ten years as a Narcotic Officer, Detective and Criminal Investigator for the Tenth Judicial Circuit Solicitor's Office.

I also taught Law Enforcement at Tri-County Technical College where I graduated. For 27 years, I was an adjunct instructor. While I was teaching, I was a Pastor at Corinth #2 Baptist Church and Crossway Community Church.

My hope for the future is to encourage those returning from war and let them know there is life after serving your country. Christ is their friend and help to a great life serving in the Lord's army. Pay attention to what is going on around you and speak up!

One thing I want everyone to know is the Hick's family, along with many others, had three sons to serve about the same time. We were raised like doorsteps and went into the service the same way. All of us were active duty overseas at the same time.

I served in the US Airforce at Kume Jima, Okinawa. Robert Lee Hicks served in US Army in Vietnam and Germany. Larry Wayne Hicks served in the US Army in Germany. He died from Leukemia while preaching in Stanford, Kentucky serving his Lord.

Our sister, Mom, and Dad were our lifeline. My parents Charles William Hicks Sr. and Mary Jane Christine Adams Hicks gave great sacrifice, their three sons. We left as boys and came home as men.

My joining Vets Helping Vets has been an outlet of sharing the memories of my service with those who understand. My family loves to see me involved with VHVA. They get to hear my stories, too.

Steve Hodge

My name is Stephen Hodge. Friends call me Steve. I enlisted in the US Air Force in 1984 at age 20, a member of 3723rd Basic Military Training Squadron, after attempting community college for art but seeing no future in it for me. I went in under the delayed enlistment program for a position in electronics. Following basic training at Lackland Air Force Base, Texas, I was stationed in the 3413th at Keesler Air Force Base in the Biloxi, Mississippi far continued specialty training as a ground radio communications maintenance technician (aka Ground Rat).

My first assignment with the 2146 ISG (Information Systems Group) was on a remote tour for a year (1985-1986) at Pilsung Range (KOTAR), and operating location assigned to Osan Air Force Base in Korea. About 60 GIs were housed with a great chow hall, video library, medic's office, gym, and of course, and NCO club. I was an apprentice technician under SSgt Dana Perkins as part of a two-men radio shop that provided radio communications for United States and also Korean Air forces.

The major function of this installation was providing a mock airfield access for training of pilots to test their skills in bombing and strafing objects on the airfield. The Air Force planes that used this field were OV-10s, F-4s, F-16s, A10s, and many more. It was incredible to see the firepower on display.

USAF personnel on this location supported this effort with electronic warfare and Televised Ordinance Scoring System (TOSS). My specific function was to work with radio equipment for range operations. Equipment included: KWM2A, which was a radio used for Military Affiliated Radio System or MARS; AN/GRR 23,24 Radio Receivers; AN/GRT 21,22 Transmitters; AN/GRC-117,211 transceivers, as well as associated interfacing equipment for communication directly to aircraft using the range.

I took advantage of learning, qualifying, and certifying on many pieces of heavy equipment such as forklifts, bulldozers, dump trucks, 18-Wheelers, M151A1 jeeps and trailers, and even the Pintle Hook (trailer hitch). One memorable duty I had was getting certified only Smokey SAM, which was a foam missile that was fired at aircraft for training and helping pilots learn evasive action of actual surface to air missiles in wartime. Although the Smokey Sam's accuracy was rarely precise once I was fortunate to get close enough to get an aircraft to maneuver around one.

Phone calls from Korea back to the states were scheduled only for a short duration, so contact with family was short and sweet. During this time, my grandfather, who was my legal guardian during childhood, passed away suddenly in a car accident. Although only an E-3, the US Air Force diverted a training mission to send a "Jolly Green" helicopter to transport me to Osan for travel back home for emergency leave. This was one of the most difficult times of my life, and I am grateful that they did not hesitate in sending me home for the funeral.

In 1987-1988, I joined the 2045th Command Group at Davidsonville Transmitter Site, operating location of Andrews Air Force Base in Maryland. We provided communications for transmitter operations in conjunction with Brandywine Receiver Site to Andrews Air Force Base using high frequency radio communications around the world. Equipment we maintained included Rockwell Collins HF transceivers using 208U3 and 208U10s linear power amplifiers, Scope Signal 3, and Giant Talk communication systems.

In some of my off time, I painted a sign based on comic strip *Beetle Bailey* with a theme of the "Outsiders," as that was a nickname given my predecessors regarding the crew assigned to Davidsonville. Some great friendships were made there including a friend, Keith Hudson, we nicknamed Radar, also J. P. McKinley and Kelly O'Brien. I just attended a Davidsonville reunion in 2020 and enjoyed seeing the old crew. I mostly hear from J.P. now, who was in my wedding and has hosted me in the D.C. area whenever I'm there on business.

Sadly, Kelly died in an unexplained drowning incident back in the1990s. I had a near fatal car accident while stationed at Davidsonville. It left me hanging upside down out the window of a Volkswagen stuck to a telephone pole. I had multiple broken bones, collapsed lung, contusions and was held in a drug-induced coma for nine days. I had strange dreams, but dreams that eventually led me to my faith in Christ. In a weakened state, I hastily married the last girl I dated but with whom I had broken up. That did not last long!

My entire family and friends, including those guys in Davidsonville, gave me an overwhelming amount of love and support so I healed physically and mentally. Doctors said I might not walk again, but I did! Several health-related consequences have resulted over the years from that wreck, but by the grace of God I have continually overcome.

I was assigned a special duty assignment in a Ground Launch Cruise Missile (GLCM) unit 38th TMW as communications technician 2141 ISS. That required extensive physical training and field living at Keesler Air Force Base and Davis Monthan Air Force Base in Arizona, which was of great help in my physical recovery. After training in Arizona for the assignment, I spent the next two years at Wueschheim Air Station in Germany. We worked with the Tomahawk Cruise Missiles. These missiles were the counterpart to the Russian SCUDS. I would later learn that this was a tactic to bring the Russians to the table for talks that would ultimately bring an end to the Cold War via Part of the INF Treaty (Intermediate-Range Nuclear Forces Treaty).

We would simulate dispersals in the field for a week three to 10 days at a time. Many Germans were friendly, such as my landlords. I didn't speak German and they didn't speak English, but we somehow built a great relationship. Some Germans were hostile to the American presence, as seen in an elaborate painting of a cow carrying an impaled missile by its horns on the entire side of a barn... just one of many examples. The Berlin Wall came down during this time, which meant the dismantling of those air stations and bases. I left in the spring of 1990.

While in Germany, I was writing to Linda, a girl back home that went to church with my dad. Letters turned into very expensive phone calls, one that was $600, so we had to set a time limit. Her letters would sometimes have lipstick kisses and perfume scents. She visited me in 1989, and we toured Europe a little bit. In fact, we visited my friend Radar, stationed in the Netherlands. We toured a diamond factory in Amsterdam, and I proposed to her on the Eiffel Tower in Paris with a ring she picked out at that factory. Although she went home to finish college at Virginia Tech, we were married in 1990, and moved to my next assignment at Kessler Air Force Base in Biloxi, Mississippi from 1990- 95.

At Keesler, I had come full circle: my new job was instructor. I really enjoyed interacting with students and seeing the lightbulb moments when electronics made sense to them! Desert Shield occurred in those years, and we would support the efforts at Keesler, loading supplies onto planes for the medical teams. One great friend I made was a retired sergeant, "Tank" Baughman, who had moved into the civilian sector. Take invested in many hours mentoring me in my career. I was able to return the favor by recommending him for a job once I moved back home. We saw each other from time to time, in which he always addressed me as "Junior," the last occurring in 2020 just before his death. Military friendship seems to have that bond that time and space cannot loosen.

Our first of three daughters were born at Kessler, and we grew a happy marriage and made many friends in Mississippi. Even now, we occasionally visit our former pastor and friends in Mississippi, as they meant so much to us and those early years of our married life. As a Staff Sergeant in 1995, I took the early-out offer, and we moved closer to home in Virginia. A job at Ericsson which became Ma/Com plus all my military training helped me build my own company in 2004: Star City Communications. Named after the place I was born, Roanoke, Virginia, known as the Star City.

Although I am now living in South Carolina to be closer to my grandchildren, I still own and operate my business in Virginia. I am finding some time to slow down, give back, and enjoy life with my wife and family with whom God has blessed me.

Although I could produce many pages of stories while I was serving, these are the ones that stick out the most. I look forward to opportunities to serve my fellow veterans as best I can.

Irv Jones

My name is Irvin L. Jones. Friends and family call me Irv. August 2nd, 1946, I was the last of six children born to a dairy farmer and his wife in a farmhouse in Forest Hill, Maryland. Mom was a housewife. Dad, now a dairy farmer, had been a licensed engineer until he was injured in an accident at Aberdeen Proving Ground during World War Two.

1957 saw us sell the Maryland farm and move 9 miles across the Pennsylvania line to a 600-acre farm. Lots of hard work. During my high school years, my life's plan was to be an electronics technician in the Navy like my brother Richard. In my senior year I quite seriously dated another senior, Gail Edwards. After graduation at 17 years of age from Kennard Dale High School, a small rural school in York County Pennsylvania, I was facing military time and possibly college. Gail was focused getting out of the area, and we broke up.

Realizing I had never learned to swim, the Navy wasn't looking so good anymore. I tried to sign up with the Air Force but failed the physical and I was told I was "1Y" draft status. They said, "Go on and live your life. 1Y is after women and children, and you can't be drafted." 1Y is a medical status as I supposedly grew too fast in my late teen years and had blackouts because of it.

So, at 17 it's off to Williamsport Tech and study electronics for a year. 1965, I found employment at General Electric's Radio Receiver Plant in Utica, New York. Within a year, I made a line leader making radios. January 1968 saw me making great money and living the "Good" life, but it was to be short lived!

Two changes were coming, in January, my brother Richard was getting out of the Navy after 20 plus years and in late January I received a letter from my Uncle Sam stating that they needed "me" of all people! It told me to report for induction at New Cumberland Army Depot in April. I said, "I can't be drafted." But the letter said otherwise. So, it was move three years of accumulations to my folk's home in Pennsylvania. I reported in at New Cumberland. Four hours later this Sergeant tells me I can't be drafted because I am "1Y" and to call someone to pick me up. I told him that I have been telling people that for almost four months, but it didn't make any difference!

So, it's move back to Utica and General Electric until I got a reclassification letter in July, changing my draft status to 1A. I had 30 days to appeal the reclassification. Why bother. On the 31st day I got my letter to report September 9th, 1968, for induction period two of the ninety-six inducted with me were drafted into the Marines. Wow, I lucked out and we were transported to Fort Dix, New Jersey for basic training. In the 7th week of basic, I found out my AIT (Advanced Individual Training) would be at Fort Monmouth, New Jersey, where I would become a 05B (Radio Operator).

Knowing that would not be a fun job, I saw a career counselor and signed up for a third year and was given orders for Redstone Arsenal Alabama where I would become a 21R (Sergeant Missile Systems Firing Set Repairman). After six months of intensive electronic school, I graduated second in my class and was promoted to SP4. I was informed, I was surplus. So, I told them just let me go home then... Ha, which didn't sit well with them! I was assigned duty in the Avionics Shop at the Redstone Arsenal Airfield. At 15 months in the Army, I was promoted to SP5. Great duty at the airfield.

I would go in at 6AM to make coffee and check the flight-line for early flights and swap out any equipment that had been written up for those early flights. All the others came in at 7AM and worked to 3PM. Because I came in early, I went home at 1PM.

Is that great duty or what? No company responsibility, no formations or even reporting. I worked for a civilian who just happened to have a 1962 Pontiac Catalina that frequently needed my personal attention. So, I would leave at 9AM and work on the car for Charlie Hendricks, my boss. I was on 24-hour call but only got called in one time that year to repair the 121 MHz emergency transmitter located on the mountain. I replaced the fuse and took the next day off as comp time.

Working there afforded me the chance to see and meet Chuck Yeager when he flew in with his personal P-51 to Redstone. Also, many of the astronauts flew in with their T-33s, and I met a few. Of course, the Super Guppy came in several times carrying the Saturn 5 Rocket motors for testing at Marshall Space Flight Center, which shared our airfield.

I never understood why they had to test those Saturn 5 rocket motors in the middle of the night. I owned a house trailer two miles from base and it would shake, rattle, and roll every time they would light off one of those rocket motors!

Redstone duty also had a most profound impact on my life as it allowed me to be introduced to the gospel, and I received Jesus Christ as my Savior while attending Calvary Bible Church, February 23, 1970.

But all good things must come to an end, and after a year at the airfield I received orders for Camp Colbern, Korea. While at Redstone, I had on-the-job-trained a new MOS, 35L (Avionics Technician) so now because I was technically on my second tour of duty and a 35L, I was able to draw $75 a month "Propay" which helped.

My duties in Korea included taking care of the ordnance platoon Jeep. It had been the Mail Jeep and was pretty beat up, so I spent a lot of time cleaning, polishing, and shining her up. The best part of Korea was volunteering for the JP4 run to Pusan. If timed correctly, we would arrive at Osan Air Force Base at lunchtime. Don't leave there too early as we needed to get to Pusan Air Force Base right around 5:00 PM so they would not load the trailer until the next day. This meant Air Force food for supper and breakfast, then stop at Osan on the way back for an Air Force lunch! That was four meals and two days of good Air Force eating! As SP5 (E-5) I would be supposed to ride shotgun with an E2 or PFC driving the deuce-and-a- half. Knowing I was responsible for I was responsible for his screwup, if he wrecked us, I chose to drive.

Not once did I have to work on the missile firing set, my trained MOS. But one time during a "Dog & Pony show," the "cannon cockers" (what we in ordinance called the firing batteries) got it up in firing position and could not get it down. It was a problem in the guidance section and not my job. But I was the only technician there, so get up there and fix it! That was the only time during my military career that I actually worked on the missile. And I got it down!

In 1971 after being in Korea for 12 months, President Nixon was reducing troops in Korea, so I was sent back to Fort Lewis, Washington to ETS (expiration-term of service) with five months to go. I was discharged honorably since the army didn't feel it worthwhile to reassign me with that little amount of time left. That was April 21, 1971, I was a free man.

Knowing that General Electric had shut down radio production in the States and now only 900 were working where 12,000 worked in 1968, I thought I would do some fixing up of the home I had in New York. I would draw unemployment for a while, just take it easy. However, I got home on a Tuesday and started working at Paolozzi's Car World, a Saab/Fiat dealership on Thursday as a line mechanic. The owner, Joe Paolozzi, had left word for me to see him as soon as I got home. So much for taking it easy.

I quickly got tired of working on rusty cars with dirty, salty, ice dripping from them and moved to Orlando, Florida, September of 1972. I started working for Central Florida Lincoln Mercury. In 1974, I took over the Service Manager's position at Bill Bryan Imports, a Fiat dealership in Orlando. January 1975, I opened my own shop, Orlando Car & Truck Repair as mechanic, owner, manager, janitor or whatever was needed.

In 1976, I started nights and weekends going to Jones College studying Business Administration and graduated in 1981. I applied for, received a Florida Adult Teacher Certificate, and started teaching Adult Education Automotive courses at Mid Florida Tech two nights a week.

By December 1989, I had seven mechanics working for me and two part time errand boys. I was pretty tired of all the 18-hour days and calls at all hours of the night, so I placed all my employees with other employers, sold my accounts, some equipment, and the real estate. I took over the full vehicle maintenance for chemical systems of Florida as an employee working 40 hours a week.

My brother Richard was living at Orange Park, Florida and was one of the founders of The Tucker Club of America. As such he restored two Tuckers, #22 and #26. I assisted with the engines, and he did all the rest. I then towed both of them to Arlington, Virginia for the owner of them, Mr. Dave Cammack. I should tell you that both of these cars were donated by the owner (Dave Cammack) to the Antique Auto Club of America in Hershey, Pennsylvania, and are on permanent display.

Now I must add in that I married my first wife in 1969. We have three children, a son and two daughters. In early 1988, we separated for the last time and that was that. In May 1989, I received a telephone call from my high school sweetie, and she was coming to Orlando for a work related seminar and could we go to lunch. During the conversation, I discovered she was in the middle of a divorce, as was I.

I suggested dinner instead of lunch and on June 15th, 1989, we had dinner at Barney's Steakhouse, then a horse drawn carriage ride around Lake Eola, and a tour of Church Street station. All in all, a really perfect evening. We continued to date long distance, she was in Fort Lauderdale, and I was in Orlando, 200 miles away. It made for really long dates! I moved to Fort Lauderdale and started working for Powell Ford as a Front-end and Brake specialist. On June 23, 1990, Gail and I were married.

Through a headhunter in 1991, I took a six-month contract to work as a Technical Advisor for Al Jazirah Vehicle's in Saudi Arabia. They are the only Ford Lincoln dealership for all of Saudi Arabia; they had thirteen locations around the Kingdom. Gail and our two dogs joined me there. It was an interesting experience, but I wouldn't want to go back.

One of my duties was hiring mechanics and body men in Manila, Philippines. 500 interviews in two weeks yielded 43 employees and I am ready to go back to Riyadh. Unfortunately, Mount Pinatubo erupted, and I was stranded in Manila for two more weeks. I must say that driving on Saudi roads was really an experience. My company car, a Lincoln Mark 7, topped out at 134 mph and the roads were perfect. And believe it or not, I was passed at that speed several times driving the 580 miles from Jeddah to home in Riyadh.

My contract was up, and I didn't renew so back to Fort Lauderdale, Florida, and Powell Ford until 1996, when we moved to Las Cruces, New Mexico. The employment I had lined up turned out to be much less than I had been promised so I ended up commuting to El Paso, Texas every day for work (100 miles roundtrip every day). A year of that and I didn't think twice when a headhunter set me up to work in Moscow, Russia for a year.

We arrived in Moscow with our dogs, June 1997. I set up a shop for the Moscow police and one for the Kremlin Medical Center for General Motor vehicles. Work involved training the mechanics and laying out the shops and parts departments. It also took us to Tbilisi, Georgia, to do some hands on work for a member of the Georgia Parliament. As things were moving along well, I took two weeks and we flew to Germany and drove around Bavaria, two weeks before Christmas. Lots of Christmas Markets!

In Moscow, we met a couple from Kentucky, who were field hosts for the Kentucky Russian Baptist Missions Partnership. Soon we would spend Thursday evenings at Red Square giving out tracks and singing hymns with the mission's teams that had come in that day. I finished up in Russia in late March and went back stateside to Tucson, Arizona.

I took a job as a Fleet Supervisor for Golder Ranch Fire District. An anonymously paid (not volunteer), fire district that had three stations and 45 paid full-time Paramedic Fighters. We covered the City of Oro Valley, towns of Catalina, Rancho Vistoso, Saddlebrook and Oracle Junction for fire and full EMS service including ambulance transports. The district was comprised partly of Pima County and partly of Pinal County. All told, we were responsible for 299 square miles. A lot of state wild land coverage is in that as well. By the time I retired in 2010, we had eight stations and 154 paid Paramedic Firefighters. My duties were to oversee the operation of the maintenance and repair shop, hire mechanics as needed, inspect and purchase fire trucks and ambulances, and other vehicles as needed.

In April 2005, we discovered Gail had stage three inflammatory breast cancer! Surgery, six months dosage chemotherapy administered in a four month time span, and six weeks of intensive radiation followed. And praise to Our God, April 27, 2021, we celebrated her 16 years of cancer free!

As retirement appeared on the horizon, and I started looking for someplace not as HOT as Arizona, much research led us to Anderson SC, and we are not sorry! Since moving here, I do a lot of automotive work for friends and church members. I joined Vets Helping Vets Anderson about five years ago and four years ago, Campbells Patriot Honor Guard. Gail and I both are active at Oakwood Baptist Church. That is 75 years condensed into seven pages! There is much more I could share, but enough for now.

Larry E. King

My name is Larry E. King, and I am from Anderson, South Carolina. I was raised up on a mill village where my dad was an electrician, and his name (James Ralton King) was well known. His fame was due to the fact he was always willing to help those in need of electrical help, even after working long hours in the mill.

I went to work while I was in high school because my dad believed in working for what you got. I worked in a Richburg Supermarket and made fifty cents an hour. While I worked there the minimum wage changed to dollar an hour. I thought I was rich. Eventually, I worked in the mill in the cloth room. I took machine shop classes in high school while working in the shop at the mill. I graduated in 1962 from Boys High School. It did not become co-ed to the next year.

At age 18, I joined the Army in April of 1963. I was sworn in at Fort Jackson, South Carolina to serve in the Airborne Infantry. After a few days at Fort Jackson, I was sent to Fort Gordon, Georgia, to begin Airborne Basic Training. After basic I stayed at Fort Gordon to continue training in Advanced Infantry. Near the end of AIT, we performed many physical and other tests to qualify for jump school at Fort Benning. I passed all the tests and was prepared to go to jump school. A few days before this, Army personnel interviewed us. During the interview, I and others were told if we would agree not to go to jump school at this time, they would send us to Germany. We would be able to go to any school we wanted. My dad had practically begged me to continue my education. After much thought, I decided to grant my dad his wish and go to school in Germany. I thought this meant I could attend jump school at a later time. I later regretted doing this and after all these years, I still do.

We were sent from Augusta, Georgia to Fort Dix, New Jersey for a few days to wait on a ship to transport us to Germany. We left from the New York Harbor on a troop ship, the USS Gordon. The ship took seven days for the trip from New York to Bremerhaven, Germany. I had mixed feelings as we passed the
Statue of Liberty. I was looking forward to the adventure but at the same time I was wondering if I would ever see the Statue of Liberty again. I went to Germany and guess what? There were no schools in Germany. The army personnel tricked me because they needed Light Weapons Infantry MOS soldiers in Germany more than airborne at that time.

A day or so after arriving in Germany I was assigned to the 1st Battalion, 19th Infantry, 24th Infantry Division. For a reason, God only knows, I was assigned to Headquarters Company. The company commander (Captain Blue) interviewed me and asked if I knew anything about maintenance. I told him I took two years of machine shop in high school and had worked in a machine shop before joining the army.

He asked me if I wanted to run the hills around there with an M14 rifle or be a mechanic. Of course, I told him I would be a mechanic. I was assigned to the battalion's motor pool. I never really worked as a mechanic, although I did help them on occasion. The battalion had recently changed to a Mechanized Infantry Battalion. My job, along with four others and the Motor Sergeant, was to keep the paperwork accurate on the vehicles in the battalion. There were approximately 88 vehicles in our unit. We had jeeps, trucks, armored personnel carriers, and M60 tanks for the Recon Platoon.

I mentioned there were four people on this job. In a month's time, I was the only person on this job. This job was not an authorized job, and it was almost impossible for me and the Motor Sergeant to keep up with the requirements. We had two machine
guns in motor pool, one was called a grease gun that fired 45 caliber rounds. I think it was an M3A1 and was assigned to the rescue

wrecker. The second machine gun was an M60 assigned to me since I had the Light Weapons Infantry MOS 111.10. I enjoyed firing the M60 and actually cut a tree down once when I was shooting targets with the M60. I was also assigned a M14 rifle.

One of the duties assigned to the 24th Infantry Battalions was to guard the Berlin Wall on a three- month rotation basis. My battalion, the 1st, did not guard the wall since we were assigned directly to NATO as an Allied Mobile Force. We, along with other NATO nations, were once placed on a red alert to go to Cyprus due to a conflict there. There have been conflicts in Cyprus for many, many years, or probably generations. The Navy moved ships close to the island. Our alert was called off after three days. A short time after this, we along with other NATO countries were sent on C-130s to some desert airfield in Turkey on a maneuver call Eastern Express.

My unit was set up in the desert next to a Belgium unit. I still have a green beret that I traded for a DX field jacket to a Belgium soldier. We carried one 3/4-ton truck on this maneuver. I don't know how it happened, but our ¾ ton truck driver ran over and killed a camel on the way to the radar site. The local Turks were not too happy about this. Tensions were high the rest of the time in Turkey.

I developed soreness in my left shoulder in Turkey. I went to a German field hospital; they found a tick embedded in my shoulder. I walked around with my arm in a sling for a couple of weeks. After we returned to Germany after our 0600-hour reveille one morning, my platoon Sergeant wanted to see me. He gave me a medal that I had no idea what it was. I thought it was looking nice looking so I put it in my locker, and it stayed there until I returned home. After a little research I found out that the medal was a Purple Heart. I never found out why he gave that to me for I was not wounded in combat. I do not and will not take away from this honor given to those who were wounded and deserve this medal. The medal is not engraved with his name or mine. The only thing I can think of, he just wanted me to have it.

I was in downtown Augsburg, Germany with my friend, a Wapato Indian, who left the guesthouse we were in. I later found out that he got in a ruckus with some German man and woman. The German community were up in arms over this incident. A short time later my friend and I were messing around with some M113 APC's (Armored Personnel Carriers). A minor thing in my opinion. Our Company Commander called us into his office and busted us, reduced us in rank for this M113 incident. The truth was they reduced our ranks so they could tell the Germans about the punishment they had given us. I had nothing to do with the conflict that my friend had with the Germans. The captain took all my keys to the Motor Pool Building. By the time I walked to the motor pool, my keys were returned to me. The leaders of the Maintenance platoon knew I had been railroaded. I did not want to throw my friend any further under the bus, so I kept my mouth shut. It wasn't long until I got my PFC stripe back. A short time after this, a blood strike became available, and this Specialist 4 rank was given to me. I would have made E5 had it not been for this incident.

I never was in combat like so many of my military brothers, and I appreciate their service and salute their efforts. I went to Germany with a Light Weapons Infantry MOS. I kept this MOS in the motor pool for about two years or so. Near the end of my time in Germany, my MOS was changed to Track Vehicle Mechanic. Although I rarely worked as a mechanic, my MOS on my DD-214 is listed as a Tank Mechanic.

I spent three Christmas seasons in Germany in a row and never got homesick like many others. Maybe because you don't miss what you don't have. One of the good old boys, a friend of mine, whom I enjoyed running around with, went home on leave. When he came back, he was just psychotic and didn't want to do it anymore. It just messed his mind up so much that the guy went and committed suicide. I guess it's not only combat that can give you PTSD.

Other than that, I enjoyed my time in the Army Infantry; it was the best time in my life. I went in a wild teenager and came out the person I am today. I didn't like the false information I was given about the schools in Germany and the reduction in rank incident. Yes, it was hard at times, the POW drills, sleeping in the snow, and eating potato peeling soup. I feel like I was a good soldier and never gave my superiors a hard time. I came home from Germany on the USS Darby, back to Fort Hamilton, New York.

I returned home to Anderson, about midnight on a Monday. Wednesday, my dad came to me and said, "It's going to look bad on your record if you are not working. I got you a job of installing equipment in the mill, starting Saturday." At Dad's insistence, I took the job. Later I took a job at Dow Badische Company where I worked for 31 years, as a supervisor for 25 of those years.

Through my life, I always regretted not jumping out of a military plane. I joined a skydive club for about a year in my late 50's. I was working most weekends and not able to jump on a regular basis. I did manage to jump eleven times from 3500 feet to 13,500 feet. I always enjoyed the thrill when you come out of the plane.

I had three uncles in WWII. Sometimes they would share stories. One was a medic who told of trying to ease the pain of a severely injured soldier. The other was in the Army, serving in Africa and through Europe. The one that was a marine died fairly early. My wife's uncle who served in Korea wrote a letter requesting a pen and a pocketknife. This was in the 50's. His mother received a letter that he was missing in action. Two years later they sent his body back in a box and his family couldn't ever feel sure that was him in there. It's things like this that makes telling our stories important. We have the opportunity to preserve history.

Dad was about 18 when his brothers went into the military. His appendix ruptured and he was in the hospital for about 54 days. The bill was 150 dollars, and more than his family could pay. It took a long time to pay the bill back then. As long as I remember, he worked seven days a week, most times at ten hours a day, proving hard work won't kill you. He lived to be 94 and kept a sense of humor his whole life.

Vets Helping Vets has helped me with public speaking. I was able to speak at my wife's funeral. The veteran's story gives different outlook on knowing history firsthand versus history read in a book. Let's continue to tell our story while we still can.

The youth of today do not know the sacrifices the veterans made for their freedom. Some show disrespect because of not knowing the whole story or from just pure meanness. Take the situation at Dolly Cooper Veterans Cemetery. We have friends buried there today and attend funerals of some we may not know personally. Why? We appreciate their importance to America's freedom and will stand up for a veteran living or dead. The very ones who vandalized their markers and try to destroy this country may get by a little while, but I'm from the old school. They need to spend their time behind bars and lose that freedom or be turned loose in a room of veterans who understand.

Bob Kapp

My name is Bob Kapp. I was born in 1947 in a very small town in Western Pennsylvania. Bad timing, as it landed me graduating from Keystone High School at the height of the Vietnam War. On the tenth day after graduation, June 1967, I left for basic training at Ft. Jackson, South Carolina. Volunteering for the draft allowed me to choose my date of entry to starting duty in the Army for two years.

Thinking I was physically fit for basic training, took on a different outlook after arrival. I was so sore the first two weeks, I wanted to cry. The rifle range where we practiced shooting was all of five miles from our barracks. We ran that distance early in the morning and started our march back in the ninety something degree heat of South Carolina's mid-summer.

Like many occasions, our Drill Sergeant gave us the command of double-time. One recruit fell out of line, claiming exhaustion quickly prompted the DI to call out column-left until the rest of us realized he was leading us in circles around the guy who had given up. At that point we knew we would be there all day. After continued name-calling and badgering we pressured the guy to get up and go, saving us and himself.

On one occasion after about four miles of running, a recruit started spitting up blood and passed out. We were warned not to drink cold liquids when extremely dehydrated, so I took a swig of my cherry Kool-aide and spit it out without swallowing. One of the guys saw the red and informed the DI, I was spitting up blood. The DI ask me if I needed to ride in the ambulance, also. I responded with a tough guy attitude and said, "No Drill Sergeant, I can make it."

After basic, I went to Advance Infantry Training and headed to a brand-new NCO Academy at Ft. Benning, Georgia. From my next set of orders, I was sent to Ft. Hood Texas. An old supply sergeant at Ft. Benning told me, Fort Hood was all mechanized. He said I would be riding in tanks and armored personnel carriers instead of walking…wrong. When I got there, they took everybody's tanks and APCs, and I was handed a M-16 and told I was going to Vietnam. Man, what a surprise.

At 11PM on March 27th, 1968, our whole battalion went over in stretched DC-8 airplanes. Our battalion had been given lots to eat and drink and the entertainment of a live band before our departure. We landed in Alaska and Japan for fuel before arriving in Chu Lia, Vietnam.

The few days spent training after we arrived caused reality to set in. I paid more attention to this training than about a year of the infantry training before. It was serious stuff, and I didn't have to be told twice.

I can't recall the reason, but I began writing down some of the things I did from June 1968 until March 1969 and counting down the days. On August 30, 1968, I bought the small journal and began writing in it at the Post Exchange. I copied notes and dates that I had kept from the scraps of writing paper. We received SP packs in the field of cigarettes, gum, candy and writing paper. I bought film as often as I could. The photos I took are priceless to me. The journal is over fifty years old and is a prized possession of mine. I've filled in the gaps with the pertinent stuff I remembered. My journal tells more of the complete story of the casualties, physical and mental, my comrades and I faced in Vietnam. This is only some of the excerpts of my journal:

- o On May 17, 1968, our platoon got our first kill and recovered the VCs AK-47.
- o On May 19th, my good buddy Harold Dean was wounded by shrapnel from a claymore mine.
- o On June 11th, I got sent down to the C-4th/21st 11th Light Infantry Brigade. On the way into Chu Lia, MPs told us to put our steel pots on. We complied but immediately took them back off only to have them chase us. (Chu Lia had a stricter protocol than we were used to.)

- We flew from Duc Pho to LZ (Landing Zone) Baldy by Caribou aircraft. As we started to land, something happens. We had just touched the runway and immediately took back to the air. The aircraft had lost its brakes on one wheel and couldn't get stopped. The second time, the pilot tried to land, we were all over the runway and just about went off the end of the runway. (I never trusted that type of airplane after that.)
- The next day we up to the mess hall and viewed *The Dirty Dozen*. (The first movie I had seen since I had been in Vietnam.) That night after the show, we walked across a dark rice paddy to get to our bunker. Guys in the other bunker thought we were VC (Vietnamese Communist). I thought we were going to get shot.
- On July 30[th,] Merasico got killed by a booby trap. Thomas was in front of him, and he is the one that set it off. I was only five feet behind Merasico. He had a sucking chest wound. We had a senior medic attached to our squad that day plus our normal medic. The mine hit many people, including Platoon Sergeant Woods. Sergeant Woods got hit and it only drew a drop of blood from his earlobe. (He seemed to be upset by this nick on his ear which really surprised me.)
- On August 1st Sergeant Woods got killed. (Looking back, I wonder if that is why he seemed extremely out of sorts about the small nick. Did he have a premonition of what laid ahead, his death perhaps? He was a Black man who had been in the Army for about sixteen years. I took his death pretty hard.)

- August 23rd was my birthday. I celebrated by shaving for the first time in about three weeks. I also got shot at on my birthday but hit the ground really quick.

  The next day I was assigned to be my buddy Pete's ammunition bearer for the M60 machine gun. Every hundred rounds were another ten pounds. At times, my backpack would weigh between seventy to eighty pounds.
- On October 3^{rd,} a priest came out to the field, and we had services. I was given a Saint Christopher medal before by a chaplain, but I had lost it. I had been spared several times and I held on to the medal for I felt it had brought me good luck.
- On October 9th, A guy named Love and I were out on flank security, and it was pretty rough going when we got back to our RON. I got a Playboy magazine from my cousin Penny and a letter from Don Husband of Mississippi, a guy I met in basic training. His family and I have stayed connected with for 50 years. I received a many of care packages from the family and him while I was in Vietnam.
- On October 16th with 157 days left, I got sent to the rear and put in Headquarters company, because I had a bad case of GIs.
- I'm at the NCO Club expecting to fill up on steak, ice cream, and all the good things I had missed. After the first bits, the cramps doubled me over in pain and quickly removed that idea. After explaining my problem to the female friend, she left and came back with a miracle drug in the form of little red pills. I was amazed, no cramp, and I could eat. I went to the PX to get more film and got

on one of those weigh scales. It said I weighed 108 pounds. Before I got sick, I weighed 138 pounds. I didn't realize that I had lost that much weight.

o (I used to joke about the only reason I went to Vietnam was to see the Bob Hope Christmas Show and to get a Seiko watch. I accomplished both.) December 23, 1968, I'm in Chu Lai at the 312th Evac Hospital for a dental appointment. (Rumor had it that the Bob Hope Show would be at the Amphitheater behind the hospital.) That night, I went to the transient tents to wait on my ride back to the field the next morning.

o In the morning on December 24th about 5AM, they came around to wake us up to take us back to the airport. Somehow, I missed the bus going back to the airport. It was still dark, and I snuck around in the dark through a muddy rice paddy to get to the mess hall for breakfast. After breakfast, about fifteen of us went to the Amphitheater and got front row seats. The hospital brought patients down and we had to move to row sixteen. I saw Bob Hope, Rosie Grier, and Miss World 1968 from Australia. The show was really good.

o I would go to the MARS (Military Affiliate Radio Service) station to call home. With a good connection, a ham radio could reach an operator in the states at certain times, if the weather was just right. The operator would call the phone number you were trying to reach. One time I tried to call Carol, a girlfriend and later wife. Her phone number and my aunts were one number different, and I was always getting them mixed up. My aunt lived next door to my parents in Pennsylvania. Our town had a party line system back in those days. Neighbors could listen in on your conversation. I called my aunt by mistake, but a neighbor overheard and told her to hold on because Carol was next door at the time visiting. In the end, I got to talk to Carol. A good turn for nosey neighbors.

- January 13th, we didn't travel very far. We were set up by 11AM. It was raining about all day, but I stayed in my tent and got all dried out. We had to go on patrol in the afternoon. All we saw was a monkey and a million leaches.

- On January 14th, I had 67 days left and we moved down off the steep hill that we were on. We went down in the valley and took resupply and went on patrol. Teddy Bear was out cutting sticks for his hooch and walked straight into a little boy. He was about eight and looked as if he had not eaten for a while. We gave him milk, and I gave him a can of beans and franks. He had something wrong with his leg and the bone was sticking out. He was really skinny, with no teeth. They sent him to the rear and found out he was twenty-eight years old and had been a POW for five years.

- On February 18, 1969, we started sweeping through a village and somebody stepped on a booby trap. Fifteen of us got hit. Ron Raker from Central Pennsylvania got killed. I got hit in the back of the head, neck, in the shoulder, and a couple of places in my back. (The PRC 25 radio I was carrying, took a lot of the blast and probably saved my life. I never wore a steel helmet until about two days before. They said my steel helmet looked like a spaghetti strainer. I still have pieces of metal in my head today.)

- The colonel was flying over us when it happened. They took us out in the colonel's chopper. All I wanted to do was close my eyes and relax. The colonel kept shaking me. He thought I was going into shock. There were two gurneys under a canopy. Two medics stared working with us. Then a Medevac took us to 6th Support Hospital in Duc Pho. Ron Raker had chest wounds, and I was with him when he passed.
- The Medevac flew me to the 27th Surgical Hospital and took me by ambulance to 312th Evac Hospital in Chu Lai. It was eleven hours from the time I was hit until I was having surgery. When I woke up from surgery, my nurse friend, Captain Mary Simons was holding my hand, wow.
- On February 21st, the nurse at the 312th came in to put me in a wheelchair. She was going to let me sit awhile before trying to get me up to walk. I said there is nothing wrong with my legs; I can stand and walk. She tried several times to dissuade me not to try yet. She eventually let me try; and when I tried to stand, I went straight to the floor. March 1st the doctor gave me permission to walk to the PX.
- I was sent to 249th General Hospital in Japan in a C141 Medivac plane filled with stretchers. I gave a Red Cross girl at the hospital the money to buy me a Seiko watch. I knew I was going home soon.
- When I got to Valley Forge General Hospital in Pennsylvania, my family drove thee hundred miles to see me. I told Mom I had been hit by a piece of shrapnel in the arm to excuse my now bad handwriting due to nerve damage. My brother-in-

law warned them I was not sent home from Vietnam for that.

I received: Army Commendation Medal, Purple Heart, AF Outstanding Unit Award, AF Org Excellence Award, Combat Readiness Award, Good Conduct Medal, Outstanding Man of year, National Defense Service Medal, Vietnam Service Medal, AF Longevity Service Award, Air Reserve Longevity Medal, Air Reserve Meritorious Service Ribbon, Small Arms Expert Marksmanship Ribbon, Republic of Vietnam Campaign Medal.

I am fortunate I did not come back as an amputee. The first time I was hit was from the shrapnel of a 500-pound bomb and the second time by a Bouncing Betty. Friendships, support and kind gestures from family and friends back home helped me make it through.

My very close friend Tim Bennet, shared the same shelter every night, pulled guard duty with me and walked the same path with me. We were hit by the same landmine and went to intensive care together, in beds across from each other.

I didn't come back the same person from all that I went through. I matured really fast. Raising my children, I was a strict disciplinarian. Trying to prepare them for life and protect them from things I hoped they would never have to go through. The word veteran took on a whole new meaning for me. I want others to know what veterans sacrificed for the freedoms they enjoy.

PTSD sometimes makes me an unhappy person. Vet Helping Vets allowed me to talk to other veterans who know what I went through, the mental and physical problems I still face now. I encourage others stay in touch with other veterans. You might meet up with old friends and you will sure make new ones.

Greg Lohning

I am Greg Lohning and I served in the United States Air Force. I have an older brother and a younger sister and brother. I grew up in the small town of Logansport, Indiana. The town was comprised of about 1500 people. My childhood was not what I would call a good childhood. My dad was a very abusive alcoholic. There was just never much love shown in the family.

My parents and I didn't get along well. Dad worked on the railroad. He'd get a call on Friday night that he was going and would be gone all weekend. As kids, we would be tickled to death because we knew that he wouldn't be home until late Sunday. We knew that things would go smoothly through the weekend. Mom was...I'm not sure how to put it...she didn't show much love...she was all about herself. We were pretty much left on our own, even at eight and nine years old. We lived a block from the city park. First thing in the morning we'd head for the park and a lot of times, we wouldn't come home until ten or eleven o'clock at night. Nobody cared. This took place back in the 1950's so it was still relatively safe to be out at that time of night.

I recall one night my mother told me to be home at five for supper. I got there about ten after and supper had already been served. I was sent to my room, nothing to eat, just go. She didn't really care. I'd usually end up getting a spanking or beating for not being home on time. The same thing happened a few days later. I looked down and it was ten past five. I thought, well if I go home for supper, I'll probably get no supper, get sent to my room and probably get a beating. And I do mean beating. So, I didn't go home at all.

I got home about ten or eleven o'clock that night. Mom asked where I'd been. I said, "At the park." I had sold popcorn or soda at the park, things like that. She asked if I'd had something to eat, to which I replied, "yes." She said, "Ok, then get to bed." At ten years old I had learned, if I don't go home at all, I'd just be sent to bed. So, I would just stay out. It was a lot more comfortable that way.

My siblings and I fought quite a bit as do normal kids. We got along ok until later in life. We became teenagers, and I was working most of the time. My older brother, who is a year older than me, went into the Air Force. It was just very hard, a strained relationship. I was working at a grocery store most of the time. At that time, we weren't allowed to sell any canned goods that didn't have labels on them. But as the stock crew, we could take them home with us. I would always write down what was in the can, and I'd usually take home ten to fifteen cans a night because we'd stock the entire store.

I was basically providing all the food for my younger brother and sister, because mom was always out drinking and running around. It wasn't good, and dad was gone. It was a strange relationship. Even today, I've made every effort to keep in touch with the family. My older brother and sister haven't spoken to me since our mom died; but my younger brother speaks with me quite often.

During high school in Indiana, I was in the Civil Air Patrol. It was during the same time that NASA was coming to the forefront. I spent a lot of time around airplanes, and I loved to fly. I often wondered how neat it would be to work for NASA. I was told by my dad, that there was no way he was going to waste his money sending me to college, because I wasn't smart enough, in his mind. My teachers and counselors at school pretty much echoed the same thing. There was no way I would ever go to college. I wasn't smart enough. That dream was pretty much out of the picture, but I still held onto it.

At that time, you either went to college, or you got drafted. Well, I didn't want to get drafted. Vietnam was heating up in 1968, the Tet Offensive was happening. My older brother was in Vietnam at the time. The chance of going to Vietnam didn't bother me. The thing is, I loved airplanes. In school, I had always loved math. Math came easy for me. Contrary to the words of the adults in my life, I did have the aptitude for college. Being around the Civil Air Patrol, we learned a lot about jobs in the Air Force. Knowing I would get drafted, I wanted to join the Air Force to become a Load Master.

In becoming a Load Master, I would be able to fly, use my math to figure out weight and balance of aircraft verses loads, etc. I talked with the recruiter and joined the Air Force in March of 1968 on the delayed entry program. Shortly after graduation, Mom kicked me out of the house. My mom and dad had divorced. I was couch surfing from that point on, staying with friends or sleeping in my car. This went on for some time. Nobody knew that I was pretty much homeless at the time.

I was at work one night at the grocery store, and I got a call from the Air Force recruiter. He wanted to know if I could go into the Air Force early. The man that was supposed to go at that time fell ill and couldn't leave then, so the recruiter needed to fill the slot. I was sleeping in my car, basically homeless, so I thought why not? At least then I will have a place to sleep and decent meals each day.

I enlisted and went in early, but because of that, the school for Loadmaster was out of the picture. It was not available at that time. The Air Force then informed me that I was best suited to be an aircraft mechanic. I didn't know the first thing about being an aircraft mechanic, but I loved planes and I knew I just needed to go in.

Air Force Basic Training was easy compared with how I grew up. I can remember a time when dad came home from work. He made cabinets on the side, and he wanted to spray varnish on the cabinets. He told me to clean up the garage, so I did. I cleaned that thing right, because I knew that if he got home and it wasn't clean, I would pay for it.

He sprayed the cabinets and then opened the door of the garage, and some dust came down off the springs of the garage door. Who would have thought, especially a young guy like me at the time? He was about half drunk as usual. He lost it. I remember getting beat with a board, to the point that I had blood running down my legs.

Basic Training was nothing compared to what I grew up with.

To me, it was like an adult playground. I had no problems with that. With my Civil Air Patrol background, I already had a good start on the discipline side of things. I enjoyed it. It was great!

There were a few catches in Basic though. The Drill Instructors would test you to your limits. If you weren't paying attention to detail, you would bear the brunt of that. They would test you to see if they could push you over the line.

I went to Basic at Lackland Air Force Base. I then attended tech school for aircraft maintenance. Back then aircraft were broken down into categories based on the number of engines they had. I went into the field of jets with two engines. I was trained on the B-52 aircraft. That's what my entire tech school was about, but I never saw one again, unless I saw one taking off from Guam or Thailand.

From Tech School, I received orders to go to Grissom Air Force Base in Indiana. That was nineteen miles from my home. I knew with my military background in jet engines, I would be working on the B-58 Hustler. It was a state-of-the-art airplane, but I also knew it would be a four-year assignment, nineteen miles from home. I did not join the Air Force to stay at home.

We were presented with an opportunity to trade in our orders for an overseas assignment. Before the man speaking could finish what he was telling us, I was turning in my orders. He asked where I wanted to go and I said, "I'll even go to Vietnam. I don't care." They took my orders and gave me new ones for the Philippine Islands. I went to Clark Air Force Base in the Philippines in 1969. There I trained on C-141's and C-133's. The entire time I was at Clark, we would get planes in with material for Vietnam. Sometimes this included entire planes of German Shepherds. They used them in Vietnam. When the planes returned from Vietnam, they would be filled with wounded, going back to rear area hospitals. A lot of them still had battle dressings on.

When you are seeing combat wounded men, coming off at a rate of 100-200 per plane, six to seven days a week, it really has an effect on you. The next plane in may be loaded full of caskets. That was tough to see. The C-133's were always out on a hot strip because they would be full of ammo going to Vietnam.

While in the Philippines, I contracted hepatitis. They transferred me to the Outpatient Hospital Squadron. I spent a total of 14 months in the hospital between Clark Air Force Base and Wright Patterson Air Force Base in Ohio, before they could release me. I was promoted twice while I was in the hospital doing nothing. From Wright Patterson, I went to Lockbourne Air Force Base in Columbus, Ohio and was trained on KC-135 Refuelers. I was there for about two and half years.

During my time at Lockbourne, I was sent to the Young Tiger Task Force. We would leave Lockbourne, go to California, Hawaii, and Guam, then over to Thailand. We would fly refuel missions out of Thailand, over Vietnam. We would also do logistics flights, taking VIPs in and around the various areas of operation. Most of my wartime experience was at 38,000 feet above the ground flying refueling missions. They did give us a parachute and a pistol with six rounds, and we were told, "Save the last one for yourself."

If you ever get shot down in a KC-135, just remember that you are carrying 186,000 pounds of fuel, so there's not much chance for you anyway. That pistol, with the six rounds was the only time I carried a weapon during the war. I entered the Air Force in 1968 and left in 1972. I actually met my wife, Pam, about the time I left the Air Force. I met her in a five-car wreck. We got married a month and a half later.

There is nothing particularly funny that I remember about basic Training, but I do remember learning something really quick. I was there, in Texas, in August. It was hot! When standing in formation for any amount of time, the Drill Instructors would tell us, "Light them if you have them." Well, I didn't smoke but I knew to go to the base exchange and buy cigarettes so that I could at least light one and go sit under the shade tree until it burned down. If you didn't have them, then you stood out in the hot sun. I learned how to play that game.

Adapting to the military was not an issue. The discipline was something that I needed at that time in my life. I learned how to function as a part of a team. Attention to detail was key. We had a demerit system, and you always wanted to stay as clean as possible in that regard. Receive too many demerits and the entire squad got punished. The whole idea behind this is to get you to function as a team. Folks used to get demerits for having toothpaste build up in the cap of their toothpaste. Every member would get demerits. We solved that by using one tube of toothpaste for the entire squad. That way, we would only get one demerit. There again, my Civil Air Patrol background came in handy. I knew how to spit-shine shoes and was super crisp on the ironing and starching of uniforms.

The first Crew Chief I had likely had the greatest impact upon me during my time in the Air Force. When I started working with Warren, we were on the KC-135's. He would drill me every day. We would inspect the airplane and he would ask me, what I thought, were off the wall questions. Things like, "Where's the only green light on a KC-135?" He was forcing me to pay attention to detail. To see the minute, little things that may not matter to someone else. That was one of the biggest things that helped carry me into my NASA career.

I was awarded a Good Conduct Medal, The National Defense Medal, Small Arms Marksmanship Badge, Presidential Unit Citation, Outstanding Unit Citation, and the Air Force Longevity Award. The important task as a Crew Chief was making sure the aircraft was ready to go. I had sixty on time launches in a row and was recognized for that with an Air Medal, at least the letter indicated I had been given the award. We left Thailand two weeks later and the paperwork never caught up, so I still haven't received my actual award for that. It's not even on my DD-214. None of my time in and over Vietnam is on my DD-214 either because we were TDY and never actually assigned to a unit there.

Jumping backwards a bit, I should relate that after leaving and being away from the Air Force for several years, my wife and I moved to the small town of Rochester, Indiana, not far from Grissom Air

Base. My wife worked for a cable company and the manager's husband worked at the Air Base. He kept pushing for me to put in for a job at the base. It was called the Air Reserve Technician Program. Just to shut him up, I filled out the paperwork, and two months later they offered me a job working on airplanes. However, you had to be in the Reserves, in order to keep your civilian job.

Back in the 1960's and 1970's, the military was not treated very well when they came home from overseas. It didn't matter where you were coming from, most people who saw you in uniform just assumed you were coming from Vietnam, so you were cussed at, yelled at, and had dog feces thrown at you. Garbage was also thrown at us. It was bad.

With that experience, I really didn't want anything to do with the military again. But just to shut him up again, I filled out the paperwork and they offered me a job. The biggest advantage in this was that as a civil servant, I could also work towards a retirement there. I did 14 years as an Air Reserve Technician. I worked on A-37's, a small ground support fighter; from that I went to the A-10 Close Air Ground Support Bird.

After getting away from the military and civil service, and after the NASA Challenger disaster, NASA started looking for people with aircraft backgrounds. I had completed an application but had no idea if I would be considered. With NASA and their applications, every word must by perfect and lined up. I had no idea of this beforehand. I just filled out the paperwork, sent it to Florida and about eleven months later, they offered me a job. I was hired as a Quality Assurance Specialist on the Space Shuttle.

I had finally reached my childhood dream of working at NASA. I had told the folks back home, when I got the job, that the next time you see me, I will be putting the astronauts into the spacecraft on launch day because I'm going to be Crew Chief on the Shuttle. They all laughed and said it would never happen. It all comes full circle. Once again, I was being told I wouldn't be able to do what

I said I was going to do.

The thing with NASA is that you walk in on day one to the Orbiter Processing Facility. It's nothing but a big hangar with the Shuttle in it. You walk in and start looking around, wondering where the shuttle is, then you look up and you're underneath it. This thing is so big that you're under it and don't even realize it. And you wonder, "What did I get myself into?"

I am now responsible for whatever job I sign off on, on this aircraft. Our job was to watch other people work, to ensure that everything was done right. It goes right back to my paying attention to detail that I had learned in the Air Force. That one small factor made me comfortable with this job. From that point on, I learned everything I could possibly learn about airplanes and the Space Shuttle. The Shuttle is a 240,000-pound glider. That's what it weighs empty. Attention to detail is crucial on the Space Shuttle.

One day we were replacing the Reinforced Carbon Panels, the light gray panels that are on the leading edge of the wings. We had taken all of them off. They had been inspected and we were given the ok to put thcm back together and then reinstall them. I was working with a gentleman, and he didn't like NASA. Nobody liked NASA quality control people to start with. For the most part, it was felt that we didn't know anything. That was our reputation. NASA pretty well deserved that reputation at the time. This was just after the Challenger disaster. There was a lady working in the cafeteria, whom they told, that when she finished her two year degree in quality assurance, they'd give her a job on the Shuttle…putting flight critical equipment on the Shuttle and signing off saying it was "airworthy."

Friday afternoon she finished her degree. Monday morning, she was putting flight critical components on the Shuttle. She didn't know the difference between a nut and a bolt. That was NASA's program. NASA had brought her on. I can't fault her though. Through my time of working with her, she became a very good Quality Assurance Person. But that was the reputation…NASA knew nothing.

I was working with Ron, and we were trying to put these

leading-edge panels back together. He was fighting with one piece, trying to get the bolt in with all the different shims. He fought it for about forty-five minutes to an hour. I finally looked at him and asked if he wanted me to show him how to do it. His quote was, "Yea, if a NASA thinks he can do anything."

So, he turns his back. Keep in mind, that when you are working on or around the Shuttle, all your jewelry must be taped to you or secured to you in some fashion. I had ¼ inch tape around my wedding band, and we had 14 shims there. I took that tape off my ring, taped the shims together and placed them into place with a set of forceps, pushed the bolt in and boom, done in less than two minutes. He looked at me and said, "Where the hell did you come from?" His exact words.

"I spent the last 18 years working on airplanes," was my response. From that point on, that man took me under his wing and taught me everything he knew about that Space Shuttle, to the very minute detail. From that, I received a pretty good reputation as a Quality Assurance person who knew what he was talking about. We had to interact with upper levels of management at times to get things straightened out, so we had to be top notch. I was able to achieve that level of reputation.

I worked for seven years in the Orbiter Processing Facility, where we handled virtually every maintenance aspect of the Shuttle. After every mission, the Shuttle would get a complete overhaul. This was so critical, that even after one mission where the engines of the Shuttle only fired for three tenths of a second and were shut down by the emergency shutoff, the engines were replaced. This was more cost effective because you couldn't always isolate the problem, and it was not an area where a lot of risk could be spared. The system itself is what shut the engines off. The computer will shut the system down for even the slightest irregularity.

Along about this time, NASA started offering some early outs and buy off programs for early retirement. That left some vacancies in the Launch Pad Crew. So, I put in for that job. The only way you get a job on the Launch Pad is if someone dies or someone retires. I was selected and given the opportunity to leave the Orbiter Processing Facility (OPF) and go to the Launch Pad Crew.

Once there, I applied for the "Close Up Crew." That's the guys in the white suits at the top of the Orbiter that are putting the astronauts into the Orbiter. It was the Crew Chief position. As I said, the only way you get that job is if someone retires. When I was selected for the Launch Crew, I was number twenty-six on the list ever, to do that job. You attend about two years' worth of training. One of the hardest parts of the training was the attention to all the tremendous amount of detail; remember, you are responsible for everything that goes into this. Shuttle and everything that comes out of the Shuttle. Even the Styrofoam camera wedges holding the cameras were your responsibility. If things are not properly accounted for, they could be floating around inside the Shuttle and cause equipment or personnel damages. If you missed even the slightest thing, you lost that position.

I conducted my first close out without incident. Several months later, as we were on a rotating cycle, I got to do my second close out. Prior to this, while still in the OPF, I had the opportunity to meet Eileen Collins. She was an Air Force Test Pilot and Pilot in the Shuttle Program. I had the opportunity to train with her and one time I asked her what it took to go from Pilot status to Commander status on the Shuttle. She told me all the requirements and I told her that maybe by the time she became Commander, I would be on the close out Crew that put her into the Shuttle.

As fate would have it, the rotation came up and on my next close out, I put Eileen Collins into the Shuttle as the first female Commander in NASA Shuttle history. During our practice launches, she came up to me and asked if I had remembered our conversation from a couple of years prior. I said, "Yes, kind of…" She said," Yep, well I'm the Commander and your putting me in."

This was STS-95. We had a lot of issues with that flight, and she saved the Shuttle and the crew. The computer system tried to kick the system off because of a coolant issue, but she overrode the computer. There were several other things that developed during that flight that she took charge of and created a safe mission for the entire crew.

I was there at NASA for 106 Shuttle launches over a period of twenty-two years. I officially retired from NASA in 2008. We moved to Tennessee. That didn't work out well, so we came back to Florida, and I ended up back at NASA again. NASA was looking for Shuttle inspectors, but I couldn't go back as a civil servant since I had retired. I went back through the Defense Contract Management Agency, an agency that inspects everything within the government from pencils to rockets.

There was a mixture of emotions when I walked away from government service for the final time. My wife also worked for NASA, and we stayed until the end of the Shuttle Program. When Atlantis landed, she would be going into retirement, and that was the end of the Shuttle program. President Bush was looking for some program that was cheaper. The Shuttle Program was very expensive. We did gain a tremendous amount from the Shuttle program; most people don't have a clue what was gained. Some of these gains can be found in the many NASA spinoffs.

President Obama was running for President and came to visit the Space Center. He promised that there would be no gaps between the Shuttle Program and whatever the next generation program would be. As soon as he was elected, he cancelled both next generation programs that NASA had been running for some time. Some eight-hundred thousand jobs were lost throughout the United States because of that. Over thirteen thousands of those were at the Space Center in Florida.

We left at a very good time, there was no job for NASA Quality anymore. With no more Shuttles, we had no direction. We were no longer producing a viable product. We went from three-hundred inspectors, down to fourteen, and the fourteen were on their way out as well. I am still very proud of the history that we made while

there at NASA. The hardest mission was when Columbia came apart during reentry over Texas. I spent fifty-three days there, picking up pieces and parts of the aircraft. We would later take them to a hangar where we would spend hours examining them and identifying them. Attention to detail came in once again in this
process. In the end, we were able to bring home about sixty-five percent of the aircraft.

My job on the launch pad held tremendous responsibility and brought enormous satisfaction. We were trained in removing the pilots from the craft in the event of an emergency and I had the authority, to stop a launch at any time should I deem things unsafe. I had the responsibility for a multi-billion-dollar craft, astronaut lives, their
families and the lives of the crews on the ground. If you made that call, you just cost NASA three and a half million dollars, so your decision better be well based. There were several instances during launches where my attention to detail prevented a launch from being scrubbed.

I think Vets Helping Vets is a terrific organization. The chance to get out and help another vet is great. While I am unable to do a lot of the physical stuff that the organization does, just being able to help support another vet is awesome. The PTSD group that meets on Mondays is fabulous. Most people do not realize how PTSD affects people. To see men, talk about what that group has done for them is a tremendous thing. I wear my Vets Helping Vets shirt everywhere I can, hoping that people will ask me about it.

Tommy P. Lowe

My name is Thomas Patrick Lowe, but friends and family call me Tommy. I was born in Anderson, South Carolina and graduated from McDuffie High School where students could learn a trade and make a good living for their family. It was a school that taught young men and women how to be self-sufficient. That was back when we were allowed to have shotguns in our trucks for rabbit hunting after school. We were taught from an early age the responsibilities of gun ownership. Almost every household kept a shotgun behind the door and children were taught the dangers. It was a rite of passage for a boy to be given his first hunting gun passed down from an older man in the family.

I took Naval JR. ROTC all three years of high school. Like many of the students, I held a part-time job to pay for tires, gas, and oil in the old beat up, fixer-ups we drove. Taking parts off junk cars at Ed Powell's Garage and doffing spinning frames in the mill helped me pay for a 1955 Bel Air Chevy, two-door post I rebuilt from the ground up. I took my graduation money and what little I saved and had her painted a two-tone Regal Turquoise and India Ivory white.

I went to Tri County Technical College right after graduation while I was still working in the mill. Two years later I married my high school sweetheart, Angela Mason. She had the smarts, and I had the humor, opposites attract, right?

This was early 1980 and the country was in a severe recession. Rumors circulated through the mill that it was closing down. I was working at Equinox Mill in Anderson and was being promoted to the shop: thinking things were looking up. One day while working second-shift, I drove to work only to find the gates locked. We were told we would get some severance pay and could continue for a little while, paying for our own insurance. We were expecting our first child.

I stood in line like everyone else applying for jobs. I took anything I could find. Worked on the frozen ground in the yard of our three room mill house, repairing cars for little pay from those who couldn't afford any more than I could. This was a mill town, and one by one the plants downsized or closed completely. Most of our family was in the same situation. I sold my 1955 Chevy to help pull us through.

In 1982, jobs were scarce, and I was still beating the pavement to find a job. I went by the Military Recruiting office. I told them I had taken ROTC in high school and had done well. The recruiter said I could go in as a PFC. I had a speech impediment since childhood that ran in the family. I was told by my family that because of my stuttering, I would never get in the military…wrong. I signed on the dotted line and took this oath:

"I, Thomas Lowe, do solemnly swear that I will support and defend the Constitution of the United States against all enemies, foreign and domestic…"

I went home to tell Angela the news: I had joined the US Army. Desperate times call for desperate measures. Looking back, we look at it more as a blessing. The door closed for a career in the mill, but the window opened for an opportunity of an education and advancement. The Army gave me an honorable way to provide for my wife and family. I also earned a degree in electronics. Young people today need to realize the benefits of serving in the US Military. There they can find purpose and receive a hands-on education that is lacking in today's education system. The Military gives a hand up not a handout.

July 1982, I headed to Fort McClellan in Anniston, Alabama, for Basic Training. I was used to long hours, hard work and low pay. Experience had taught me all about mind games. They found out I was good at repairing almost anything. This kept me out of pulling extra duty, and I was getting to do things I enjoyed. I can't vouch for the truth of this, but a buddy once swore he had to wake me up during our Class A inspection while standing in formation. He punched me with his elbow and said I was snoring.

It was on to Fort Gordon, Georgia, for Advanced Individual Training as MOS 36K, technical wire operation specialist (my first of several). First Sergeant saw the potential in me of getting things done and recommended me for Drill Instructors Academy. I barely completed the course, but I received my hat and badge. That makes me a winner! Between BNOC (Basic Noncommissioned Officer Course) at Fort Benning, Georgia, and ANOC (Advance Noncommissioned Officer Course) at Fort Bliss, Texas, they spit and polished this ole country boy and made him look and act like new money.

I applied for an AGR (Active Guard Reserve) job with the South Carolina Army National Guard and served with the 2-263rd ADA (Air Defense Artillery). We provided help when natural disasters struck such as Hurricane Hugo. The Federal mission of the National Guard is "To provide properly trained and equipped units for prompt mobilization for war, national emergency or as otherwise needed." Our Battalion received one of the US Army's high-tech weapons that was first used during Operation Desert Storm. During Desert Storm/Shield, I trained at Fort Bliss on the outskirts of El Paso, Texas, on the Hawk Missile Systems. I was MOS 23R40 (Hawk Master Mechanic).

Everywhere I went I made friends with the finest of people of the Military. Their character showed self-confidence not egotism. They were willing to teach and share their knowledge. They lead by example. I could not have made it through without some of these leaders. I decided not to name names, for my memory might leave someone out by mistake. I can only hope I had the opportunity to tell them face to face.

The military took good care of my wife, our two children and me. Once I had injured my lower back and was flown to Walter Reed Medical Center, Washington, DC. The surgeons repaired me and eventually I was back on duty. Years later, after a physical at Fort Gordon, the surgeon informed me I was having emergency surgery on my neck. Unfortunately, after this surgery, I was placed on TDRL (Temporary Disability Retired List) and eventually I was medically retired from the Army.

Throughout my life, I have heard the stories and seen the casualties of war from family and friends. I learned to be a good listener and gained a better perspective of the sacrifices the men and women make for our country. I, like others, would stand up today to protect America and my family.

Veterans never meet a stranger when they meet another veteran. I was sitting in a restaurant eating breakfast when veteran (Gene Cromer) was telling a group of us about an organization called Vets Helping Vets. He told us if we were veterans to come and check it out. I showed up the next Wednesday and I've been there ever since. I never pass up an opportunity to tell other veterans about the support and fellowship we share with each other.

I met Gary Acker at the Chick-Fil-A in Anderson at the Greenville Street location. I saw his 82nd Air Borne hat and told him about our Vets Helping Vets-Anderson meetings. Gary showed up the next Wednesday and sat with his back to the corner at the door. Always having our back, he became known as the Corner Man. I enjoyed listening to the stories he and the others told from week to week. When God called Gary home, there was a void. Remembering those stories that meant so much to me reminds me he is not forgotten.

I asked my wife how we could help the veterans put their stories on paper to share with their family and friends. There is real history of men and women who served in the military, and it needs to be preserved. I'm thankful I have found a place where I can continue to serve in my own way. I am thankful for my wife who has a heart for veterans. Angela found a way to fulfill my request and compiled this book for Vets Helping Vets.

Ron Lupperger

Ronald Paul Lupperger is my name, but I am called Ron. I was named after my biological dad, Paul Lehman Harkins. I was born in Columbus, Georgia. My dad was killed during the Second World War. I was two. He was in the army and was killed in Italy while on maneuvers. He was classified as missing in action for a long time. Later they found that he had run an errand and was blown up in a bank. They found his dog tags, maybe a wallet. He was buried in Italy in a temporary grave site for a while.

The Italian government gave some property for a cemetery and then they transferred the deceased soldiers to the cemetery. His remains could have been brought back here for burial, but by the time I was grown and married, the statute of limitation would not allow it. My wife and I got to visit the cemetery in 2012, along with two first cousins on my mother's side. One cousin was a history teacher and planned the whole trip to Italy. My cousin Glenda was a history teacher, so we went to all these museums.

I would have given anything to bury my dad next to my mom in Jasper, Alabama. The place she was born is now under the water in one of Alabama's man-made lakes. My granddad bought about ten burial plots in Jasper.

I didn't have to go into service because I was a sole surviving son. When I enlisted in the military, I was living in Philadelphia, Pennsylvania, and not doing good in school. My grades were failing so they figured the next best thing was to sign me up for the military. I guess the Navy, at that time, was easy to get in without a high school diploma. I eventually did a correspondence course and received my high school diploma.

I was cold during Basic Training in Great Lakes, Illinois. When I first arrived at the boot camp, we were housed in the old World War Two barracks. They were in the process of building brand new barracks. I think I was in the old barracks maybe two weeks before I was transferred into the new. The ironic thing is, I was only in for 10 months and 10 days.

A funny thing about basic training, I had to guard the dumpster at nighttime, and it was cold. I must have guarded it well for no one ever bothered it. I adapted well to the military life for a seventeen-year-old kid. My first duty was to the USS Sierra which is a destroyer tender. It was an auxiliary ship designed to give maintenance support. It was tied up to the dock and I still get seasick. Then I reported to the USS Holder which was a destroyer submarine chaser. I was a fireman apprentice.

At the end of my service, my ship was going in for modernization. They gave the crew a choice of either having ship duty or shore duty. I took shore duty and was assigned to the bakery, stationed in Norfolk, Virginia. My job the first day was to deliver this great big cart full of cakes, cookies, and pies. The head baker told me to be careful with ruts going to the mess hall. Believe it or not, I hit a rut and the cart started going over. I pulled it back and I had cakes, pies, and cookies all over me. The Chief wanted to kill me. Well, I ended up with a broken foot and in the hospital with a cast in on my on my right leg. That's how I got out of service.

I came out with the cast, and it took some time for it to heal. When I turned 21 years old, Mom gave me the money she had been saving for me from the money sent to her for Dad's death. My stepdad was the best dad you could imagine for a stepdad. I cherished him and he treated me right. Mom was very protective. He adopted me and gave me his name, too. I lost him in an automobile accident.

I put a down payment on a truck, went to a school in Indianapolis, Indiana, and went to work with Mayflower Van Lines because my stepdad was a truck driver. I was owner operator of a stub nose GMC gas truck with a single axle tractor. I hauled furniture all over the United States for two years. I was a young man living the dream, not a care in the world. Hauling furniture, loading, and unloading will make an old man of you quickly, especially being on the road four weeks in a row with no end in sight. I eventually bought a burgundy freightliner with chrome, end to end.

I have been married to my wife, Arlys, for fifty years. She was a farmer's daughter, still in school and working as a waitress. It was a long-distance romance of writing letters for a while. We married in the Lutheran Church of Waco, Nebraska. I stayed on the road for 39 years. I bought property to retire in South Carolina because I had relatives here. Truck drivers are the lifeline of America. Everything can be hauled on the railroad to a certain extent but then it has to get from the rail to the little train town that doesn't have the rail system.

My granddad and uncles on my mother side were carpenters and contractors. I enjoy woodworking, too. A talent handed down. My mom was given a handmade table by my Granddad. He used Tennessee redwood with wedges and a lazy Susan in the middle. I passed it to my son and daughter-in-law as a wedding present. Granddaddy turn the legs on a homemade lathe and chiseled it off. He was an invalid in a wheelchair, and he was proud of that table.

As I mentioned, I did not have to be in the service because I was the sole surviving son. I got an honorable discharge with mention of medical terms attached. I may not have liked the Navy but I'm proud to have served. Jesse Taylor of Vets Helping Vets noticed my Navy hat and invited me to my first meeting. I visited and joined. I feel we are all brothers and sisters, and it doesn't matter what branch, rank, or length of service. We, as veterans, can make a difference in each other's lives.

Something life taught me: ask the questions to grandparents and parents now while you still can and encourage others to ask questions. If it is something that you don't want to answer, tell them why.

Norman Mason

I am a native of Oconee County, South Carolina. I live at the same location now. My name is Norman Cleveland Mason. Levi was the nickname I had in high school because of the blue jeans I wore, with the cuffs rolled up. I graduated from Pendleton High School in 1957.

I enlisted on November 22, 1961, in the U. S. Air Force to keep from being drafted into the Army. I wanted to learn a trade that the army didn't offer, and I wanted to keep from sitting in foxholes with water up to my waist. Basic Training was different from civilian life or any job I had worked. I became more involved with other boots and learned how to cooperate. The Air Force welded us into a unified group. I laughed at the things that happen to others on the obstacle course. In between the fun, I learned to respect and salute officers, obey NCOs, and carry out orders.

In January 1962, I was assigned to Chanute Air Force Base, Illinois, to attend Tech School to prepare me for working on an aircraft's electrical system. From there I was assigned to a permanent base at Donaldson Air Force Base in Greenville, South Carolina. I began OJT (on the job training) to work on aircraft and their components.

I left Donaldson AFB in March of 1963 and went to Hunter Air Force Base in Savannah, Georgia. Donaldson's base was closed and the whole unit transferred. I served four years. Other places I was deployed for TDY (Temporary Duty) was Rhein-Main Air Force Base, Germany; Myrtle Beach Air Force Base, South Carolina; Fort Sill, Oklahoma; and Belgian Congo, Africa.

On November 22, 1965, I reenlisted. In 1966, I got orders that assigned me to Takhli Royal Airforce Base in Thailand. I worked on F-105s and a little on EB-66s (Electronic Bombers). We had two crews. If I got bored, I'd go help the guys on the other crew.

I also worked at the Battery Shop charging batteries and

building silver zinc batteries. We'd go to Japan for technical training for the F-105 and visit the Philippines for a couple of days. Undoubtedly, they didn't know we had received OTJ (on the job training) for them, which is better than a textbook any day.

I was assigned to the 355th Field Maintenance Squadron (FMS). The aircraft at my station were fighter bombers used as support during Vietnam, flying missions in North Vietnam and the Ho Chi Minh trail. Aircraft often came in with battle damage. One of them that come in took an artillery shell through the wing, cutting a fuel line. This forced the aircraft to hook up to a fuel tanker to keep enough fuel in it to keep the engine running. They made it to the base until the end of the runway and disconnected as planned. We went to check logs for work orders and noticed the pilot had written the last item in the log, "Thank God for this aircraft. It brought me home." A prayer answered.

As an Airman First Class, I was chosen for Escort Duty for Lyndon B. Johnson and Lady Bird (the President's wife's nickname) as they entertained at the palace in Bangkok. I received a bronze Presidential medallion with these words engraved: "On the occasion of the Asian-Pacific visit October - November 1966 - To continue the search for peace on every front, however long the road." Lyndon B. Johnson, President of the United States of America. I was also given a silver-colored Zippo lighter, embellished with the presidential seal and President Johnson's signature.

Meeting Frank Sinatra, Jr. and seeing Ann Margaret, Patti Paige and Phyliss Diller perform at the Bob Hope Show was exciting at the time but was not the only excitement. We were issued electric fans to cool our barracks or Quonset huts. The fans did not relieve the heat but proved to be a determent for the mosquitoes. Many times, we saw footlong rats crawl across beds making grown men such as me spring out of bed to attention. One of the crew headed back to the barracks from the latrine had a Siamese Viper snake strike his leather boot. From then on, he received the reputation for being the best two-step Charlie of the crew.

Often, I headed to chow, not feeling excited about the prospects. I had checked into sickbay for the excruciating stomach pain. The doctor looking over his glasses and speaking in a half serious tone explained that I should avoid the chow hall. Of course, that was not an option, so he dispensed a huge bottle of "horse pills" for me to take for indigestion.

Two-hundred ninety-five days later I got orders to transfer to another PCS (Permanent Change of Station) in Pease Air Force Base, New Hampshire. It took me sixteen hours from Bangkok to Travis Air Force Base, California. I caught a bus from there to San Francisco International Airport. I caught a plane to Atlanta, Georgia. I rode a bus to Seneca, South Carolina, to take some leave time back home. I was anxious to see family, before traveling with my wife and two kids on to New Hampshire. February 1967, I got housing for my wife and kids on the base and went to work in the 509th Field Maintenance Squadron's electrical shop. Later that year I went TDY for more technical training to Chanute Air Force Base, Illinois.

In February 1968, I had surgery in Chelsea Naval hospital, Massachusetts for kidney stones. I stayed at Pease until July 23, 1969, just four months of my official military discharge. The Air Force medically discharged me for a back injury and sent me back home to South Carolina. I kept my interest in new aircraft and have lived to see amazing machinery.

In a way I was glad to be home, but it was harder now because I had to find a job, find housing for my family, and settle into civilian life. I am thankful for how the military gave me more confidence in myself and the ability to solve problems. I have enjoyed being part of the group of Vets Helping Vets Anderson. It is like old times when I had the support of my buddies, their friendship and conversation.

The military is set up to run efficiently by all the ranks and MOSs. Example: It takes at least eight different personnel to operate one aircraft. It's only as strong as its weakest link. I'm reminded of the story of the little boy who had a bunch of sticks and tried to break them together. He could easily break one maybe two, but he could never break all of them at the same time. I want to see everyone get along, respect each other's heritage and history, and not destroy it. Together we can keep America the strong nation it has always been.

.

Larry Morelock

I was about five years old when my dad took me for one of those orientation flights in Indianapolis near the local airport. Right then, I knew I wanted to be a pilot. My name is Larry Dean Morelock, and I was born in 1949. When I was in college my fraternity brothers called me Larry Dean. I really didn't have a nickname in the Air Force. Flying tankers like I did; we didn't have tactical call signs like the fighter jocks. I ended up with one from doing some ground projects at one of my bases and for some reason it was Ramrod, but it didn't stick

I wanted to fly, and I didn't know how I was going to be able to do it. My dad wanted me to go to college. I chose to go to Purdue University in Lafayette, Indiana. I was in the class of '67 in high school and went to see the counselor at the university on high school day. I told him how I really wanted to become a pilot. He sent me over to talk to the Air Force ROTC detachment. I enrolled in ROTC in my freshman year, the fall of 1967 and continued until I graduated February 1, 1972. I had to stay an extra semester to get done and that's when I met my lovely wife, Susan.

I was commissioned, February 1, 1972, and entered pilot training May of 1972 in Del Rio Texas at Laughlin Air Force Base. I graduated in April 1973 and got my assignment. I chose the KC-135 tanker to do inflight refueling, and I was assigned in those years to Strategic Air Command. From there, I went to another school at Castle Air Force Base in California and got my Copilot training on the aircraft and then after that survival training at Fairchild Air Force Base in Washington State. It was in the summertime, so I didn't have to deal with the Washington winters. Then I went to Water Survival Training in Florida at McConnell Air Force Base.

My wife and I got married April 1st, 1972, so she was with me the whole time and was a blessing. She helped me study, and she encouraged me to get through all these schools. I was stationed at Barksdale Air Force Base in Bossier City, Louisiana, for about six years. The nearest big city, Shreveport, was right across the Red River. It was during the time when the Vietnam War was still going on. Tankers would be going over on what we called Young Tiger Temporary Duty Assignments for three to six months. I wanted to go but every crew that I got put on had already been there and they didn't want to go back right away. I finally was sent over around March 1974. I think our government administration had declared that it was no longer a war zone.

I didn't get credit for a Vietnam tour. As a copilot, I flew tanker missions out of Kadena Air Base in Okinawa, Japan, Andersen Air Force Base, Guam, and out of U-Tapao AB, Thailand. I got a taste of what it was like as far as the air side of it. The one thing about tankers is anywhere they send fighters or bombers or any other aircraft that's capable of being refueled, inflight tankers are there. We've been called the force multiplier; always giving fuel prior to whatever mission they're probably doing, and that allows planes to get there and do their mission. Tankers are right there in the mix of it.

In the six years at Barksdale AFB, I went from being a copilot on the aircraft to being an aircraft commander. I became an instructor pilot and then an evaluator. I worked my way up through that in different schools. That brought us back to California on a temporary basis to go through some of those schools. My wife, always traveling with me, kept a job and the house. We've been married for 50 years. I would like to give Susan the credit she deserves.

I had several TDYs (Temporary Duty) to the Tanker Task Force based in the Pacific, Europe, and Alaska. The crews refueled aircraft in those geographic areas. The military thought any war was going to be fought with heavy bombers and nuclear weapons. SAC was commissioned in March 1946.This continued until 1992 after the Soviet Union's fall in 1991 when they finally took the tankers and bombers off of alert status. We had B52s and KC135s on standby at every SAC base (Strategic Air Command).

The main job in SAC, especially after the Vietnam, era was sitting on alert. If the horn went off and there was any kind of nuclear conflict, the bombers had targets all over the world. We were tasked to refuel those bombers. For the six years I was stationed at Barksdale AFB, every third week I was assigned to a crew ready to respond to an alert, besides other flying duties. In our case, we had to be sitting on alert, ready to go to war in seven minutes. That's how quickly we had to be off the ground. We still have missiles and missile silos that are on alert. Plus, support for any other conflicts.

When I received Permanent Change of Station (PCS) to go to Castle Air Force Base, California as an instructor, my life got to be a little bit more normal. I got picked for a TDY in Naples, Italy for a big exercise with Allied Forces as part of NATO. We would be picked up from our hotels every morning and taken out to the mountains where we worked out of old WWII bunkers that were drilled back into caves. About a mile back into the cave was like a whole city guarded by big blast doors. Representatives from NATO nations, side by side, not all of them friendly with each other. We would be back there for days during this exercise. I was doing things associated with tanker business like planning and developing where we could refuel when they came with a mission. It was interesting to see the construction of such a place and know all over the world places like this exist.

I was promoted up the ranks and while I was at Castle AFB, I was promoted to Major. Most of the time, you stay two to three years at a base. I stayed six because the change of command kept us longer. I almost had an assignment to Zaragoza, Spain to serve on the Tanker Task Force there. Someone must have wanted it a lot more and it fell through at the last minute. A job came open at the Illinois Air National Guard flying a KC-135 in an active duty position. An active duty Air Force Advisor was assigned to each Guard unit in SAC. They wanted a pilot which is logical. I got the job. The navigator that I had flown with at Barksdale AFB, Mike Seymore, was at this Guard unit. It was the 126th Air Refueling Wing Illinois Air National Guard at Chicago. Mike and I had been was and how to have better crew coordination.

He had been sent there to instruct Guard Navigators when they were transitioning from their previous plane to the KC-135.

The Guard unit would ask me to go TDY with them and support a variety of assignments. I traveled all over the world. Germany, Iceland, Italy, England, wherever they needed a tanker. Eventually that took me to Desert Shield and Desert Storm. I always wanted to go to Australia but that's one place I didn't get to.

The Guard unit was flying missions out of Iceland at the time the Soviet Union was still in existence. We would be up there for two weeks with two crews and one airplane, and we would rotate. I had one crew and another pilot who was an American Airlines captain had the other crew. Our job was to support the F-15s that they had at that base. Their job was to intercept the Russian bear as it would come down through the gap. It would be heading over towards the United States and down our coast and into Cuba.

Once they got word that one of those was coming that way, they would scramble the fighters. We would launch right behind them and follow them. Basically, as soon as they got within a certain range of the bomber, they dropped back on us and refueled. Then, they would go up and be on the bomber's wing tips. Actually, we were a kind of escort, letting him know we are here. Tankers knew how far we were supposed to stay behind the bear. The fighters could just drop back from us about two miles. We used radar and our navigator made sure we were there flying in formation. I ask an intelligence officer at a briefing why the two miles. He said he figured that was the range of their gun on their tail. It was a great joy to fly with the Guard unit for those years. I was there to evaluate them, also with their mission.

I was at the Guard unit as their advisor when Desert Shield/Desert Storm happened. We deployed right away. I flew a whole lot of missions as we were building up and doing training. We were based in Moron, Spain for the tankers and were fueling, going through the Mediterranean. Later, they moved our entire wing to Saudi Arabia at the port of Jedda on the Red Sea. The entire unit was mobilized, the airplanes, mechanics, and support. Before Desert Shield was totally over, they moved our wing over to Abu Dhabi in the United Arab Emirates, which is on the Persian Gulf. We flew the entire war out of there. I got tagged to fly the first mission of the first night of the war. That night we refueled four F-4 Wild Weasels with targets in Kuwait.

One day, the flight crews were assembled under a big tent out in the desert, watching a televised interview. President Bush was asked why not just bring everybody home and get out like you did in Vietnam. He said, "No I'm not doing that to our military personnel. I'm letting them finish the job." You should have heard the roar that went up. I think we had the right general as the commander, General Schwarzkopf.

My navigator and I had served together for two years, and we flew about 126 combat hours supporting all kinds of fighters. We had a lot of Vietnam Veterans in our unit that had flown fighter type aircraft and airline pilots as well. They made a great team and built up our confidence. When it came time to come home, we flew formation all the way from United Arab Emirates to the United States into Chicago O'Hare International Airport. The tower let us make a fly-by and the four tankers spread out together, came around, landed, and taxied in.

Everybody including family members, and officials from the Governor's office was there. The press interviewed us. I was asked what the difference in coming home from Vietnam. I will tell you; it almost makes me cry now, knowing so many guys that were in our unit that had Vietnam background. They didn't get anything like we experienced when they came home from Vietnam. A few weeks later Chicago had a ticker tape parade and who do we see on the sidelines but Vietnam Veterans who came out to show their respect to us. Knowing what they went through made me wish they would join with us to march together. I was reminded of the time, while in ROTC at Purdue University, when we were told not to wear our uniforms to or from campus. Sad times for what had once been a conservative college. At another parade, we decided to break rank and go over and shake the Vietnam Veteran's hands who had cared enough to support us. We knew the sacrifices they made for our rights to march down Main Street America. We got our chance to say thank you, and they should have had these kinds of parades.

Before I retired, I received a humanitarian trip with the Guard unit. It was to go and assist with our Medical Unit to Senegal, Africa. We spent two weeks out in the jungle in villages and such. The Medical Unit was providing medical treatment to anybody there. We were on the support side of the mission which included flying, security, MREs (meals ready to eat) and taking photographs.

I retired from the Air Force the 1st of June 1992. At the same date that the Air Force retired the Strategic Air Command (SAC). We now have what's called Strategic Command and it is a combination of the Air Force and the Navy. The US Air Force has the bomber side of the nuclear and missiles, while the US Navy has the submarines with their missiles. If they ever have to go to nuclear
war, then they all come together under that one command at Offutt Air Force Base in Omaha, Nebraska. They still have the underground command post there.

I moved back to Castle Air Force Base after I retired and went to work in a job with Flight Safety International. They had won the contract to do the ground training and simulator training for the KC 135, so it was all Air Force guys, and some of us knew each other. I did that until they were closing that base and moving it to Altus AFB, Oklahoma. I got a job with Reno Air flying out of San Jose, California, which was just about a two hour commute from where we lived in the Central Valley. I flew for Reno Air for five years and went from being a copilot to an aircraft commander. A captain on the MD 80. McDonald Douglas 80 series aircraft is a commercial airliner. By August of 1999, we all became part of American Airlines. I flew as a captain right away at American Airlines, for six months, until they merged our seniority list.

Most all of the captains I flew with were younger than me and still learning. They would listen to me because they knew I was older and had been through a lot and trained a lot. Some were Navy guys, and they didn't land the airplane very well because they were used to slamming down on carrier decks. All I've ever done is fly big airplanes, landing on the ground. I retired from American Airlines at 60 years of age, May 2009. My wife gave a speech at the retirement ceremony. She said to be careful what you wish for because it may come true. She explained how I had joined the US Air Force and stayed in at the ten year point, but I wanted to fly the big silver jets of American Airlines, and I did.

We stayed in California from 2009 until 2018. I served on the board of directors of the Castle Air Museum. In 2019, we moved to South Carolina to be near nephews who were living in the Greenville, SC area. When we visited, we really were impressed. We moved into our house on Lake Hartwell, Seneca, February 2020 just when COVID hit. I am a member of the Order of Daedalians (military flyers fraternal organization), Military Officers Association of America, and the Elks Lodge. I visited the Anderson, SC Elks Lodge and was invited to attend the Vets Helping Vets meeting. At the first meeting, I saw what VHVA stood for. It was impressive because as the name implies, they are about helping other veterans with their needs. They are people who want to contribute to veteran organizations monetarily or with their labor where they can see the benefits.

Today's younger generation could benefit from John F. Kennedy's statement, "Ask not what your country can do for you, but what you can do for your country." I am a big believer that high school graduates not going to college immediately need to go and serve our country. The rewards would be earning money for college and a better understanding of what it means to work for what you desire.

Doug Moses

My name is Douglas L. Moses Sr., and this is my story. In June of 1972, a day after I had landed a job since I left college, I received a notice to report for a physical at the Federal Building in downtown Cleveland, Ohio. Three months later I was drafted into the U.S. Army. It was an event that changed the trajectory of my life.

Growing up in Cleveland in the 60's was not easy for me as a young black man. I have seen first-hand my share of injustices and being drafted to protect this way of life seemed counterproductive to me. Yet, being in the Army started me on a path of self-awareness and self-discipline. I no longer had my family and friends to fall back on; I had to learn to stand on my own.

My first airplane ride was from Cleveland to Fort Polk, Louisiana for basic combat training. Upon arrival to the Reception Station, I had decided to put forth my best effort so that I could learn how to survive. The leaders back home always preached to us to take advantage of every opportunity placed before us and I had hoped to be more than just a "bullet stopper."

My junior high school gym teacher used to tell us that many of us would wind up in Vietnam so he would march us around the neighborhood. He told us that if we knew how to march and call cadence that chances were that we would be offered a leadership position. His words were prophetic. My squad leader made me his assistant and when he fell out of one run too many, the Drill Sergeant made me the Squad Leader. From that moment, I knew that I had to set a good example for my squad, platoon, and company.

Basic was a challenge for me because I had never fired a weapon or run a mile. I didn't know what a compass or a protective mask was. The Gas Chamber, filled with tear gas, was particularly memorable for me because when "gas" was yelled out, we had to don our protective masks in nine seconds. In my haste to put my mask on and clear it, I tossed my helmet and hit my CO on his ankle instead of placing my helmet on the barrel of my weapon. My CO picked it up and told me that I could get it back from him inside the chamber. Once inside, I had to remove my mask and state my name, rank, serial number, and any other information he requested before I could walk out. I never missed the barrel of my weapon again.

Rewards in basic training were few. Our platoon had neither made Honor Platoon nor Goon Platoon. We were always average. We kept working and making improvements and towards the end of the cycle, after an in ranks inspection and a barracks inspection, we were finally the Honor Platoon. We were marched down to the local auditorium where we saw Jeannie C. Riley in concert. I didn't know who she was then, but I appreciated the time off.

Waiting on orders for AIT (Advanced Individual Training) was stressful for draftees because unlike the volunteers, we had no say in what our job would be. I was ordered to Fort Sam Houston in San Antonio, Texas, to begin training as a combat medic. AIT was an education for me. Protecting the patient was paramount, which meant learning how to dress wounds, to reduce infections, to give immunizations, to assist doctors and nurses as needed, to evacuate the wounded, to recognize illness, and to start IV's and catheters. Most of the wounds I saw were either simulated in the classroom or on film during training.

A memorable event in AIT was the Criminal Investigation Division busting several medics for drug abuse. Among them were a high school classmate and my next-door neighbor. I never saw either one again as my orders came down for Germany. My permanent duty station was O'Brien Kaserne, Schwabach, West Germany. I was assigned to the 1st Armored Division, the 2 Battalion 59 Air Defense Artillery.

It was March of 1973 when I arrived in Schwabach. Before I could claim my bunk and wall locker, I was sent to supply to draw my TA50. As soon as I had signed for the equipment, I was put on a truck and taken to Grafenwöhr training site where I spent the next two-weeks as a field medic. We supported the artillery batterie in the field by holding sick-call, treating sprains, frostbite, and other field related injuries. After the field exercise, I signed in at HHB 2/59 ADA. Headquarters had eight medics including me, and since I was the newest, I was tasked with maintaining the medical records for both units on post. Maintaining medical records was not covered in AIT so I had to read the regulations. To maintain the skills I learned in AIT, the Clinical Specialist would allow me to take TPR's (temperature, pulse, and respiration), dress wounds and observe some procedures.

Shortly after my arrival, the doctor assigned to the Battalion Aid Station received a PCS'd (Permanent Change of Station), and a new doctor arrived to replace him. His arrival would change the course of my career. The Army needed to get a handle on the drug and alcohol abuse problem. Community Drug and Alcohol Centers (CDAAC) were set up on various posts with the intent of giving the soldiers a place to go for help. The doctor assigned me as the intake clerk for the soldiers seeking help.

Most of the soldiers volunteered but some were ordered to get help. Included in the program was random urine sampling. There were strict guidelines for gathering, storing, and shipping the specimens. I was involved in the program until Congress declared it unconstitutional shortly before my ETS in September 1974. My time on active duty was toward the end of the Vietnam War and I never saw any combat. However, while serving in Germany, I saw some of the effects the war had on the servicemen, and I did what I could to help them cope. I'd like to think that the 1 year, 11 months and 21 days on active duty made a difference and I believe that the Army did too since I was up for promotion to SGT E-5 when I got out which was virtually unheard of for a draftee.

I got to know several soldiers during my time in Germany. Since I was one of the last draftees, most of them either PCS'd or ETS'd (Expiration-Term of Service) before me. I did stay in touch with one friend after he and his family moved home to Virginia

After about 15 years, I went to visit them and to meet their child that I had helped name. That was almost 30 years ago, and I haven't heard from them again. That is indicative of my time in the. service both active and reserves. It is a tight knit group until people start to leave. I'm sure there was more I could have done to keep in touch but so could they.

My wife left Germany about a month before I did. A few days later she called to let me know that we were expecting our first child. The marriage didn't last but we had 2 great sons of whom I am very proud. When I got home, I knew that I had to find work and fast. After about 2 weeks of looking, I found a job in Columbus, Ohio. That entry level job as a machine operator started me on my career in manufacturing in the oil pipeline, aerospace, and automotive industries.

My grandfather served in WWI. My uncle served in WWII. My brother served in Korea. None of them ever spoke of their experiences in the military. Once I was drafted, the only option I had was to serve honorably. My time in the service was not always good but I managed to make the best of a bad situation. But once I was out of the service, I realized how much I missed the comradery and discipline. In 1983, after being out of the service for nearly 9 years, I joined the U.S. Army Reserves.

I held several positions in the reserves including Medic, Patient Administration Specialist, Reenlistment NCO and finally First Sergeant of a Transportation Company. In 1990, the 2291st USAH was mobilized to Kenner Army Hospital, Fort Lee, Virginia during Desert Storm. During the drawdown after Desert Storm, my job was to find units for the displaced reservists or help them transition out of the military. The First Sergeant position was the most rewarding because I was able to pull a fragmented and undisciplined unit together through NCO development and have meaningful training for the soldiers. I retired from the Army in 2001 before the big event of that year.

In 2003, I married my current wife, she has been the one constant in my life. She keeps me on the straight and narrow because I need it. She is the blessing that I will never understand, but maybe I'm not supposed to. Hopefully, she knows how much she is appreciated and loved. She brought a beautiful daughter into the marriage who is just like one of my own.

Joining Veterans Helping Veterans Anderson has given me an opportunity to get to know vets from different walks of life. I have had the opportunity to help veterans with the challenges of growing old to the challenges of dealing with the horrors of war. All veterans should be treated with respect.

One nation, under God, indivisible, with liberty and justice for ALL.

Mathew Muth

My name is Matthew Todd Muth and as a kid, I had a nickname – Turkey. The backstory to that nickname came about in this way. In November of 1965, I had to have an operation for intussusception, because my small and large intestines were intertwined instead of laying out normally like they should be. So, they had to go in and take care of that. No one knew what that was, they only knew that I was born in June and by November, I was starving to death. Every time I ate something, I threw it back up. My brothers, who are all older than me, said "Our turkey weighs more than he does." So, they started calling me Turkey. That nickname just stuck with me. I didn't lose it until I went into the service.

I served in the Marine Corps for thirteen years, then I did a couple of years in the Navy Reserves. Following that, I went into the Army National Guard, and I retired from there. I enlisted into the Marine Corps in September 1983 right out of high school. I had gone down to the MEPS station because I wanted to go into the Army and into Special Forces, but they told me at the MEPS Station that my eyesight was too bad, and I could not go into Special Forces. So, I simply said, "I'm not doing it," and I left.

I had a buddy at the same time who was going into the Marine Corps, but the time for me to ship off to boot camp had already passed, so they put me on the delayed entry program. He was a year behind me, so they put us together and we would go to boot camp at the same time the next year.

I started taking some college courses at the time, but I began to get restless, and they decided they needed to get rid of me. To take care of this, they sent me off to boot camp. My mom took me to the bus station on Christmas Day, in the evening, to catch the bus to the MEPS Station in Beckley, West Virginia.

Marine Corps Basic Training was not all that difficult for me. I had played sports all through high school, so physically, I was prepared for the challenge. At that time, we didn't have all the video games of today, so we were always outside doing something. Physically, I didn't have a problem with it. For me, it was more the mental aspect of being told where to go, when to be there. For me it was the trick of learning how to stay out of the eyesight of the Drill Instructors.

But try as I might, even that didn't work. My bunkmate, whose name was McCormick, from Long Island, NY., was always into something. He couldn't march in step and was always just messing up. They called him "Captain Quarterdeck." When he got into something, the drill instructors would always call out, "Captain Quarterdeck, come here and bring your two Wonder Friends with you." Since I was his bunkmate, I was always called with him, along with another recruit who had joined on the buddy system with him. Of course, I didn't want to do that, but it was the nature of basic training.

We had another guy; his name was West. He was this big, muscular guy who felt that he wasn't getting enough of a workout, so he would be across from us in line in the squad bay and he would be cutting up, laughing, and making jokes causing us to laugh. The drill instructors would ask why you were laughing and of course we would point to Private West, and they would call all of us out. West loved that because he wanted to extra physical training. We didn't!

I still remember my Senior Drill Sergeant. I can't tell you his name, but he was short, and I always remember him talking about being a machine gunner in Vietnam on Hill 881. He got wounded on Hill 881 and he always talked about that. In our squad bay, he had a little table set up and it was all about that battle on Hill 881. The other two Drill Sergeants were these two huge guys. It was quite hilarious because the Senior Drill Instructor was probably 5' 5" and these other two guys were 6' 4" – 6' 5". I remember the Senior Drill Instructor because he was hard, but he was caring. He understood where you were coming from. I mean, he had been there, and he would take the time to work with you one on one to assist you in overcoming your shortcomings.

McCormick is the one boot camp classmate that I remember the most. The funny part about that was that he and I were both infantry and we graduated together. We both went home, came back, and checked into Infantry School together. We went to our first duty station in the Philippines together. When we completed that and came back stateside, we checked into the same infantry platoon together. He stayed in for four years, and I reenlisted, but for those first four years we stayed together the entire way. I am happy to say that we are still friends. He went back to New York and became a police officer, and we still connect on Facebook.

For me, one of the major lessons I took away from the Marine Corps was the discipline. Prior to boot camp, I was young and got up when I wanted to get up, did what I wanted to do, within reason with my parents. It was during boot camp that I learned why that discipline was needed and was always present. It was the discipline of blind obedience. You learned to react from memory, from what you had trained so hard to learn. You didn't have to think about things, you simply reacted from memory. That discipline has stuck with me for all these years.

My family's history with the military is rich. My dad enlisted in the military in either 1944 or 1945. He, like many others, had to fudge a bit on his age to enlist. He wanted to be a Marine. He went down to enlist in the Marines, and they wouldn't take him because he was too short. He was only five foot five, so he ended up joining the Army. He was initially stationed in Panama, because he had four or five brothers who were already serving in the Pacific at the time. My grandfather migrated from Germany, so they were first generation Americans, and they were not allowed to fight in the European Theater because they still had relatives fighting on the German side. With this in mind, they sent my dad to Panama, and he continued to serve until he retired in 1975. My dad was originally an artillery guy until he went into Special Forces, in the early sixties, just when

Special Forces were being given the recognition they sought. My dad was part of that standup of the Green Berets when they first began. After that, all my brothers served. They served in Special Forces as well. I was the only one who went into the Marine Corps. Me and my son is now serving in the South Carolina National Guard. He's the last one of us that is serving.

At the time I enlisted, I was living in Huntington, West Virginia. That is my home. I was always going to join the military. I was simply following my dad's footsteps. I had seen that tradition. My dad was my idol, and that's the whole reason I joined.

There is not one particular moment in basic training that sticks out in my mind as funny. However, there is a memory that does stick out, but it took place closer to the time I was set to retire. We were flying into Albania in 1995. We had the four-man tents and all the other equipment we would need because we were going to be there for an extended period. I had the four-man tent, and a five-gallon water-can strapped to my rucksack. When I came down the ramp of the helo, I hit an ice patch and ended up on my back. I was like a turtle…laying on my back and couldn't get up. My teammates had to come get me up, my feet couldn't touch the ground. I was in quite the predicament.

I did serve in other branches of the military as well. While I served most of my career in the Marine Corps, I did serve as well in the Navy Reserves. For the Marine Corps and the Navy Reserves, there really is no comparison. I didn't like the Navy Reserves; there was no real structure to it. We'd come to our weekend drills and sit in a classroom and talk about all the special training we were going to do the next time we came together, but we ended up not doing it then either. It was all just really boring so I got out of it as soon as I could.

When I first transferred over to the Army, I was assigned to an Anti-Aircraft Battery. I was not MOS qualified for that unit, being an infantryman, but once I got over to the Infantry unit, it was much like the Marine Corps with the discipline and training. It was a lot more focused and structured.

This broad experience within multiple branches of the military showed me that within the active-duty side, there are not really a whole lot of differences as far as discipline and all those types of things. Every branch has their discipline. There are different rules and different terminologies, but after I had joined the Army and went overseas, all the skills from the Marine Corps came back. It was just muscle memory. The skills I relied upon just kept clicking.

Over the last twenty years of this Global War on Terror I served overseas in Iraq from 2009 – 2010. I was in the "Triangle of Death" just south of Baghdad. We ran patrols everyday…two, three, even four times a day with the 30th Infantry Brigade, 1/120th, Bravo Company. I was a sergeant, E-5, so I was a team leader while there. I also deployed to Afghanistan, but that was at a later point in time. When I deployed there, it was with the Signal Brigade Headquarters because they were short on people, and I was just a warm body working in the supply shop. I didn't leave the Forward Operating Base while in Afghanistan, so all my combat experience came from my time in Iraq.

My thoughts on my first actual combat engagement came during a patrol in which we had lost a Raven, a small drone like device. We had been given orders to go to a cache site to dig it up. We took the Raven and put it in the air for extra security. Over time, the Raven decided to go its own way and flew off into the distance. The military, in their great wisdom, said, "That thing is worth thirty-five thousand dollars, so you need to go find it." Given those orders, we attempted to determine just how far the aircraft would have flown in that direction before it lost radio contact and crashed.

We moved into that area and began searching for this thing in the middle of the night. Sometime around early morning, we took some sniper fire from a nearby schoolhouse. With the Rules of Engagement as they were, we were not able to return fire because it was coming from a schoolhouse. We got out of that situation by simply turning around and walking away. very effective anyway, they couldn't hit the broadside of a barn, so we just went back to the vehicles, called it in and left the area.

My two deployments overseas were vastly different. In Iraq we were out doing patrols and other combat related operations. I never left the security of the Forward Operating Base in Afghanistan. I tried to find ways to get off the base and into other outlying areas, but it was simply not to be. Iraq on the other hand was a different story. There we were always on edge, we were on patrol every day, something was always going on. We worked the Main Supply Routes, the villages, and public areas. One night as we were preparing to leave the base area, another company from our unit was also scheduled to meet with a group of elders from a local village. Enroute to this meeting, they got hit with an IED. They were ambushed. It destroyed the HUMVEE and killed the four soldiers inside. Since we were "on deck" if you will, we proceeded straight out to the spot where this occurred. We spent the entire night there picking up the remaining pieces of the vehicle and the soldiers who were killed.

I cannot say that this overwhelmed me. It did shock me, but at the same time, you expected those things over there. You knew it would eventually happen. You're just dealing with it. The loss of these men didn't affect me immediately. I mean, you're still out there, on edge, and you are doing what you must do. The part that affects you most is that before you can actually begin picking up all these pieces, you have to wait for the cycle of destruction to end. The vehicle has been hit and was on fire. The ammunition and rockets onboard the vehicle continued to go off and you had to wait for that to clear.

When you're out there picking up the pieces and a medic tells you, "Hey, that's not part of the vehicle. That's actually melted fat and pieces of one of the soldiers," that's when it hits you. You're out there and you're picking up pieces of a body and there's just nothing there. That sticks with you.

When I found out that my combat tour in Iraq was drawing to an end, I wanted to stay. I wanted to stay because I felt like I could do more. I still had gas in the tank. This was something I had prepared all my young adult life to do, and when that time came, I just felt like I wanted and could do more. I had a sense of guilt. When you are there, life is a lot easier. By that, I mean, you are in that zone. You know what you are going to be doing from day to day. It's repetition. It's acting from muscle memory. The guilt comes from knowing that you are going home, and three or four other guys are not. You feel that there is more that can be accomplished. Many of the Iraqi people that we worked with were good people, and they just wanted to be free.

Returning home for me was kind of unique. It was just me and my wife. My younger kids still lived with my ex-wife and the older ones had moved on. For me it was the battle of knowing that I am here doing this, and yet others can't, because they are no longer with us or remain deployed overseas in a combat zone. I sat down with some friends and others, and I learned that I couldn't live my life in a state of regret or guilt. I learned that I needed to live my life for those left behind or gone, because they can't. One big thing that aided me in this transition from combat zone to everyday life was that I was a National Guard soldier. That means, I went right back to work. I didn't have empty space and time to fill. I was right back into the daily routine of going to work and earning a living.

During my combat deployments, my friends and I did have things we did to combat the stress and pressure. We played practical jokes on one another. While they were out on patrol, we would set up little surprises for them for when they got back inside the wire. One prank that sticks out in my mind was a prank we did to a guy that had been recalled from college back to active duty. He was a real "dick." So, one night while he was out, we went into his sleeping area and painted all these little explicit symbols all over the walls of his space. We even used glow in the dark paint for some of them. They were everywhere.

I retired from the military on July 15, 2015, as a Staff Sergeant (E-6). Getting out of the military was a pain in the butt. Getting my retirement paperwork pushed through the National Guard system was a nightmare. It took forever and I had to finally resort to getting outside assistance. My packet was simply not moving forward in the system. But in the end, we got it all worked out.

I still miss the military at times as I reflect back now, being retired. I knew that I was older than most of the guys in my unit and came to the realization that it was time for me to go. Many of the friends that I had made in the early days of my military career, had served their initial terms, and gotten out. I told them at that time that they would regret leaving the military, and here I was, making that same decision after having served an entire career in uniform. Since I retired out of the National Guard, there was a bit of regret, but I thought, "Now I have my weekends back again!"

When I first left the service in 1996, because of the Clinton era draw-down, I was angry. I felt like the military was simply telling me that they no longer needed me and was throwing me away. It was not my choice to get out at that time. It was something that was forced upon me. I was not ready for that. I had only seven more years before I could officially retire. That event, as I was single at the time, forced me to move back in with my mom for a time while I sorted things out. I had to learn quickly how to become a civilian again. That whole experience really made me angry. My brothers tried to talk me into going into the Army at the time. But my mindset was, "Screw the government. I've done thirteen years and they don't want the rest of me, so I'm done with them." I had a bitter attitude about the military up until about 2001. I felt like I had given the military everything for thirteen years, and all they gave me in return was the shaft. That mindset for me changed after 9/11.

Today, with the pullout of combat operations that we are seeing, there will be another drawdown in forces. The hardest thing for me leaving the military in that way was finding a job. I worked in the restaurant business and sold shoes, which I didn't like, but I needed a job. I needed the income, so I did what I had to do.

I feel that the time I spent in the military has made me more demanding. I'm getting better at this, but when I ask someone to do something, I expect them to do it. It has led to me holding myself more accountable. It was a challenge at first, but I am slowly overcoming that.

I learned from the military that I could do far more than I ever thought I could. Even at times when I thought I was done, I could always find that little extra something inside me to keep going. My combat engagements taught me that I am not alone. I don't have to try to do everything on my own. I learned how to control my emotions instead of letting my emotions control me. I learned to push past that.

Some of my hopes for the future include my being able to fully retire and travel with my wife and see some of the great sights of this country. I'd love to go see all these beautiful things our country has to offer before they are gone.

My wish for the civilian population in this country, in regard to the military, is that I wish they could understand that every day, these men, and women of the military are putting their lives on the line, whether it be in training or in combat situations. Training in the military is realistic, and they are constantly putting their lives at risk for this country. They are putting in the time, efforts, and energy so those civilians can do the things they love and enjoy doing. Even despite the differences in the way soldiers have been treated upon coming home from war, I don't think the civilian population really understands the sacrifices these men and women have made.

Like almost every other veteran that has served, I miss the level of comradery found in the military. You build relationships. You gain friends and these bonds you have are just different than those found in civilian life. In the military, it's a Brotherhood and a sense of belonging. In society today, everyone is focused on themselves and their immediate families. While in the military, if something bad happened, I always had someone I could call.

I haven't had the difficulty in sharing my military experiences with others as many have had. My wife doesn't want to hear them. She doesn't want to relive what I went through. My son on the other hand, is someone that I can talk to, so I have an outlet when needed. My brothers were all in the military, so there is an added level of support for me there as well.

If my kids ever get a copy of this book, I hope that they will be able to see that I sacrificed many of the good years of my life so that they could have a good life, and so that they could make decisions in life without a government dictating to them what they can and cannot do. I hope they learn that they can live free not only because of my own personal sacrifices, but because of the sacrifices of so many others as well.

I first became involved with Vets Helping Vets – Anderson in 2016. Sammy Lewis, a member of Vets Helping Vets, was the Veterans Service Officer here at the time. I had just come to work here, and he wanted to put together a Marine Corps Ball. My first interaction with VHVA was in my approaching them to invite them and to sell tickets to this function. Slowly, over time, I spent more time with the VHVA group until Sammy retired. It was then that I became more involved with Vets Helping Vets after I became the director here. In my current position as VSO, Vets Helping Vets has really become a resource for me. I get vets in here all the time from that organization and we can work on their issues together. Vets Helping Vets is a place where I can send veterans that need a place to tell their story. Vets Helping Vets has also given me a place where I can go to tell my story and regain some of that comradery that I miss.

My message to Vets Helping Vets is simple…keep doing what you're doing. Keep pushing forward. We need places like that.

The VFW and American Legion type organizations have a great place in our history, but VHVA is more hands on. On the outside, these other organizations seem to be more political, whereas in the trenches, VHVA is right there with the veterans on a more personal basis. That's what I like and that's what I've seen from them. VHVA is a more grassroots program. We are assisting people daily directly into their lives.

Donnie Nix

I am Donnie Eugene Nix. I served in the United States Air Force. People used to refer to me as "Lefty." I am left-handed and when I met someone or was offered something, I always used my left hand. I used my left hand when talking to others and in making gestures. From there, it just evolved into a nickname, I guess. The nickname never bothered me. I am left-handed, so it just stuck.

I enlisted in the Air Force. I served as an enlisted man, not an officer. At the time I left the Air Force, I had achieved the rank of E-7. When I signed up in 1954, the military was unlike what it is today. They did a series of tests to determine where you would best fit according to your aptitude and the needs of the military. This was done in basic training. As a result of this testing, they gave me four options to look at...

1. Aircraft and Engines
2. Electronics
3. Cook
4. Heavy Equipment

I wanted to be an aircraft engine mechanic, so I applied for that. From basic, I went to Amarillo, Texas for the mechanic schooling. After completing six months of mechanic schooling, I was then sent to Roswell, New Mexico, to Walker Air Force Base. I was assigned to the Strategic Air Command (SAC) and worked on C-47's. I was on the ground there, and I became a Crew Chief on a C-47. Within two years, I was promoted to Staff Sergeant. Shortly thereafter, I received orders to go to Japan.

When I went to Japan, they had the C-130's. When I got there, it was cold, I mean, cold! I was working on the flight line, and I said, "There's got to be something better than this!" When the Flight Engineers came out to get on the planes, I talked with them. I decided to volunteer as a Flight Engineer and was sent to school for that. That position was only for that unit though.

After my time in Japan, I came back to the States and was

assigned to Dover Air Force Base in Delaware. I ended up right back on the flight line. I told them that I wanted to be a Flight Engineer. I was told that I would have to go to school once again. But they asked me what grade level education I had. I didn't graduate. I didn't even finish the 8th Grade. So, I went and took the GED test and maxed it out.

I was congratulated by my superiors, sent on to school and became a Flight Engineer for the Military Airlift Command (MAC). I started flying the C-133's there and served on the crew for C-133's for nine years while there at Dover. From there, I was sent to McCullen Airbase to work with the intelligence gathering planes that were used in Southeast Asia. I became a Flight Engineer for those planes.

When I attended survival school, they checked us for tuberculosis. My test came back positive. My plans were changed, and I spent a year working until I was assigned to the Spector C-130 gunships. In 1970, I was sent to school for training on these planes. I was sent to Southeast Asia as a crew member aboard the C-130 gunships, Model E. The A model C-130s were already in country at the time. I flew the E model for two years. I flew it for a year over there until I came back to the States. I spent about six months here, then I volunteered to go back to the same outfit in Southeast Asia and spent another year doing that. After my second tour in the region, I came back to North Carolina and Pope Air Force Base. I retired from the Air Force in 1975 while assigned to Pope Air Force Base.

I was born and raised in North Georgia, in the mountains. My father passed away when I was three years old. My mother never remarried, and I was the only child. My mom raised me by herself. She used to tell me, that while I was a baby, and her working in the cotton fields, she would lay me on the bag of cotton and drag me around the field as she picked. As time moved on, she eventually moved from the cotton fields into the cotton mill itself.

Time came for me to start school. What I found out soon

enough was that I just didn't have the discipline for school. I should have had it, but I did not. I just did as I pleased. When I finally reached the eighth grade, I didn't want any more of it. School that is. So, me and a cousin of mine started hanging out…we'd go fishing and hunting, things like that. School went by the wayside. I did work during this time. I had several jobs. I worked at a truck stop washing dishes and I even delivered ice on a horse drawn wagon. Many people didn't have refrigerators back in those days, so we delivered twenty-five-pound blocks of ice to their homes to put in the icebox.

My mom and I had a good relationship. We were close, but our relationship didn't just happen. It developed over the years. The relationship grew closer after my father died. He used to work in the talc mines. In North Georgia there are many talc mines. They use the talc in a variety of different products. Back in the 1930' when he was working these mines, dust was a big problem. The miners didn't pay it much attention because they had no masks or respirators in those days. They just breathed the dust in. That dust is what eventually took his life. After his passing, I became the main thing in my mother's life, and she took care of me.

I was living in Chatsworth, Georgia, right at the foot of the mountains at the time I enlisted. The primary reason I joined the military was that I really didn't want to go to jail. The guys and the young people I hung around with at the time were not the best of the bunch. They were like me; they didn't care anything about going to school and were getting into trouble. Homebrew at the time was a dollar a gallon, so you could buy all you wanted of that junk. The drinking and carrying on was leading us nowhere. We weren't doing anything serious, but it could have easily ended up that way. The local cops chased us around town and kept an eye on us.

I noticed that things were escalating, and it was no longer childish games that we were playing. I was getting involved in things that weren't necessarily criminal, but they were out of character for me. I knew that, sooner or later, I would end up in jail.

So, I had a conversation with my mother. I was only seventeen at the time, so she would have to be involved in me joining the military. At the time, I was working at W.F. Nolan's farm. I told my mom that I have to go into the military, I just don't have a choice. I don't have an education, but they will take me like I am. We went down to the recruiter, but I didn't have a birth certificate. My mother, my aunt and I had to go to the courthouse to sign some documents to get a birth certificate. Once that was accomplished, I could then talk to the recruiter.

This was not long after the Korean War, and people were leaving the service; leaving vacancies that needed to be filled. With this happening, the military was taking just about anyone who volunteered, regardless of their education level. I had a good mind, my problem was, I was just borderline stupid. I was making bad choices. I didn't have any problems learning; I could learn about anything if I applied myself.

I had a fascination with planes. That was in large part why I selected the Air Force. Back then, there was a lot of "barn-storming" going on across the country. I loved that. What I didn't realize at the time was that I would not be the pilot. I would not be the one doing the acrobatics, tricks, etc. But I would be part of it, so that's what I wanted to do.

Basic training was a challenge for me. No matter what I did, I had two left feet. It seemed like it always got me in trouble. One time, I even had to wash the barracks steps with a toothbrush. Every time I turned around, I was in trouble for something. It was never anything big, the Drill Instructors were just on my case the entire time. It may have been as simple as; he saw potential in me and was trying to get it out.

An example of this was when I worked on the Nolan Farm. When I was about fourteen years old, Mr. Nolan bought me an old A-Model truck. He gave thirty dollars for it. I got it home and kept it for a while, then I started messing with it. I tore it down and rebuilt everything on it. I feel that doing things like this before the military, really helped me with the mechanical side once I joined the Air Force. Basic training was strict, and that was something that I wasn't used to.

One of the funny things that I recall about Basic Training was my shoes. They didn't issue us any clothes or uniforms the first few days we were there. The mud in Texas is not much different than what we have here or back in Georgia. We were marching all over the place and one day we went through the mud. All of a sudden, my shoes weren't on my feet anymore. They had gotten stuck in the mud and had come right off my feet. I'm marching around barefoot. I hollered to the rest of the group and the Drill Sergeant chewed me out. Then he looked down and realized that I didn't have any shoes on. That was a funny moment for us all.

I didn't have any troubles adapting to the military life, and I really don't understand why, based on my activities before I enlisted. I learned that I had people in authority over me; I was there to learn and obey those orders. That was my job, to obey those orders.

During the Vietnam war, I was stationed in Thailand. That's where our planes flew out of. In the nine years I served at Dover, we made two trips a month into Vietnam. We flew into just about every air base in Vietnam. We were bringing in equipment and loaded coffins to transport back home. I was never actually stationed in Vietnam. We flew into Laos, Cambodia, and Vietnam from Thailand.

When we flew into Vietnam and some of the other places on a C-130 Gunship, you would see things. Things that were taking place on the ground with the troops we were supporting. We flew mainly at night. I only remember conducting two daylight flights the whole time I spent in Vietnam.

On one of the daylight flights, we were orbiting overhead at a rubber plantation. There were two gunships on station, offset 180 degrees from one another. We got a call that told us to move back because Arclight was coming in. They were preparing for a B-52 strike on the area. We continued our orbit over the target, but we expanded the orbit so we would be out of the way of the incoming B-52's. In an instant, the rubber plantation vanished in a cloud of smoke.

It was just gone. We never did see the B-52's because they flew at much higher altitudes. When the smoke cleared, there was nothing there. Nothing. Total devastation.

We were circling this plantation because we were supposedly supporting troops in combat. But there couldn't have been any of our troops in there. They would never have called for an Arclight strike if our troops had been in there. I don't know for certain whether it was South Vietnamese troops involved there, but its highly likely that North Vietnamese troops were.

Our other daylight flight was around Saigon when the Tet Offensive started. We conducted aerial patrols to prevent enemy movements into the city. We took out things like bicycles and such that were carrying munitions.

Our missions at night would originate in Thailand. We were on the Yellow River there, and in the river was an old barge. We used that barge to boresight our guns before we left the area. The enemy wasn't stupid, they knew what was going on, and they set up Triple A guns near the area. One night as we were bore sighting our guns, they lit the sky up. We returned to the base and got things in order, then took care of the anti-aircraft guns. There wasn't anything left there but us. That gunship was awesome once it got started.

We were on a mission over Cambodia one night. We picked up some trucks, and we started firing on them. The whole world blew up. We were right over what appeared to be an ammo storage facility. We were in the area for six hours, and when we left, it was still blowing up. There is no telling how much ammo was in that place.

From a gunship, we had a whole different perspective of what was going on. In some cases, we couldn't actually see what was taking place on the ground unless it was along a road, clear terrain, or if we used the IR System. Now this was in the 1970's, but the IR (Infrared) System we had would allow us to see a man smoking a cigarette under a tree. We had cameras aboard the plane that fed into monitors that would allow us to see what was taking place on the ground. We could

see well in most cases. But when you look down at those trucks, or whatever it was that you were about to
shoot at at…God have mercy if you saw people and you knew what you were about to do to them. You were killing them. It didn't matter what their age bracket was or anything. You tried not to think about it. You knew what was about to happen, but it happened anyway. You'd see this and you knew that you didn't want to do it, but you had to.

We would start firing, and God have mercy, the people would die on the ground. I've never talked about this. I've never talked about this to my family because I know they won't understand. How could I do such a thing and feel like I do?

We did what we were supposed to do. It wasn't good because I know that the people on the ground were doing what they felt they were supposed to do as well. I didn't like what I did. But I did it because my government wanted me too. We were supposed to be saving democracy, but sometimes, I just wonder, "Why?"

We never fired on villages, but the VC set up Triple A guns all around the villages. They opened fire on us as we came across their path. Then we turned the guns on the area. There were children in that place. Every night I get on my knees, and I ask God to forgive me for what I've done. I knew there were women and children, slaughtered by us, in that village.

When I came home, it was beautiful. My wife was waiting on me, and my family. When I got off the plane in the States, we took a bus to the train station. People wouldn't talk to you. I even got spit on. We had heard about the reception men were getting when they came home, but I just wondered, "Why?" Riots were going on. People were marching against the war and everything that was taking place. I just didn't let all that dampen my enthusiasm for coming home.

Later, I began to think about what I was doing. I wondered why I was doing what I was doing, if the people I was supposedly doing it for, didn't care about me at all? Why throw me under the bus because I did what my country had asked me to do? Not everyone was that way, but the ones that were, just left a bad taste in your mouth. I never did think about harming any of them because I thought, "This is my country, these are my people."

Richard Cole is a man from my days in the Air Force that I remember well. He was a Flight Engineer like I was on the C-130 gunships. His plane went down and the whole crew was lost. I remember him because we were good friends. He and I were on different planes. The SA-7 rockets the enemy used are what took them down. You could see them once they were launched from the ground. The fire and exhaust from the rocket made them very visible. The SA-7 was a heat seeking missile, and they homed in on our engines. We lost several planes over the course of my time there. Eventually, the Air Force put bubbles on the ramps of the gunships so a man could lay down in there and see all the way to the front of the plane on the underside. He could then look for and alert the crew to a missile launch.

The guy manning that position on our plane created a funny moment on one flight. We began taking fire and he saw a missile launch and hollered over the radio, "Stop!" Can you imagine a 165-thousand-pound aircraft coming to a dead stop in mid-flight? It wasn't funny at the time, but it was funny once we got out of the danger zone.

After a flight, one of the first things we wanted was a beer. The ground crews were good. They would usually meet us at the aircraft with a beer. We'd go to the debrief and then hit the NCO Club. The Officers generally came with us, because they had more fun at the NCO Club than they did at the Officers Club. Eyes were watching them at the Officers Club, but at the NCO Club, they could get away with about anything.

The gunners on our birds were a rowdy bunch. They had a compound off the base, all to themselves. If you went down there, you had better close your eyes, because there was no telling what you would see. Some of the Officers, whose wives had come over to see them, took their wives down to this compound. These gunners were auctioning off women from the stage that were completely naked. They were auctioning them off to members of other crews. The Officers couldn't get their wives out of there fast enough.

Those gunners were always into something. That was their down time. Once they hit the tarmac again, they were truly professionals. Our gunners could have one 105 Howitzer round hitting the ground, one in mid-flight and one on the way at the same time. They were that fast and that good. It was awesome watching them work.

I left the military for the last time in August 1975. Right around the time when Saigon fell. That event caused me to think that we had wasted our time and resources over there. We wasted a lot of lives and gained nothing for it. Nothing at all. We made the mistake of allowing politicians to run this war instead of turning it over to the military like they should have. It always bothered me that we bombed Hanoi with the intent of getting the parties involved in peace talks. Then they just stopped the bombing. If they were really interested in doing something, they should have bombed it out of existence. The politicians hamstrung the Generals and other leaders. This was a politician's war, nothing more. It happened in Korea; we didn't learn anything. It happened in Vietnam; we didn't learn anything. We are in the process of doing the same thing in Afghanistan today. We haven't learned a thing.

In my first few months away from the Air Force, I was kind of lost. I had been used to the military for twenty-one years. You always had people around you. The same kind of people you were. No matter where you went or what you did, these people were around you. You were never alone.

When I got out of the military, I found myself alone. I had my family, and they were a stabilizing force, but I found myself outside the gates with no way to get back in. It wasn't a good feeling. I applied at the hospital as an orderly in Gainesville, GA. I got the job. That job proved to be like the military for me. I had the same people around me all the time. This gave me the stability I needed at that point in my life.

For folks leaving the military today, I would have to tell them to remember that they are going into an environment that they are not used to. It's different back in the civilian world. You'll be apprehensive; looking for things. As odd as it may sound, you will need a job that affords you the ability to be around the same people, day in and day out. Your family is good, and will no doubt be a huge factor, but you will need an outlet. You're not going to be able to simply hang around family all the time. Immerse yourself into your job, it will help you tremendously.

Overall, I'd say that my time in the military allowed me to grow up; to become a better human being than I ever would have before. It gave me the ability to be stable. I've carried the lessons from the military with me my entire life. In the military, I learned that I had the capability to do about most anything I set my mind to.

My hopes for the future focus on the people leading this country. We put them into office, and then they think we are supposed to become their slaves. That's not how this thing is supposed to work. Yet, that's the way it's happening. We must straighten this mess out. We must put people into office so that they realize this country is sinking. We're going down the tubes…bad. I don't want to see anyone go without food and necessities; but all these people coming in from other countries are siphoning off the very things that people in this country need. Our citizens are coming up short. We put people into office who make all sorts of claims on the campaign trail, then the minute they hit the office, they are back-pedaling on everything.

If we don't change, we're not going to make it as a country. I feel and even fear for my grandchildren and great grandchildren. They are growing up in something that is becoming an absolute mess. Our schools and education systems are a joke. Things being taught in schools today, should not be allowed. I get mad when I see how things are progressing in this country with no end in sight.

I miss the camaraderie of the military but have found it again with the Vets Helping Vets organization. Leaving the military was like being pushed out a door into the cold, with nowhere to go. Even though I have made friends and built relationships since leaving the military, they are just not the same. It's strange. The camaraderie was always there in the military, and I miss that more than anything else.

I never really talk to my family about specifics of my job in the Air Force. Instead, I would tell them about the places I've been and things I've seen, but not my job specifically. The nightlife in the military didn't get publicized either. My sons have all been in the military and I have talked with them some, but the rest of my family never really seemed interested.

If my family picks up this book at some point in the future, I want them to understand that the military was something I needed to do in growing up and becoming the man that I became in order to provide for them. They will see that there were bad things, but that was part of the situation at that time. We as the military, were part of that and had to do it. I don't see anything within my story that would lead them to condemn the military or me. It's not pretty, it's not something that I would want them to identify as the "best part" of my story. I would want them to read it and understand that this is what happens when we are engaged in a war. Not only do soldiers get killed and maimed for life, there are others that pay the consequences also. Whatever was done, was done because my country said it needed to be done. That's why we need to put a reign on the politicians.

When I found out about Vets Helping Vets, I didn't really understand what they were all about until I came. It took me a couple of meetings to really figure it out. I had been without the camaraderie of people like me for so long, it took me a while to realize that this was what I had been missing, for years. Vets Helping Vets is the best thing that could have come my way. I wish that it would have happened sooner. I believe if vets would simply come by and sit in on a couple of meetings, they would realize that this is what they have been missing for so long. Vets Helping Vets is a beautiful thing.

Roland Ocampo

Roland Ocampo is my name, and I earned the nick name, Scrappy, because I used to get into a lot of fights during libo (slang for liberty, time off). I was never one to back down to anyone, even higher ups. My dad was in the Army during the Vietnam era, but he never got deployed. He was in college at the University of Missouri. I think Dad was a Reservist. I remember seeing him in his uniform and seeing his dress uniform downstairs in the basement.

To be honest, I never thought the military would be a good fit for me because I dislike rules. I followed the urge of wanting to fight in the Gulf War and tried to enlist in the Marines. The Marines said no for they did not accept anyone without a high school diploma. Although I did have my GED, I did not have my high school diploma. I walked at my graduation, and nobody knew. I talked to my high school back in Minnesota. They told me I could get the five credits I needed by doing correspondence courses, and by taking my final exam at the high school. A year later, I did and passed. In my high school teacher's office, there was a diploma with my old graduation date on it, May 3, 1988. My official transcript now reads: Graduation Date, 1990.

Boot camp was fun. My recruiter gave me the best advice. He said, "They are going to yell at you about everything. Just remember they do not know you." So, when the DI yelled, I did not care. I just did my job. I loved training and working out. A funny incident I remember from boot camp was listening to the Squad Leader, who carried the guidon (platoon flag) during drill, yell and scream while he was sleeping. Funny pranks included the boot one, go get me a box of grid squares, and go tell the gunny (Gunnery Sergeant) I need the keys to the Humvee.

I would get in trouble "re-directing" other recruits, getting in to fights on the way back from chow. I have kicked recruits up and down stairs. Another time, I ignored a DI from another platoon because he was not my DI. The Drill Instructor found me later and asked my DIs if he could take me for some enlighten PT thrashing. They said yes. I went down two decks to his platoon and got thrashed for an hour in front of his platoon. Inside, I was laughing.

My favorite time while in boot camp was listening to taps as the colors (American Flag) came down and hearing the boom. It reminded me I was doing something great, and I was at home. I thank the Marines every day for making me go back and get my high school diploma. The first mission accomplished was making me better for the future. I was living in Kansas City, Missouri, when I enlisted in the US Marine Corps, March 13, 1990.

Thinking I was going into training to get ready for combat, I soon realized training was not just physical. It included academic training on navigation, equipment, radios, and weaponry, all part of a well-organized system. In the classrooms, you learn to do the job and then take that learning out to the field right away. You learn as much as anyone going to college, but it is much better. You can then apply it the same day or week in the real context. Performing it with hands-on makes sure the person does it correctly.

After about a year and a half, you are instructed how to start teaching your fellow team and recruits that come in after you. Right away the Marine Corps teaches you how to be a leader in instructing your men, what to do and how to do the job as a team, effectively. I made it a point to learn all aspects of military training, including weapon systems. If a situation arose, I would be capable to complete the mission.

Many awards were given out in formation to the whole group. My first was the National Defense ribbon in Boot Camp. I remember saying to myself, "Why are we getting these? We have not done anything yet." In retrospect, I see we all signed up during wartime to be sacrificed for the greater good if need be. We signed a blank check to defend the Nation which could cost us our lives.

Later, I received awards for two times Overseas Deployment, Presidential Unit Citation, Combat Action, Humanitarian, two times Southwest Asia, Armed Forces Expeditionary, and Desert Storm. Three of them I received after I left the Corps.

I enlisted at the tail end of Desert Storm. We patrolled the waters, but because of Somalia, we did not go inland. Instead, we were asked to do the initial landing in Somalia, which took our time away from doing actions in Desert Storm. My job was 0341 Mortarman for Echo Company 2nd Battalion 9th Marines. Somalia was the worst, best, and exciting lessons I ever experienced about the world. Our unit did not have any casualties during combat. Unfortunately, another unit did while patrolling Mogadishu, a city of Somalia. Later in the 2nd Battalion 4th Marines, I earned a new MOS 0861, Forward Observer with 4th Angico.

McCowin was my best friend in the Marines. We were in the same platoon in boot camp; however, we did not talk until Marine Combat Training and the School of Infantry. Then we would hang out, grabs some drinks, and explore the cities. I would listen to him talk about his mom and dad; plus, his sister whom I knew. We still try to stay in touch by talking every week. We were called Heckle and Jeckle after the Two Crows cartoon because we were always getting into trouble together our first two years. Later, it was only me.

My most terrifying event was not in combat but while training in Japan. We were firing live, with the SMAW (Shoulder-Launched Multipurpose Assault Weapon) and one LCpl (Lance Corporal) fired, hitting the target, and blowing it up. Suddenly a Gunny noticed a projectile coming straight back at us. There are like eight US Marines in our group and the Gunny yells, "Move!" We spread out in all directions. I unfortunately got hit by the fragments. It blew me back so fast and hard, hitting me in the left leg, flipping me on my head. I hit the ground screaming like a baby for the doc. The fragment was

10-12 inches long on one end and all jagged metal. On the other end was a flat open circle. It was basically the propellant end of the rocket. The flat end hit my leg. The doc said I would have bled out if it had been the jagged end. The fragment hit me and bounced another fifteen feet in the other direction. The Gunny retrieved it for me to keep. He said it was my good luck charm.

There are important things the Marine Corps teaches, and you are expected to learn them. How to discipline yourself to learn and then put it into practice. Learn how to teach. Learn how to listen in order to help guide. It is important to know your team inside and out. Know about their family life. Any problems that might affect their job when put in the situation of combat. A leader guides them to be a better Marine, leading the way, not dragging them through their problems. As in life in general, they must choose their own path, and hopefully they choose the right one. The military does a good job teaching you to overcome.

I left active duty August 9th to go on terminal leave ending September 9th, 1995.It was a surreal moment in not having to do anything No one was there to meet me. Being on my own, and not knowing what was ahead, was a little scary. Yet, I told myself I am a Marine and I can handle anything--wrong. Civilian life was what I was not prepared for. The Marines had prepared us on how to enter the workforce, with resume prepping and how to go out and get employment.

For a while felt like I was on vacation, not having to wake up at a certain time. I would hit the beach, swim, workout, and then go to work. My mannerisms are still military, verbiage, too, and I still dislike rules. I miss the job, the training, the team, the adventure, and the excitement. My advice to others thinking to transition out of the military is: Stay in and make it your career.

Unfortunately, in civilian life, we may not have a good team around us, and we need that buddy on the left or right to ask for help and guidance. When the problems arise, the team is no longer there.

Sometimes we think we are invincible, and we find we are not.

The depression mode sets in, and we get down and out. I've been there. I share this to help others. I attempted to end it myself with gunshots to the chest and stomach. I survived somehow twice. When you have spiraled down the hole of despair in life, it is hard to ask for help.

Surround yourself with people who know you and know how to give a hand up when you start sinking into the hole. I learned that in any direction you will find difficulty in accomplishing your goals. I learned freedom is not free, it is earned. Be there for others to guide them, that is what I am working on right now, to grow my A Grunt's View: (podcast) agruntsview.com and (blog) agruntsview.net. My hope for the future is to learn to cope with the struggles endured in everyday life which includes sharing our stories. Vets Helping Vets meetings is a place where you can relate with other veterans.

Jeremiah Palmer

I was born and raised in Belton, South Carolina. My name is Jeremiah Ezekiel Palmer. As I grew older, I attended Geer Gantt High School through the eleventh grade. I was always called by my initials, J.E. Palmer. My parents called me that, and so did everyone I knew in Belton and in school. I stopped using that as my name in the Marine Corps, yet many still call me by my initials.

During my senior year, I transferred to Belton-Honea Path High School. It was the first year the school was opened, and I also ran the first touchdown recorded by the school. This was in 1966. I received two scholarship offers to play football in college when I graduated in 1967. However, my father did not want me to attend college. He wanted me to stay home and help him work. He said that's what he had done for his parents, and that I should do the same. I told him that he would not have to pay for anything and that I could do more for the family by going to college.

I told him that if I didn't go to college, I would risk being drafted into the Army and being sent to Vietnam. He still wanted me to pass on the opportunity to go to college. I cried at this lost opportunity, but I did as he wanted.

Later in 1967, I went to have a physical. Everything was fine and I knew then that I was going to be drafted into the Army. I asked my buddies Marvin Dotson and Columbus Moorehead, to come with me and join the Marines. We signed up on the buddy plan to go in together, but we weren't supposed to leave until after my birthday, on March 21, 1968. However, there was a change in our plans. Columbus and I were called to enter earlier. I was hot, because I had planned to celebrate my birthday, and now, Marvin wasn't going in with us. He did follow later, in March.

I called the recruiter and asked him why we were being separated. He told me that Marines were being killed in Vietnam and they needed to be replaced, and that Marvin would catch up with us later. I knew then that my attitude had to change; I would either end up in a military prison or be a good Marine. I changed for the better and became the best man in my platoon.

I left for Marine Corps basic training at Parris Island on February 29, 1968. I became the best man in our platoon, graduating the Most Outstanding Man in our platoon. I won the dress blue uniform and was awarded the rank of Private First Class. From there I attended ITR (Infantry Training Regiment) at Camp Lejeune, North Carolina, where I acted as the student Platoon Sergeant. My final training station before going to Vietnam was Camp Pendleton, California.

From Camp Pendleton, it was off to Andrews Air Force Base in Maryland, and then over to Alaska. The next destination point was Japan, where we were allowed off the plane for a short time. The next stop was Okinawa. We stayed there for a few days then we were off the ground again; this time, headed to Da Nang, Vietnam in August of 1968.

My first week in Vietnam found me in the jungles and hills southwest of Da Nang to protect it from enemy patrols. The first week there, we had a large operation where many Marines were killed or injured. I was assigned to Lima Company, 3/7th Marines. Our job was to patrol and protect many of the bridges and hills in the area. I witnessed many of my fellow Marines being killed or wounded.

I was soon after promoted to Lance Corporal, then later, to Corporal. On my last night with the squad, we spent the night in the field. The next day, February 23, 1969, we were told to return to base. Corporal Cole, a close friend of mine, asked me to change places with him. I did so. I took his place, and he took mine in the order of march. That move put me closer to the front of the patrol.

We were ambushed by a North Vietnamese Army Patrol. I was shot in my right calf, and while on the ground, I was shot again in my right thigh. While lying on the ground, I asked the Lord which way I should move. The response I got was, "Back to the Corpsman." I crawled back to him, and he patched me up.

I thought we were receiving friendly fire from our left since the first shot hit me in the lower inside of my right leg. We called the Marines on our left, telling them we were coming towards them on their right. My squad was being killed and wounded so I was going to crawl back over the hill.

I crawled back up the hill and found two NVA (North Vietnamese Army) soldiers looking at me. I was surprised to see them, but quickly ducked my head and rolled back down the hill away from them. I went back to the Corpsman to tell him, and he yelled to the others that it was the NVA that was shooting at us.

Other Marines came in to get us out of that situation. It was then that I learned, Corporal Cole had died in the ambush. He had taken my place. It could have been me. The first helicopter arrived to take us out, and I was carried to the bird by Jim Trenam and Eugene Doodey. We were in an open field where other dead Marines were gathered, and the helicopter took off without us. They were receiving too much ground fire. And we were still in the open field.

The next helicopter came in about 1 a.m., February 24, 1969. Rudy Antonucci placed flashlights down in holes in the ground so the helicopters could identify our location. These Marines risked their lives helping me, and I will always be greatly appreciative.

We were taken to the hospital at Da Nang. They took the AK-47 round out of my thigh, and then sent me to Japan. The hospital in Japan was where they closed the wound and stitched me up. It was there that I saw Corporal Cole in a dream. I remember telling him in that dream that he was dead, so how could he be here? In the dream he simply smiled and didn't respond. After he walked away, I never saw him again.

After some time in the hospital in Japan, I was given a choice as to where I could go next. I chose Charleston, South Carolina. That was soil in South Carolina, and that's where I wanted to be. I don't recall the exact timing of my return, but I do know that because of my injuries, I couldn't walk, so I couldn't get off the plane at the various places we stopped on the flight home.

We left Japan, flew to Alaska, then on to Andrews Air Force Base where it all began. We stayed at Andrews for the night. The next morning it snowed. We stayed over again, and the next morning one of the plane's motors was not functioning. So, we stayed one more night in Maryland. Finally, the next day, we made it to Charleston.

After leaving the Naval Hospital I went back to Camp Lejeune where I was Honorably Discharged on July 10, 1969. I carried a sore leg with me for some time after that. I left Belton, South Carolina and moved to Detroit where I got a job on July 30, 1969. My leg still hurt, but I went to work. I am so proud that I served in the United States Marine Corps.

It was an honor for me to have Rudy and his wife Celeste Antonucci visit my home, church, and the Vets Helping Vets Barbeque this year. It was an honor to have my first squad leader in Vietnam, George Adams, be with my family this summer as well.

I am happy to be the Chaplain of the Vets Helping Vets – Anderson. I am happy to be the Marine Corps League Chaplain of South Carolina. I am happy to be the Lima 3/7 Vietnam Veterans Reunion Chaplain. Happy to be the Chaplain of the Military Order of the Purple Heart in Anderson, SC. I am very happy to be the Pastor of New Broadmouth Baptist Church in Honea Path, where I have served for 35 years.

Semper Fi!

Jim Pierson

Most people know me as Jim, but my full name is James Leroy Pierson. While I was in the Army, people called me Deacon because I was a Chaplain's Assistant. I was drafted in August of 1968. I went from Lake Placid, Florida, on a bus to my inception center at Fort Jackson, South Carolina. I was there for one week, for induction, then they sent me to Fort Gordon, Georgia.

It was at Fort Gordon that I attended Basic Training. At the time I was drafted, I was no longer living at home. I was living on my own. I was a retail milkman for Borden's dairy at Avon Park, Florida.

I was raised on a farm. We farmed a thousand acres, but only about eight hundred was tillable. That was a lot of land back in the 1950's. You can imagine the type of equipment that we had to work with. We had one hired man who only worked part of the time. So, it was me and my family that did it all. I have a full brother and a stepbrother whom I grew up with. My dad, later in life, had two more children with the same lady.

My relationship with my parents was excellent. Unfortunately, they divorced when I was twelve years old and that really tore me up. We were a "Leave it to Beaver" family. We were a good Christian family; we were in church every time the door was open. My parents even belonged to a young Christian's married group that met once a month. We went on camping trips, and they would stay up all night playing cards. We would fish and other fun stuff. No alcohol was involved. The group even put on a play at the University of Illinois. They were always active in something. They square danced, and my mom even made her own dresses. But something happened, and they ended up divorced.

My mom was the reason behind the divorce. She had been on some type of nerve pills back in the day. She asked him to leave. My mom was really sorry and wanted my dad back, but he would not go back. But we moved on and I had a good life. Mom struggled because she ended up marrying a guy who was thirty-six, going on eighteen. He didn't work half the time. In the eighth grade, they moved to Carmi, Illinois, which I believe, that middle school had taken the state championship in basketball, for the last twenty years. I was in the eighth grade and had been playing since the sixth grade. I was the last guy on the second string, I made the team, but I had to quit to help support my family.

Mom needed help and I took a paper route. I made something like thirteen dollars a week, and I gave her ten of it for groceries. After about a year of that, she got a job as an Avon District Manager and moved to northern Illinois. I went with her during my freshman year and part of my sophomore year. She made good money, and things were going pretty well then. Back in 1961, she made thirteen thousand a year, and that was good money for those days. In the middle of my sophomore year, I returned to live with my dad in southern Illinois.

I went back to farming and ended up getting a girl pregnant during my senior year in high school. I tried to join the Marines and they wouldn't take me because I had a dependent. They told me to get a divorce, then they'd take me. Well, I didn't, and we hung on for a couple more years and moved to Florida. She ended up moving back to Illinois, taking the baby. I had the job at Borden's Dairy and was making good money. I had built the route and it was starting to pay off. The girl called and wanted money. I told her I had a little cottage on the lake, I'm making good money, bring the baby and we'll patch it up. She said, "I don't want you; I just want your money. If you don't send me money, I'm going to turn you over to the draft board." I told her to do whatever she thought was right.

Shortly thereafter, I received a questionnaire that asked if I was living with family and supporting family. I checked, "Yes." I returned it, and they sent it back with red ink underlining the penalties for lying. I responded, "No, no, no!" and within a week, I was drafted. I didn't care because I really wanted to go in anyway.

My first job was just Basic Training. Once there, they gave us aptitude tests to see what we were best suited to do. I had a motorcycle back then, and when they asked me what I wanted to do, I said, "I think I'd like to be a motorcycle policeman." Well, that didn't happen, of course.

Remember, I was a guy who had been in church all my life. We were at a gathering one day, and we were told that out of five hundred men, whoever wants to volunteer to be a Chaplain's Assistant, we're going to pick two of you. Two men out of five hundred will be selected.

Of course, everyone who is drafted thinks this would be better than the Infantry, so everyone raised their hands. They called me in for an interview. They narrowed it down from fifty men to five. They interviewed us again, then had us write a paper on what we felt the relationship between a Chaplain and a Chaplain's Assistant should be.

I wrote the paper and at the end of Basic Training, they had a posting on the board outside the company commander's office which listed what MOS you were going to be trained in. Mine was listed as 71M20. I looked it up and learned that it was Battalion Chaplain's Assistant.

They shipped me to Fort Dix, New Jersey, to clerk typist school. From there it was off to Brooklyn, New York, to Chaplain's School. On the first day of Chaplain's School, there were fifty-one of us, and they asked if there were any of us that did not have a four-year degree. Two of us raised our hands. I had taken a few college
Courses. The other guy was merely a preacher by calling. They told us that we were not supposed to be there without a degree, how'd that happen? They had assumed I had a degree. My fate would be in the hands of the head Chaplain the next morning and whatever he chose to do.

We both reported to him the next morning, but he did not know how we had gotten there. He was going to put us on probation for two weeks. This was a very rigorous study, and everyone here has a four-year degree, and it is still difficult for them. Even with them, we still have a high wash out rate. You will be allowed to stay for two weeks to see how you are cutting it. If you're not, it's not the end of the world, you're still a clerk typist.

I made it and the other guy, the preacher did not. Fifty out of fifty-one of us were shipped to Vietnam. The preacher, whose dad was a full bird colonel, was assigned to the Pentagon. I don't know how he managed it, but the preacher went to the Pentagon.

Basic Training was hell. I didn't think it was fun at all. After about five weeks, I called my dad, he was a veteran of WWII and Korea. I told him, "This is hell." He said, "You'll be alright." I think it's like a woman having a baby, they forget what birth was like once it's over. When you're finished with boot camp, you seem to forget how bad it was. Dad told me, "If they tell you to stick your head in a bucket of crap, do it. Just do it and push forward. You will make it just fine." I did, but I've never forgotten how bad it was.

I look back at it now, and I didn't realize how structured everything was. There was this black sergeant, about forty years old, and a big guy assigned to break us. In my opinion, somebody is assigned to break everybody in there; to see how far they can push them and make a killer out of them. We're just street boys, farm boys, and they're gonna make killers out of us.

This guy would do things. When we were off in the evenings, he'd have one of us get him a pack of cigarettes. He say, "I don't have any money, so get me a pack of cigarettes." So, I'd go to the PX and buy him a pack of cigarettes.

I recall a time when we were doing some medical training. The dust was thick. It was dry and hot. They had us low crawling, then dragging a guy through this pit. This sergeant said my head wasn't low enough. So, he came up to me and put his foot behind my neck and shoved my face down into the dirt. I was choking and I thought I was going to suffocate.

He let me go, had everyone stand and then let's us fall out. He wanted to know who wants to volunteer to go through this again. I'd learned it was better to not volunteer. He was not happy. In fact, he made all those who didn't want to volunteer do it again. He put me through the same thing once more. He got me to the point where I was almost lifeless. He finally allowed us to drink some Kool aide, sit under a tree and cool off. I thought, if they gave me a gun and told me I could shoot him and get away with it, I would. I hated him so bad.

I remember after that we were doing bayonet practice. They used to hang tires and you would practice your long thrust and whatever. I was doing a long thrust into that tire and this sergeant stood behind it. He knew that I wanted to stick that bayonet all the way through that tire and get him. They are screaming at us to sound off. I swear, I must have had blood in my eyes, because he looked at me as if he were thinking, "There it is. You are finally there." I look back and I think about it; he accomplished what he was supposed to do. He broke me.

The one thing that got me through Basic Training was the fact that you have a job to do, and you just don't walk away from it. You make it work. Whatever it is, you don't quit.

I remember the beer hall at the Clerk Typist School. We'd all go down there and drink the cheap beer then get up the next morning and go to school. It was mundane. Once I arrived at the Chaplain School, it was a bit different because I was dealing with some guys who were pretty smart. Some of these guys were top of the class, college graduates. Some even had master's degrees. It was kinda like Catch 22, because they just made a joke out of the Army. We were dealing with E-6's and E-7's who barely got out of the eighth grade and they're telling us what to do.

I remember living in the barracks. We had two-man rooms and Saturday inspections. On this day, the colonel would come through. We each had a footlocker, and everything had to be in order. We had one guy, who occupied a room to himself. We had an odd number in our group, so one man was left to himself. This guy didn't have a partner, so we thought it would be funny to make one up before the inspection.

We got a footlocker, and put Smith on it with tape, shined some boots and even made him a bunk. We got everything we needed from Supply. When the colonel came though he asked this lone man where Smith was. "He went home for the weekend, Sir." The colonel was upset and replied, "Oh he did? Write this down Sergeant." I think they're still looking for Smith.

I served during the Vietnam War and served in country. I spent a year and five days there. When I went to Vietnam, I was assigned to the 577th Engineer Battalion. They primarily built roads, and I spent my entire time in country in that unit.

I flew into Long Binh in a commercial aircraft. We left Fort Dix, New Jersey, and I remember they had us take off our winter clothes and put on jungle fatigues. It was cold at the time. They loaded us onto the plane and flew us first, to Juneau, Alaska to refuel. From there we flew to Hawaii, then on to Long Binh. We circled Long Binh, and the captain of the plane calmly comes over the intercom and says, "looks like we have a little skirmish below, it appears that the Vietcong are mortaring the airbase. We have thirty minutes of extra fuel, so we'll be OK, and the Marines will get this cleared up shortly. Sit back and relax and enjoy your last few minutes of the flight." We eventually landed Ok after everything was cleared out.

I remember the heat hitting me in the face when we off loaded the plane that night. You could smell the latrine burn pits and marijuana. Everywhere you went in Vietnam, they burned the latrine waste in diesel fuel. We got on the bus at the airfield because they were going to transport us into town, and this lieutenant comes on the bus to give us a quick indoctrination. He tells us that we are going to go through this village on the way, and the windows on the bus have screens over them. If anyone puts anything on the screens, knock it off and get low. We're going through the village when suddenly, we hear bang, bang, bang. It was the bus backfiring.

We got to our destination, and we had no idea where we were going to be assigned. Finally, they told me I was going to Phou Hip, and I am going to be assigned to the 577th Engineer Battalion. We were only at this first location for about a week, but it was right on a beautiful beach. We were told that we would be moving to the Central Highlands, building roads up there. My first week there, I received my military driver's license so I could drive the trucks and help with the move. It was so different there. It wasn't all spit and polish like it had been in Basic. We were living in the field.

As the Chaplain's Assistant, during that first week, we were trying to get as much packed up from the Chapel as we could. We had this beautiful cross. It was stained glass of different colors, built into the wall. The Chaplain wanted to take it and he got it out of the wall. We put it between two mattresses and got it to where we were going. He had some guys build a box for the cross, put it in the box, and put lights behind it. We then hung it in the chapel. There was nothing out there when we first got there. We were pitching tents and living out of them. It was like a firebase of sorts. We had howitzers overhead. It was an artillery base. We were just an outpost for building roads.

On the base, we built bunkers and showers. We built revetments around the plywood buildings we built for protection. We filled sandbags and placed them everywhere, even overhead on the buildings. I often wondered if they would take a B-40 rocket. I found out. It did!

We saw action a couple of times a week. I had a Chaplain that wanted to kill a "Commie" for Christ. He wanted to get medals. He always wanted to be in the field, and I drove him. I drove over ten-thousand miles all over Vietnam. I drove him in an old jeep pickup. In the bottom were sandbags and, on the sides, we had armor plating. If you were fired upon, you could duck and continue driving. I also had an M-16 hanging from the window and an M-79 grenade launcher beside me. We also had a M-60 machine gun mounted in the back. This Chaplain was out after "Commies." He wanted to be a Combat

Chaplain. All I wanted to do was to get in there and get out safely.

On Sunday's we held six services. We didn't have a Catholic Chaplain, so we hired a civilian who was running an orphanage. His name was Father Lager and he'd never been to the US, he was German. He gave the rest of his life building this orphanage for boys, aged 11-14. He spoke several languages fluently. I really respected the guy, and we gave him ten dollars a service. He drove an old yellow jeep and part of our agreement with him was to keep that jeep running. If he could get it there on Sunday's, our guys would go through it and make repairs. Everyone knew him because you could see his jeep coming from ten miles down the road.

On Sunday's, I was responsible for a number of administrative tasks. I'd load up the song books, cut the bulletins, and make sure everything we needed for the services was in place. I guess on the average, I was shot at, at least twice a week while on the road. I got to the point where I just considered it harassment; because if they wanted me dead, I would have been dead a long time ago. Thirty days before I came home, I got in a firefight and was shot. I then thought, well maybe these guys are serious.

I had mixed emotions about these engagements. Sometimes it was scary, and other times I was just pissed off. There were times when I thought, "Just come at me, I need a piece of you." At other times, I was afraid; there were times I felt sorry for them.

I remember a time, there was a road that came down to our compound. The officers couldn't drive in Vietnam, they were not allowed to drive. They had to have an enlisted man drive them. I'm driving the Chaplain and we're coming down a mountain, and it was very narrow. There was a civilian convoy coming the opposite direction. One of the other drivers came over so close that he clipped my mirror, and the glass broke, landing in my lap. The Chaplain asked me how that made me feel. I replied, "I feel bad for him. He doesn't know me. This is totally impersonal. Someone had probably nearly run over one of his kids in the village and thrown candy or something else at him. They may have treated his daughter badly, and he just hates Americans. I have nothing to do with that." The Chaplain said, "You're finally growing up."

We only had six casualties in my unit. We did have other guys that were injured and shot up though. One casualty was killed by one of our own. The soldier came in and killed the company commander, then ran off into the field. We surrounded and captured the shooter and shipped him off the Long Binh. I don't know what ever happened to him. The young company commander was ten days from coming home.

Two other guys were sent to Cam Ranh Bay and were bringing back two trucks back filled with beer. They were racing around the mountain. One went over the side of the mountain; the truck rolled over on him and killed him. I felt bad for the families, but these casualties didn't have a great effect on me. I didn't know those guys personally.

The next casualty, at one of our outposts, a guy had gone into the village at night and raped a fifteen-year-old civilian girl. He was out on a road crew the next day when an ARVN armored car pulled up looking for him. They were taken to the individual and he was shot in the head. The young girl in question was this ARVN Major's sister. They shot him in the head and drove off. That was the end of it.

I would write the letters home to the next of kin, but the Chaplain would sign them. The colonel said," Make him a hero. We're not taking this to court. It happened. Tell his parents that he was killed in action along a road. You don't have to lie, but don't tell them exactly what happened." Writing those letters didn't bother me too much. I was just careful as to how I worded them, to give peace to the families the best I could, because I knew it would be really hard to take.

Two other casualties that occurred were accidents. Several other guys were injured by mortars and small arms fire. One generator operator was hit by a B-40 rocket and killed as well. I was hit on the road. I took a bullet across the cheek. My replacement told me that after I left, it really got hot in our area along the Ho Chi Minh Trail. They were getting hit every day after I left.

For my time in Vietnam, I was awarded a Purple Heart, Good Conduct Medal, Vietnam Service Medal, and the National Defense Medal. When I came home, I was just thankful to be alive. I was thankful to be living in a country where I didn't get shot at running up and down the road. I heard people complaining about their jobs. These were people who were sitting in air-conditioned offices, and I couldn't understand it. I really appreciated coming back to a free world. I really did. Yet I was somewhat jumpy. I had developed defensive measures to keep from getting killed. Near my dad's farm was a rock quarry. When they'd do blasting over there, I just assumed we were shelling something.

I worked on a hog farm for a short time, then I became an Illinois Farm Bureau Insurance Agent. In becoming an insurance agent, they had me in this back room studying at a desk. There was a lawnmower shop behind us. They started up a lawnmower and it started sputtering and backfiring and before I knew it, I was under the desk. I thought it was machine gun fire. I was so embarrassed. I looked out from behind the desk, and thankfully, no one saw me. I had a few instances like that. I was at my brother's apartment in Oregon one day and someone fired off three shots with a pistol down the street. Before the second round fired, boom, I was flat on the floor.

There is a guy named Benson that I remember fondly from my time in the service. He was an older guy to us, he was twenty-six, very smart guy who worked in personnel. We came to be very good friends. He visited me after I got home and stayed a few days. He eventually got a government civil service job as a historian. He ended up in Missouri and on one of my trips to Colorado, I stopped and stayed a few days with him. He served as our point of contact for guys in the unit, but I haven't heard from him in many years. Another friend, our company clerk in Vietnam, ended up becoming an actor in Hollywood. His name was Dennis Janes. He was born with a silver spoon in his mouth and very cocky. Everybody hated him but me.

My first few months home were really different. People didn't really appreciate us being in Vietnam. I didn't catch a lot of flak like some city guys did because I lived out in a rural area, but I did get some. In fact, I had a dark tan when I returned, and people would ask where I had been. I just told them that I had been down in the Bahama's for a couple of weeks. I also couldn't believe the guys walking around with long hair, looking like girls.

I'm seeing the transitioning from military to civilian life in my own son. He's retiring from the military. He has taken steps to get schooling under his belt and certifications that will help him with employment on the outside. He currently has a national company courting him for potential teaching and instructional positions. I do see a bit of anxiety in him, which I guess is to be expected. He must constantly be on the move.

The military was good for me in a lot of ways. I didn't understand PTSD until I got older. I think the older we get, the worse it gets. I just didn't realize what it was. I have a close friend that has severe PTSD. He was the one who helped me realize my own battle with this issue.

I wish civilians understood that the military is necessary for defense. Without the military, it would be like the battle we are currently in, a country without borders. This is a very serious situation we are dealing with on our southern border. To let hundreds of thousands of people just come across our border illegally; we're not going to be a country much longer. I felt that through my service to this country, I secured my right to vote.

My view of Vets Helping Vets is this: I think it's great, not simply because we're all vets, but because we are helping other vets. We know we can't help the whole world, but we are helping one another, and it's a good brotherhood. I am really impressed with just what we can do to help others. We need to stop looking to the government for help and look for organizations like ours. That's what it's all about, helping your neighbor. All these guys have big hearts.

John L. Price

My nickname is Leroy, but don't ask me how I got it because I don't know. My full name is John L. Price. I grew up in a small community, a brickyard community. Here in the South, they refer to them as Mill Villages, but ours had no mill; instead, we produced bricks. The brickyards built homes for the workers much like southern mill villages. I attended grade school in this small town. But later, I had to travel across the river to Mount Union where I attended high school. When I enlisted in the Navy, I was living in Kesler, Pennsylvania.

I enlisted in the Navy right out of high school. The thing that attracted me to the Navy was the fact that I would not be sleeping on the ground like the Army or Marine enlistees. I wanted to serve, but I also sought a bit more comfort while doing so. My choice of branch was really a toss-up between the Navy and the Marines, and I just decided that the Navy was probably a better fit for me.

My job in the Navy really stemmed from my time in the Boy Scouts as a youngster. Back then, we learned Morse Code in the Boy Scouts, so when I entered the Navy and they began to test us, I did very well in the radio portions of the testing. The Navy used Morse Code heavily in those days and I had a good background in that prior to entering the Navy. That's how I became a Navy Radioman.

I attended Navy boot camp at Great Lakes, Michigan, in January. We plowed through the snow quite a few times while there. Navy boot camp was not particularly difficult for me because I had been well disciplined at home. The Navy just fit with me, and I was eating regularly.

The funniest thing I remember about boot camp was the "Great Lakes Shuffle." We had to put steel wool on the bottoms of our boots and shuffle across the floors to get the heels marks off the decks and floors. And that is the "Great Lakes Shuffle."

Being in the Boy Scouts really helped me adapt to Navy life, along with my strict upbringing at home. Things in the Boy Scouts and around my home were regimented so boot camp and adapting to military life was rather easy. My being somewhat bashful and not very outspoken also afforded me a bit of protection from added attention in boot camp. I simply did what I was told and got along well.

I served in the Navy during both World War II and Korea. I was part of the Flotilla staff, working for a Commander that oversaw a fleet of ships. I was assigned to an LCS Ship – Landing Craft Support. It only drew three feet of water and was seventy-five feet long. We sailed to Pearl Harbor, of course, and all my time during WWII was in the Pacific.

On one of our trips to the Philippines, our engine gave way, so we had to conduct repairs. While there, we missed the real storm that hit Okinawa, Japan. Once repairs were finished, we headed to Japan and strafed some of the islands along the way, clearing the harbors of mines and such. The minesweepers would move into the harbors, cut the mines loose, and we'd fire at them with a 20mm cannon to blow them up. You could always tell when that happened because you could hear the loud "ping" on the bottom of the ship. We continued our way, and I don't recall exactly where we were, but we began training for an invasion of Japan. Fortunately for us, the Japanese surrendered before we launched that mission.

After WWII, I was told that I could join the reserves and receive my discharge faster. Then Korea came along, and they simply went through the files of those who served in WWII. When my name came up, I was recalled to active duty. Unlike in WWII, I served on a destroyer during the Korean Conflict, DD-643. I quickly found out why it was called a "tin can." When it reached the open seas, it rode the waves just like a can would. It crested the waves and then dived straight down into the following wave. We had waves that went clear over the bridge at times. I didn't see any active combat since I was a radioman on the ship.

One of our ship commanders I remember very clearly. He was the commander of the destroyer I was on during Korea. It was his first command. We took a destroyer out of mothballs in Charleston, South Carolina, refurbished it and put it back into service. We took it out to sea and dropped depth charges to ensure that the hull was seaworthy. Then we went into drydock, and they rebuilt the entire ship.

Once we began operations, this Captain brought us into port where when doing so, we would throw what we called "A Monkey Fist" onto the shore, and they would secure this to help tie the ship to the dock. This captain failed to do this. Instead, he pulled the ship in like a car to the dock and simply stepped off the boat. Unfortunately, too much line had been released and it began entangled in the screws of the ship. We had to send divers down to clean the ropes from the screws. When we moved on to refuel, he almost ran us into the fueling dock.

We left the port there and headed to our home port of Newport, Rhode Island. Along the way, we stopped in Norfolk, Virginia, to spend the night. Off in the distance we could see a big communications ship headed our direction. Captain orders that one blow of the ship's horns be blown, indicating that we are going to continue on the path we have set. For some unknown reason, our ship turns fifteen degrees left rudder, right into the path of the oncoming ship. Captain then says, "we'll tell them we are going the other direction. Sound two blasts." The ship approaching us returns with one blast indicating that, "No, you are going the way you said you were going." Our Captain and Executive Officer were at the helm trying to get us turned around. I had just come off radio watch, and here we are, the fantail of the other ship was just passing our bow. We just missed the other ship.

As we traveled further up the East Coast toward our destination, the radar onboard reports that one-thousand yards ahead, we have land. Captain looks at the gyro, the maps and so forth. He says that the radar must be broken or not working correctly since we had just taken the ship out of mothballs just a short time ago. The radar then warns, "Land, 500 yards ahead."

Captain says, "This can't be…" My being on current radio watch, the next thing I notice is the ship shaking like crazy as we're trying to back up. Out the front windows, we saw this mountain we had almost run directly into. That was pretty much my experience with this new Captain.

Getting out of the Navy. Really left me with no feelings at all. It didn't bother me or cause problems. I had no misgivings whatsoever. I was fortunate to have served on several ships, because as a member of the Flotilla Staff, wherever the Commander went, I went. After leaving the ship, I landed with an LST in San Francisco.

My hometown didn't even know that I was coming home. They probably had no idea that I was even in the service. It was just a small community. It was a brick making community that made bricks for the steel mills in the area.

There is one instance that sticks out in my mind as regards to people I met in the Navy. Once when I got on a train in Chicago, my two cousins were on the train with me. I didn't even know they had enlisted. Come to find out, they were going to the Great Lakes with me. However, we never saw each other there because we were assigned to different training companies.

On the various ships, we played cards after the supper meal as a form of entertainment. We played poker, which was a bit unusual, but our Captain played with us. He had grown up through the ranks prior to becoming an officer. He was like one of us, but he was the captain of the ship. Eventually we weren't allowed to play anymore because Captain became tired of losing money.

I enlisted in the Navy on December 31, 1943, and left the Navy in May of 1945, then went back in for Korea in 1951 and ended my time in 1953. Upon leaving the military, nothing really stood out or struck me as strange. Back home we had a soda fountain or soda shop that all the high school kids hung out in. That was the most popular place in town where folks gathered. In the town was a place called the 5220 Club. They gave us $20 a week for 52 weeks. That was our spending money. Jobs were pretty hard to find. I ended up working in a military ammunition supply factory. I loaded 5 inch 50's for cannons all day long. We loaded these into freight cars to be transported to various military bases. I ended up working there for quite a while.

While in high school, I had attended welding school, they bused us over to the next town, twelve miles away for this school, and we learned how to weld. I saw a notice on one of the job boards that a place was looking for a welder, so I applied. I went down and took the test and became a welder. The job I ended up in was fifty miles away from my home, so it was fifty miles to work and fifty miles home, after working ten hours a day. This became too much to handle.

My dad worked in the brickyard, and I found out they had a job opening. I quit the welding job and took the job in my hometown as a brick layers tender. I'd go get the bricks he needed to rebuild the kilns where they baked these bricks. They used a steel frame of sorts to put the raw brick material into, and then push that into the kiln. You made six bricks at a time, then put them onto a cart. I tried that for a time until the Foreman said, "This job's not for you." I was a small guy, and the weight was wearing me out. It was tough, but I did it. They had a brick layers tender job which I then applied for and got.

My whole life was destined to be in the brickyard, but I had the GI Bill and determined that I was going to get out of the brickyards. I went to school for electronics. I went to Temple University in Philadelphia. This was between WWII and Korea so I ended up having to get a deferment so I could finish my degree before returning to active duty.

I don't really think the military affected me that much at all. I was in the Boy Scouts prior to the military so I was already well disciplined when I signed up. I was in a family of eleven children, of which I am the oldest. My dad was a weekend alcoholic. He'd get paid on Friday and head straight for the bar. He worked hard. He was a good worker and hardly anyone could keep up with him. But come payday, he forgot about us and went to the bar. Eventually, he would come home smashed, and I'd sit at the table with him and if I said anything that he didn't like, he'd just slap me in the mouth. After a couple of those incidents, I just refused to talk anymore. It wasn't until I joined the Navy that I began to talk openly again.

My family never heard about my military service. I had left home and lived on my own after I got out of high school, and I never went back home. There was never anything for them to celebrate once I was discharged. They didn't even know I was gone. I didn't receive any special awards while serving, and I maintained the same job during both WWII and Korea.

I remember the phrase and cartoon with the words "Kilroy was here" that originated during WWII. My hope for the future is for world peace. I wish civilians understood about the role of the military. It's for everyone's security and for some it was a requirement. I enjoy the Vets Helping Vets meetings. I think we have a good club here.

Mike Pruitt

My name is Michael Alda Pruitt, and I was known as Mike around my hometown of Belton, South Carolina. I enlisted July 15th, 1966, in the US Army. I had just graduated although I had been working in the yarn mill for two years. I got off my shift that night and was in the poolroom drinking a cold beer with my friend. Neither one of us had ever been out of Belton, South Carolina, except around Christmas we might go to Anderson, SC, to get a new pair of blue jeans or something. My friend, Tony Reeves, had married while he was in high school. He had just got a divorce. Tony said to me, "Mike, let's get the heck out of this town and join the military." I answered, "Let's go join the Air Force." A decision we thought would give us an opportunity for adventure and ensure a better future.

We went over to the recruiting office in Anderson, SC, to join the US Air Force. He couldn't join the Air Force because he had quit school. I could have but decided we would stick together. We would go Army and then Airborne. This was on a Tuesday, as well as I can remember. The Recruiter filled out the papers and said," Y'all be over here Monday morning, and I will have your bus ticket for Fort Jackson, SC." We asked him if we could leave before then. The next morning, Wednesday, we went to Fort Jackson to be inducted into the US Army.

The Army sent me to basic training at Ft. Gordan, Georgia. I had a ball in basic training and thought it was a piece of cake. My dad was a WWII veteran. He had what they now diagnose as PTSD. He was a pretty tough old man who didn't play around much with his three boys and two girls. So, when I went to Basic Training, it wasn't much different to my home life. I had become tough and could take just about anything.

I was more of a goofball and always screwing up such as laughing at something I thought was funny. Tony was more athletic, and they picked him to be squad leader. One day, we had just finished policing up the grounds when someone took a drag off a

off a cigarette, tossed it at the butt can, and missed as we went back in. Here comes the Drill Sergeant asking us who it belonged to. No one admitted to it, so the Drill Sergeant had us low crawl back and forth under the barracks (the barracks were not underpinned back then). It was hot in July. We did that for a while before he gave us a break, maybe he got tired of seeing us crawl. He said he'd be back soon. I told the guys that I'd take the wrap if they each would give me a quarter apiece.

When the Drill Sergeant came back, I took the blame for the group. He took me to the orderly room, gives me a razor blade and instructs me to start scraping wax off of the floors. He let me perform the task about thirty minutes before calling me to attention and asking me again who threw down the cigarette butt. I said I did, but he told me that he knew I didn't, because if I did, I would have told him straight up. He asks me why I took the rap. I explained about the money. He laughs and takes me back down to the barracks. We were instructed to start low crawls again. This made me mad at first, and then I found it a little funny.

As I explained before, I was mischief looking for a place to happen. When we finally started getting breaks, they prepared our passes to be handed out. When they were given out, I always got one because of my buddy, Tony. The other guys left wondering how I was getting a pass after I stayed in so much trouble.

I got orders to go to mechanic school (MOS 63B) at Aberdeen Proving Grounds, Maryland. From there I got orders to go to Ft. Benning, Georgia, to Jump School. There, you do not walk, only run, everywhere. Our motto was, "Airbourne before Christmas." We all made it through weeks before Christmas. I jumped out of the first five planes I ever flew in. Then I got orders January 1967, to go to 1st/325th HQ Co. 82d Airbourne Division, Ft. Bragg, North Carolina, assigned to the motor pool.

I was a good soldier and managed to stay out of trouble except for a few fights here and there. Nothing serious. Then I was assigned to B Troup 2/17th Cavalry 101st Airbourne Division, Ft. Campbell, Kentucky, August 1967. I was made a clerk in the motor
pool. I kept up with the vehicles when they needed wheel bearings changed, and preventative maintenance. It was a cushy job and they treated me well. Our Unit went to Vietnam, December 1967, with what was left of the 101st Airbourne Division of Ft. Campbell. The vehicles left in plane after plane. Their destination, Vietnam!

We stopped over in Anchorage, Alaska. A bus took us over to a building. The whole place was covered in ice. The driver looked as if he was going to run straight into the building. He slid that bus up even with the door of the building while lining it up with the bus door. This amazed us. We refueled in Japan.

When in Vietnam, The Bob Hope Christmas Show was held at Long Binh. We decided to borrow two Jeeps from the motor pool after being told we could not go. By the time we arrived, patients from the hospital filled the rows, leaving us so far back it was like watching dolls. We could hardly see it, and of course, we got caught up with for taking the Jeeps. I got an article 15, busted in rank, and put on a helicopter to go out in the sticks to join the 2nd Platoon.

We were dug in foxholes covered with sandbags with incoming mortars nearly every night. On January 8, 1968, we were attacked during the night but held our position. Mortars wounded fourteen of our group on January 15th and some were medevacked out. Here I am pounding the ground, and I was given a M16. The weapon I used in basic was a M14. I learned how to operate the M16 quickly. We would go out on slow trips called search and destroy. Huffing it through mountain trails, jungles, and the Cambodian border looking for enemy. We come across a small creek. I grabbed some water. Platoon Sergeant said, "You going to die drinking that water," I said, "I'm going to die if I don't." I lived. We went out on an ambush, a first for me, setting up claymore mines. We killed eleven enemies that night.

We received six M113 Armored Personnel Carriers (APCs). Because I had been a mechanic, I was assigned to drive one. It was like a big green box with tracks on it like a bulldozer. It had a 50 caliber machine gun mounted on top and could aim in any direction and two M60 machine guns. We got called to Nui Ba Ra Mountain to protect a signal company on top surrounded by Viet Cong. We took out a multitude of enemies by artillery at Binh Phuoc before they escaped.

The Viet Cong created what we called "spider holes," a network of tunnels and well-camouflaged. They would pop up and start shooting and then disappear in them. We spotted spider holes in a large field. The six APCs lined up toward the field. My APC was assigned to pull up beside one spider hole and drop a hand grenade in it. It was thrown in, exploded. The APC pulled back and waited a few minutes. We went back since there was no activity. My M60 machine gunner got off the APC and looked into the hole as his body was filled with rifle fire.

The enemy started popping up everywhere. I was attempting to get off the APC to assist our gunner, and that is when I got hit with grenade fragments. I had blood covering my face and eyes. I lost some of my vision and could not see. My Track Commander drove the APC, and I manned the 50 Cal. until we could get out of the area to a medevac location. I was transported to a field hospital; from there I was sent to Tan Son Nhut Air Base in Saigon. They were trying to transport me and many other wounded on stretchers to fly us to 249th

General Hospital in Japan. While trying to board us there would be incoming mortars and we would be rushed back to a Conex (huge metal boxes covered with sandbags. After several attempts we finally were boarded. Away we went.

I got promoted to Specialist E-4 while in the hospital. Fortunately, they didn't have a record of my getting busted for going to the Bob Hope Show. I didn't get to go back to the Airborne unit because I couldn't see out of one eye. The sent me to work in the Post Office at a Navy Base with all Army guys in Yokohama, Japan. At the end of 1968 I got promoted to Buck Sergeant E-5.

May of 1969, my career took a bad turn and so did I. I was arrested for tearing up a sign outside a bar. Japanese witnesses supposedly said I didn't do it, but the court didn't pay them much attention, if indeed they did. At the end of my enlistment, I got a plane ticket to go to Oakland California.

I was awarded a Purple Heart, National Defense Service Medal, Vietnam Service Medal with one silver star, Combat Infantryman Badge 1st Award, Republic of Vietnam Campaign Ribbon w/Device, Expert Badge with Rifle Bar, and Parachutist Badge-Basic.

I got out of service in June 1969, and married Beth Gambrell in March 1970. We have done good together and had two children. Marriage takes two people, and you have to have an understanding spouse. They have to contend with the bad ghosts that show up from time to time.

My advice to the young veteran getting out of service: Check and recheck your DD-214. Mistakes are hard to fix if you wait. Go see a Veteran's Administrator right away. If you have a problem and you feel like you are hitting a brick wall, keep going back. Don't let it aggravate you enough to make you give in.

When I got out of service, I attended Greenville Technical College and used up my GI Bill on an education receiving a degree in Mechanical Engineering and a degree in Business. I went to work for Duke Energy and retired after thirty years. Veterans back then never talked much about their service. We didn't discuss the dreams and stuff that causes us to spiral down the hole again. We were too busy trying to make a living. I was a supervisor before I retired because I learned through life how to get something done. I had very little patience with those who always ask what to do.

For a while I didn't want to have anything to do with the military until I attended a reunion of the 217th. Our group served together around the middle of 1967. At the reunion, I met my sergeant and the guy that put me on the helicopter when I got wounded. I didn't remember names but after I got to meet some of them, names started coming back.

Vets Helping Vets gave me some place to go and not be alone. The older I get the more I like my privacy. It is good to be around others who have some of the same issues. Each of us had reached a milestone in our lives and had actually reached out for some help. I am part of the original group of fourteen that continued to meet with Jessie after the VA decided we didn't need to meet. I would encourage others to attend veteran meetings and reunions. Build relationships that are worth your time.

Rock Reinhart

My name is Rock Alan Reinhart, and I was raised on a farm in Northeast Indiana. My wife calls me Rocky when she is upset with me. I get called Rocky a lot. On November 23, 1959, I enlisted in the Navy when I was seventeen, because I wanted to see the world as the ad said. I was tired of the hogs and chickens. I was excited to go to San Diego, California for boot camp.

Basic Training was fun, and I enjoyed it. Much of it passed up because I was picked as a "go-fer" for some officers by what I guess was luck of the draw. I got out of just about all of the drilling on The Grinder, the close-order drill on the endless parade ground for recruits where sailors can't march very well. I was even worse at marching, but I did go through the firefighting part. It was tough. There was a small building that you could not stand up in where you were instructed to go into with all your fire equipment on. The small unit was angled on one side and covered with oil. They would light the oil and it was full of smoke. You went in one way and came out another after putting the fire out.

When I finished boot camp, I was given test to see what job I would be eligible for. I was offered three different schools, but I did not take any of them because I was not sure what I wanted to do. I went upon the ship as a striker. As a striker you can watch other people and see what they do. You can then ask them if you can be in their particular division. I picked supply and became a storekeeper, ordering all the food for the ship. Whenever we refueled another ship at sea, I would measure the number of barrels the ship received, type up an invoice, and send it to the other ship.

After boot camp in San Diego, I got to take a two week vacation. I took a train named El Capitan and traveled thirty-nine hours to Chicago to take another train to go to Indiana where my parents lived. When I got to Chicago, they had lost my bag. All I had on was my Dressed Blues and no jacket. The temperature was freezing, and I had to go from one train station to another on a bus. Somewhere along the way, my bag showed up, and it was delivered to me in Indiana. I rode another thirty-nine hours back to San Diego.

At San Diego, I was put on an Aircraft Carrier that was going through a shakedown cruise (a test or trial journey to declare the craft operational). They were going to drop me off at my new home port at Pearl Harbor, Hawaii. I was assigned almost four years on the USS Ponchatoula throughout the Western Pacific region. The fleet oiler would refuel a Destroyer on one side and an Aircraft Carrier on the other, pumping oil to them at the same time. It was so big, as a comparison, it would not fit in the Death Valley Stadium of Clemson, SC.

While assigned to the ship USS Ponchatoula, I was picked as Petty Officer of the month and another guy for seaman of the month. We had to make a choice between taking our dates out on the town, spend so much as the Navy Exchange, or spend a weekend on the main island at a military camp in the mountain. We choose to go over to Hickam Airforce Base where we would get a free ride to Hilo, Hawaii. An Airforce guy decided to play a trick on two swabbies. Swabbies was a slang term for sailors. He tells us to run out there and hop in that plane. We go to the pilot and tell him our names. He looks at his manifest and can't find our names. He asks us where we are going, and we replied to Hilo. Then he remarks that his plane goes to the French Frigate Shoals out in the middle of the Pacific once a week. At least it was a prank that didn't work.

I saw a lot of beautiful places and ports. While steaming the sea, the bow of the ship divides the water. Porpoises like to play in the fast water and are fun to watch. When flying fish jump out of the water, sailors like to bet on how far they go. All this is very entertaining for sailors. There are three or four initiations in the Navy. One is crossing of the equator and going through these horrendous initiations. You become a shellback. The purpose of the initiations is to test physical and mental toughness while reinforcing teamwork.

Our ship, the USS Ponchatoula, was part of Operation

Dominic 1962. We were waiting for scientists to have perfect weather conditions in order to give their approval for nuclear

weapons tests. This ship was 656 feet long and carried ten million gallons of fuel. When the atomic test bomb went off, the ship moved. It split the air so powerful that it created a vacuum, and then there was another movement in the implosion. We saw the red and black column of fire go up and the white cloud at the top. The air blew the top off the mushroom cloud. When we got back to Pearl Harbor, Life Magazine had the same picture that we had observed. The Navy had us wear dosimeters to measure any radiation we were exposed to, and we had to keep track of that awhile. I didn't have any problems, and my wife says I don't glow in the dark, so I'm safe.

I served on eight different ships throughout my career and traveled to eighteen different countries. Once while serving on the USS Denver, we were steaming in the islands of Japan. These islands have electricity because of the overhead cables feeding the islands. We know how high our ship is and we know how high the cables are because of our navigational charts. Someone forgot about the difference in the tides. We went under the cables and knocked off seven antennas but did not break the cable. At least it was not an international incident, but it was a mess. On the USS Denver there was an amphibious transport dock that lowers itself into the water to land and support the Marines amphibious track vehicles. When the back of the ship comes down, the big gate comes down and hits a piece of steel. The marines use this to enter and exit the floating ship.

We had been selected to do a burial at sea for a chief who had died with the request. We left Long Beach, California. No family or press was on board. We headed out from the coast three miles through the sea, very slowly, because it was foggy. The casket is wrapped, and steel bands are place around it. They march it to the back of the ship where it put over and out to sea. The casket hit the piece of steel on the amphibious transport dock and breaks open. The body floats to the surface. We did not want the body to float to shore. It was foggy and did not want to lose sight of the body. A guy is instructed to keep watch of it from a whale boat (small boat) they

lowered to the water. They big ship was around. Heavy pieces of steel from the machine shop were used to wrap the body in and sink it.

When I was in the Mediterranean, I got to see some great places. Once I saw something unusual on the radar. I was on night watch, and the radar showed three flying targets. We could not identify them because they were moving too fast. As we watched they suddenly disappeared, and we did not see them again. I t was kind of spooky. I do not have an answer for it, but I know what we saw.

During that time Russians complained about the United States following ships around. It was during the Cold War, and they were doing things to us that they complained of us doing. We would turn off our emitting signal equipment antennas and sneak around to the Russians for observation.

One time, I was on a ship with two anchors that weighed at least 22,500 pounds each. A disastrous typhoon came out of the Philippines and worked its way around to our ship near Hong Kong. The typhoon was so strong, the ship was pulled backward with the two anchor dragging ground. The ship was going flank speed (maximum speed) toward the anchors, and we were still being drawn back. It passed over us and flattened the Hong Kong Island. Big freighters and ships were packed up into the islands. The captain got on the loudspeaker and thanked us for saving the ship and his career. We survived.

The Navy decided sailors need to be trained on how to act if they were ever caught and put into a prison in a foreign country. The Army made this mock prisoner camp and had Asians dressed up like Chinese with guns. The sailors would be taught how to behave and what to do if captured. The sailors were put in a cattle car (a no frills bus) to take them up to the Army's post where the training was supposed to take place. Well, the sailors knew if they were captured, they were to escape the evasion. As soon as the doors where opened, the sailors ran in all kinds of directions into a pineapple field. The sailors had a weekend of liberty.

There was a policy in the Navy, if you enrolled in college, you could get out of your enlistment three months early. I wrote to my parents and ask them to sign me up to go to Purdue University. I had changed my mind and didn't like the "Canoe Club." I bought this big motorcycle in San Francisco, California, and rode cross country to start college. I didn't have any goals except to get out of the Navy. I was more interested in chasing girls and riding motorcycles than school.

I got a job working in a warehouse at a candy factory in Kendallville, Indiana. The guy I was working for had fourteen years seniority, and I had more authority as an E-5 after four years in the Navy. About that time a recruiter came to see me. He said if I went back in the Navy before ninety days, I could keep my stripes. So, I decided I had seen the Pacific and wanted to see the Atlantic. I went back in. My parents drove me to Washington DC. I am in the Receiving Station to receive my orders, and they ask me would I like shore duty. I asked where I would go and what would I be doing? They told me it was secret, and I had to get top security clearance to go. I decided to throw my hat into the ring because I knew I should be able to get top security clearance.

In the meantime, the White House is flooded with correspondence because President Kennedy had been assassinated. I am sent to the White House Executive Officers Building to help with the correspondence. I met a young lady over there in correspondence and begin to date her. I didn't have any money, so our first date is a bus ride to a free Navy concert. I have been married to this lady for fifty-seven years, and her name is Bonnie.

While I was dating her, we would go over to Andrews Airforce Base to see a movie. The base was close by, and the movies were cheap. One time, we had an hour to kill, and we went for a walk. On the sidewalk we found a traffic ticket book that belonged to a MP. For about an hour, we had a great time writing tickets and putting them on windshields designated as an officer's car. I can picture the next morning when they ran into the Provost Marshall's office asking what was going on.

The secret mission I was stationed at was Camp David. My wife was stationed at the White House. We were both part of the White House Staff. Between the both of us we have five White House Christmas paintings that we received for serving on the staff. While I was at Camp David, I and other sailors got a letter telling us to change from non-critical skill jobs to a critical skill job. My last job had been in supply, so I changed and went to electronics school and made my E-6. I spent fourteen years in electronics and crossed trained, working my way up to a Warrant Officer. I was on a ship in Charleston as their electronic maintenance officer.

I retired on October 5, 1979, with twenty years of service and about a year of constructed time. Before I retired, I was assigned to a two year tour at the Naval Station in Key West, Florida, as ground electronic maintenance officer. Jet fighter pilots could train at Key West. They did not have to go far to international airspace, and this saved fuel. One came to me about an issue. Knobs had been turned on an instrument panel in the radar trailer, and there were bare footprints inside the trailer. The trailer with the radar equipment was located in the middle of an airstrip between the runways. I recalibrated the equipment and got it back online for the pilots and reported what had happened. Later that day, a guy was caught running naked down the runway. When the air maintenance caught him, they asked him why. He said, "The devil made me do it."

I was sent back to school to be an instructor in Great Lakes, Michigan where I had attended before. Now I was teaching electronics in the same room where I had gone to night school. When I started college, I was able to challenge a lot of courses because of the training the Navy had given me. This meant that I could take a test and if I passed, I did not have to spend time taking the class. I was able to get a Bachelor of Arts and Science in industrial management in three years instead of four.

The United States now has an all-volunteer force and at one time we had the draft where men were drafted through the Selective Service Registration. We have a lot of crime in our society of young people. Maybe if they were forced to spend time in the military, they could learn to channel that energy into something positive. Learn teamwork, set goals, and receive the education that will help them accomplish the goals.

My wife and I eventually retired to South Carolina where our two daughters were living. I talked my wife into RV living. I like the mountains and the lakes of South Carolina. We are part of an organization called Campers on a Mission. Campers go around to different churches and help build handicap ramps or remodel the churches.

Vets Helping Vets is a good organization. It gives veterans a place to let off some steam if they want to talk. There is no pressure if they don't want to. There are no big requirements, and it gives us an opportunity to help someone who needs it. I like the way we pull together to help another veteran.

John Roe

I am John Fain Roe. I was born in Gordon County, Georgia in 1948. My dad was a sawmiller and my mother was a housewife. They eventually built a chicken house that held ten-thousand chickens, and my mother raised the chickens. The house that I was born in, only had one bedroom. Me, my mom and dad, my sister and younger brother, all slept in the same room. It was a big country house, but it only had that one bedroom.

My sister was born with partial paralysis. She had to go to Shriner's Hospital to have surgery on her leg so that she could straighten her foot out and walk more easily. We didn't have indoor plumbing. While she was in the hospital, an indoor bathroom was put in so that she wouldn't have to go out to use the bathroom. She spent about eight months at the hospital. They divided this extra space off and made a bedroom for her, but the rest of us still slept in the same room.

I grew up that way. The only heat we had was a coal fired stove and wood cook stove. We had a well at the back porch and that's where mother washed clothes. We always kept meat; we always had pigs, chickens, and an icebox. Somewhere along the way, I guess I was about seven to eight years old, we got electricity and a phone…a party line with three other people on it.

We never wanted for anything. We always had a place to sleep, food to eat and clothes to wear. There were people in the community that were worse off than we were. When I was about 10 -11 years old, my parents sold that place. My dad had quit sawmilling and started operating heavy equipment for the county. We moved into what I call town, into a neighborhood. At twelve years old, I had relatives that were still sharecropping, growing cotton and corn, so I went to live with them. I spent two years there, picking cotton, picking corn, hoeing corn for spending money. I got three-cents a pound on cotton, thirty-five cents an hour chopping cotton…but at 12-13 years old, in that day, it was good money. By the time I was fourteen, the man that owned the land where they were sharecropping, had also gotten in with the chicken hatchery. He recruited us to catch chickens when they were ready to be sent off.

We'd start on Friday night at dark and catch till Saturday morning at daylight. We'd then come back Saturday night at dark and catch until Sunday morning. If school was out, we'd do the same thing over again on Sunday night. We had to go into that chicken house and physically catch the chickens, then carry them to the truck, where they would be put into a cage to transport them to the processing plant. I was coming to Vets Helping Vets not long ago and passed one of those trucks, and I got cold sweats just remembering those days.

My relationship growing up with my parents was good. Honestly, I know my dad loved me, but I don't remember him ever telling me that. I was kind of a momma's boy, even though I had a younger brother. I don't think my mother ever told me she loved me until I came home on the way to Vietnam. My parents took me to the airport in Atlanta. She hugged me and told me she loved me. My little brother told me later that when she got home, she sat down at the kitchen table and cried for two hours. After that, she never shed another tear.

One of the biggest mistakes of my life was dropping out of high school at sixteen years old. Education didn't have a high priority. My dad had a sixth-grade education and my mother had to drop out in the seventh grade. My mother's dad had been in the Navy and was on disability. Well, Truman came along and stopped all disability. My mother went to work in a cotton mill and supported herself, six brothers and sisters, along with her mom and dad. My mother did this at twelve years old.

My younger brother was so much younger than me, that by the time I left home, we really didn't have a lot of interaction. My sister and I had a brother/sister relationship. Once she was old enough to start cooking and cleaning, she took over that and me

mother went to work. My sister took care of the cooking, cleaning and took care of us. She had as much to do with raising my younger brother and I as my mother did at that point. When my sister got married, our relationship changed dramatically. I stayed with her and her husband a lot. They had their first baby; I would babysit for them. My sister and I are very, very close. My brother and I are close, but not like my sister and me. Today, my sister is my support, other than my wife.

Somewhere in this time, I went to work in a carpet plant. I turned 16 in December of 1964 and went to work in this plant in January. I started at the lowest paying job they had, second shift. After about six months, I was running one of the carpet machines and was making more money than my parents were, and I was only sixteen years old. I got interested in girls, cars, and alcohol. After a few months, I started dating my sister's husband's sister. We fell in love, automatically, and I was wild. We got engaged and tried to get married but couldn't find anyone to marry us, and I thank the Lord for that now. That would have been bad. If I had gone back there after getting out of the Army, I would now be an alcoholic, in jail or dead.

Working in a carpet mill, I quickly learned that I didn't want to spend the rest of my life doing that. I came from basically, a Navy family. So, a friend and I got to talking one day and decided, let's just join the Navy and get the hell out of here. My friend, Ronald, said OK, so we went over to the next town, and the Navy recruiter was out for lunch. So, we said, we'll just join the Marines. We went and knocked on his door, and he wasn't there. We then decided that we'd just go grab a hamburger then come back.

We started out and the Army recruiter caught us. We enlisted in the Army. I was seventeen. My mother had to sign for me. The recruiter came to our house; he came to Calhoun once a week because it was such a small town that there wasn't a permanent recruiter office there.

He came to the house, and my mother started to sign the papers, when she looked up at me and said, "Johnny, I'm going to sign this, but don't ever ask me to sign anything else." She then said, "I'm going to sign this, but if you come back home crying, I'm going to whip your ass and take you back." Those were her exact words.

On February 7, 1966, Ronald, my friend, and I, joined on the buddy plan. It was a holiday, so the recruiter told us to wear our clothes and take one change of clothes with us. We ended up spending a week in the reception center. We stayed in the old WWII style barracks. It was so cold that when we'd wash out our underwear at night, we'd wake up to find them frozen solid the next morning. We were later sent to Harmony Church. They came around asking for volunteers for the Infantry. I didn't know what the Infantry was, so my head Drill Instructor explained that to us. I said that's what I want to do. He was also Airborne, so I told him that I wanted to jump out of planes as well. Ronald and I went to basic, then Advanced Individual Training (AIT). I went on to jump school, but Ronald didn't. In jump school, I made three successful jumps, but on the fourth jump, I broke my ankle. The nature of the break prevented me from being able to jump again.

They sent me to Fort Gordon to Radio School. After Radio School, I thought I could go back to Fort Benning. Instead, I got orders for Germany. I was seventeen years old when I went to Germany. I went to Germany on the last troop transport ship ever, the USS Geiger, containing twenty-six hundred GI's. Our ship left on a Sunday. The following day, the USS Rose was due to depart with my two cousins on board. They pulled them off the boat and flew them to Germany. We spent nine days at sea with a bunch of sick GIs.

Arriving in Germany, I ended up in the 3rd Cavalry, Charlie Company, a recon company. It was nothing like I would later see in Vietnam. We had a tank platoon, mortar platoon and an infantry platoon. We were all cross trained in all the skills. I got there in

August, then we rotated to border duty in September. We came back from that, and headed to Grafenwoehr to qualify on the tanks, mortars, and other weapons. We spent about four weeks there and two of those weeks were in the field. When we went back to the old barracks, they billeted us in cramped quarters barracks. It was cold as hell in that place. Instead of going outside to the latrine facilities, at night, we would just step outside the back door and relieve ourselves there. It was so cold that it would freeze right there on the ground as you were going.

I woke up one morning and I couldn't get out of bed. I couldn't move. The Platoon Sergeant, Sergeant Roland came around and said, "Roe, get out of bed." I said, "Sarge, I can't get up." He asked what I meant by "I can't get up?" I said, "I can't get up." They called a medic and took me to Nuremburg, did a spinal tap and kept me for two days. They sent me back and notified us later that I had meningitis. I don't think I did, but I became a very popular individual because they quarantined the entire company for ten days.

When we got back to Baumholder, two things happened - I was engaged to that gal back home. I had asked her to marry me. I had bought a ring. I knew that the only way I would be able to get home to marry her was to volunteer for Vietnam. A couple of other guys in my squad had done the same earlier. So, I went down and volunteered for Vietnam. It would take about six weeks for the orders to come through. Two weeks after I volunteered for Vietnam, I got a "Dear John" letter. The girl I was supposed to marry was dating someone else. But it didn't bother me. For some reason, it didn't upset me. I simply wrote her a return letter wishing them both the best.

Backing up a bit, let's look at Basic Training. The first morning, at Harmony Church, we fell out for formation. I didn't run. The only sports team my high school had at the time was a basketball team, no track or anything like that. We fell out and they ran us a mile. I got back and I sat on my footlocker, and I said, "Boy, you have really made some stupid mistakes in your life, but you have really screwed up this time."

Basic was not that bad. We did the fire watch, we did the road marches, we went to the classes, we worked with the bayonet, and we did the gas chamber. Drill Instructors were tough. Yes, Basic Training was tough, but it was a good time. AIT was fun as well and I loved jump school, except for the running. I've never been a good runner. The funny thing was, that after I got out of the Army, I started running. I ran three to five miles a day, five days a week.

For fun, during basic training, we slipped off to the beer hall one night. About eight of us. It was that night that I met a guy from Alabama named Roe, whose name, years later, I saw on The Wall in Washington. Coming back from the beer hall, we were all three sheets to the wind, but I had them all in formation. We were double-timing, and I was calling cadence. We walked back into the barracks, and a drill sergeant caught us. We picked up cigarette butts, pulled extra duty, suffered through extra running and extra PT, just whatever he wanted us to do. Thing was, he was just an acting sergeant. He was only an E-4 but assigned as an acting sergeant. His antics went on for a couple of days, then Sergeant Goldsmith put a stop to it. The acting sergeant was abusing us. We'd lay in the dying cockroach position, with an M-14 across our feet. When Sergeant Goldsmith found out about that, he put a stop to it. We got even with that acting sergeant though. One morning in formation, they called him out, took his stripes away from him and shipped him out.

At about week six, we got a guy that was a recycle. We did the forced march and bivouac for three days. We did the crawl infiltration course and the confidence course; and we were just nasty when we returned to the barracks. We all showered, except for this recycled guy. He slept in the bunk above me, and you could smell him. After two nights of that, we took him down and gave him a scrub brush shower.

One of the fun things we did that I remember was the "Slide for Life" at the Ranger Lake, just down from where we had our barracks at Harmony Church. I think we were the only company in our training battalion that did that. That was fun, I enjoyed it and

wanted to do it again, but they wouldn't let us. That's about it for basic training. It was stressful and tiring, just like AIT and jump school. The thing I hate most is that I never got the chance to finish jump school.

As I've already mentioned, I left basic, AIT and jump school and went to Germany. When I came home from Germany on leave, about three days after arriving, some buddies asked me if I wanted to go to the lake with a bunch of college girls. I mean, what am I going to say? "I think I'll stay here and talk to momma and daddy." No, I'm eighteen years old, on my way to Vietnam.

I met my wife that very day. Two weeks later, we were engaged. I borrowed the money to buy her a diamond from my parents. After becoming engaged, I met her mom and dad. My wife was then at Berry College at Nursing School. After meeting them, her father called her and told her that if everyone she dated was as nice as that young man I met, then I don't have anything to worry about. If ya'll still feel the same way when he gets back, then I guess it's permanent. Two and a half weeks later, I left for thirteen months. I went to Vietnam.

I flew into Bien Ho, in Vietnam. When we started exiting the airplane, the stewardesses and flight attendants were standing there crying. When I came to the door, the first thing that hit me was the heat and the smell. I looked at the guy behind me whom I had been sitting with and I said, "Ten thousand years of buffalo **** is what I smell."

We went into these big open buildings that had sandbags knee high all around them, and we waited on the buses. I got on the bus and saw the wire caging on the windows. I asked the driver what the deal was with the wire. He said they had had instances of hand grenades being thrown through the windows, so they put that there to prevent that. My thought at that moment was, "I've screwed up once again."

At the 90th Replacement Center in Vietnam, we spent about two or three days there. We had a couple of formations a day where

they would call out names of men to ship them out. Another guy and I had been sitting and reading the Stars and Stripes paper, and on the front page it had an article about the 199th Infantry. It showed a picture of them crossing a stream with water up to their chests. I looked over at my buddy and said, "I hope I don't get assigned to that unit." Four names later, they called out my name to go to the 199th.

They picked us up in a deuce and a half and carried us over to Camp Fresnel Jones, to where the 199th's rear area was. Once there, we attended a ten-day orientation course. At that point, I'd never had any jungle training. For that matter, I had never even seen an M-16 until I arrived in Vietnam. They took us and trained us on C-4, det cord, claymore mines, flares, and so much other stuff. They'd take us right outside the wire to practice ambushes, or into a couple of local, small villages for training. After these ten days, we had a formation and they started calling us out again. I went to HQ's Company, 3/7th Infantry. I stayed there a couple of days, then was assigned to Bravo Company, 3/7th Infantry as an E-4. This was the middle to end of May 1967.

The unit was in the field, and the Battalion was at a river crossing. A ferry was at this river crossing; and our duty was to protect this ferry and conduct patrols around the area. We were there for about a month, and I thought, "This isn't bad at all." We never had any enemy contact there. I was writing letters home telling everyone that things were cool, things were good. After about a month, they pulled us out of there and sent us up north of Saigon, into an old banana plantation. That was where I had my first firefight.

After being at the river crossing location, thinking that my tour was not going to be all that bad, we were out on patrol and ran across a VC camp. I won't tell you that I wasn't scared, wasn't nervous, yet when it hit the fan, I seemed to calm down. Unfortunately, that day, a guy about three feet away from me was shot and killed. I'll never forget him. I'll never forget his face. I don't know that I shot anyone that day, but the VC had a habit of dragging their dead off the battlefield. You could see blood trails, but no bodies. That was my first time experiencing enemy fire directly. It was then that I realized that what I was in was real.

When the buddy next to me was hit and killed that day, at that moment, I didn't think about it. We were under fire and that's where my focus was. Afterwards, to be honest, I puked. And I cried. Not for the danger I was in, but for him and the family he was leaving behind. It could have been me; the guy was three feet away from me! The casualties did bother me, in fact after many engagements, I would get physically ill and throw up. The thing that bothered me the most was knowing it could have been me, yet it wasn't. That's the guilt I've carried all these years. I really can't explain that guilt and why I have it. A few years ago, I visited the Wall in DC. I've been there three times. And each time, I stand there and cry. I don't care who knows or sees me. I just feel that guilt.

In September of 1967, I was promoted to E-5 and given a ten-man squad. I lost people, yet I feel that if I'd have had more training, would I have done the things I did? I feel I had those emotions because of the lack of training that I had up to that point. I had no jungle training except what they gave us in country. I knew nothing about the country, the jungle, or how to fight in it. I knew how to read a map. I've asked myself more than a million times I know. "Why them and not me?" I've come the realization that God has a plan for me, and I haven't gotten there yet, and I won't die until I do." There are other things that bother me that I will not discuss. There is no reason. There are no answers. At the same time, I was writing everyone at home, telling them that things were ok and that I was fine.

We'd later run into another VC camp, and we were in this ditch, this ravine, and there sits a newsman with his camera. He got me square in the face. I begged him not to publish that film footage. Yet he did. And everyone back home saw it. My sister had written me and told me that all momma and daddy do, is come home, eat, then watch the news, looking to see if they saw pictures of me. That news reporter didn't cut it out, and my mother saw it. Since that day, I've had no use for the media.

Tet came along and we were down south, south of Saigon in the Bien Chon area. We'd been there about four weeks. We'd have one company in for security, and three companies out in the field. The Battalion Commander, for some reason, called everyone back in. The night before Tet. Colonel Chandler just had a feeling about something. Sure enough, the next morning, up to Saigon we went, up to the racetrack in the Cho Lon district. We were there for a week. Alpha Company went in first and they caught it. They were chopped all to pieces. My company went in to relieve them. Over several weeks, we had secured the racetrack, gone back to our original location, only to come back and have to retake the racetrack again. The VC had set their headquarters right on the racetrack. From there, it was house to house fighting. We were not involved in a lot of that, but that was what was taking place there. That was a nerve-wracking time.

We moved out of the Bien Chon district over to the end of the longest runway at Tan Son Nhut Air Base. What we didn't realize was that we had moved here, right in the middle of a retreating regiment of NVA, and we were surrounded. They were retreating, but we were surrounded. That's the place where I saw an NVA soldier get up and charge an Armored Personnel Carrier, equipped with a .50 caliber machine gun. My memory of that was that I lost three men wounded. I received orders to ETS back to the states. I told the First Sergeant that I didn't want to leave like that, not right now. I asked him if I could stay over. He was going to look into it for me.

One of the things that haunts me about Vietnam comes from our being at a firebase, and along comes this APC (Armored Personnel Carrier). A man had been killed, and the crew had simply thrown him onto the hood like a deer. I stopped them and said, "You aren't going to do this. I'll shoot your *** before I let you do this." Someone finally took him down and moved his body inside the APC.

I stayed in Vietnam almost four weeks longer than I was required. Then came the day, the First Sergeant and the Sergeant Major came looking for me. "Sergeant Roe," they said, "You will be on the next helicopter out of here even if we have to knock you over the head and throw you on it." I flew back to Brigade Headquarters that morning, and on an airplane home that afternoon.

I was on a Capital Airlines flight out of Vietnam. We flew through Japan and picked up some dependents, then flew into Alaska. I tried to call home from Alaska, but no one was at home. Everyone was at school or work. We eventually landed in the States. I flew out of Travis Air Force base in California and through McGuire Air Force base in New Jersey on my way home. At the time, I didn't feel too bad because I was with many other guys who had also just left Vietnam. One guy, who had arrived with us, didn't have money to fly home. I had money because I had a month's pay in my pockets. So, I loaned him the money to fly home.

When I got home, I hadn't spoken to my parents since leaving Vietnam. They didn't know I was coming. My sister and her husband picked me up at the airport, and I walked into my parents' home at five o'clock in the morning. My mother was cooking breakfast, and she dropped the frying pan.

I was uncomfortable at home. Some of my friends, who had not been in the military, I just wasn't comfortable around them. I just wasn't. I had grown up a lot. I grew up a lot in Germany. My Platoon Sergeant in Germany made me grow up. He and my First Sergeant in Germany taught me a lot of things. I was a smart-assed seventeen-year-old when I got there, but I grew up.

I sent most of my money back home for my parents to save until I got out. So, I had written them and told them to buy me a good used car for when I returned. It needed tires, and I had taken it to have those tires put on. My mother was taking me to pick it up.

We went under an overpass at the same time a tractor-trailer crossed overhead. It sounded just like a rocket coming in. Of course, I flinched, and my mother said, "Johnny, you have changed a lot." Before I could even think about it, I said, "Momma, if you had lived like an animal for a year, you would too." I would never have said that to her before Vietnam.

I didn't have a real hard time, but I still had time on my contract, so they sent me to Ft. Bragg, North Carolina. They assigned me to the 3rd Army Armory. They didn't know what to do with me. I worked with the Special Forces then, checking out weapons and then checking them back in later in the day. I had been there about four weeks, coming home to Belton South Carolina on the weekends, when the Sergeant Major told me they were looking for people over at 14th Airborne Corps and wanted to know if I wanted to go over there. He noticed that I had been to jump school. I told him that I hadn't graduated jump school, but he persisted in asking if I wanted to go. So, I said yes. I was asked by the Sergeant Major where my jump wings were and I told him, I didn't graduate. That's when he found a pair of jump wings, tossed them to me and told me to put the **** things on my uniform and not take them off.

I never had them sown onto my fatigues, I just wore the ones he gave me. I had those, but never bloused my boots except for inspections. I was there a few weeks and went to NCO School because I had never attended and once, I graduated, I was made a Platoon Sergeant. It was there that I was assigned to what I called, "Death Detail." We were responsible for meeting the bodies of dead soldiers returning home and escorting them. I did that for about three months. I was a nervous wreck. I begged to be taken off that detail. I never did jump at Bragg. I wanted too, but never did.

The day I signed out of Ft. Bragg, the Captain that signed me out told me to change out of my uniform before I left the base. They are having a demonstration downtown and you don't want to get mixed up in that. I knew he was afraid of what I might do if I was around those folks. So, I did. I took my uniform off. When I got home, I packed all my stuff into a duffle bag. Everything, including my medals, awards, and uniforms went into the duffle bag, and I stored it. To this day, I don't know where it is. I don't know who got it or what happened to it, but I'm still looking for it.

Kathy and I were married in August after I had gotten home in June. This past June was 53 years. We were both just nineteen years old when we married on August 4, 1968. I am proud of the fact that even though I dropped out of school at a young age, I was able to earn my GED in Basic Training. Then after leaving the Army, I attended college and earned my degree.

I don't talk to my family about Vietnam. Much of it they simply wouldn't understand. My son and I have had some discussions because he spent time in Iraq, but as a whole, I don't talk to them about it. One of my greatest regrets about Vietnam was the amount of collateral damage caused by combat operations. As in any war, innocent people will be affected in great ways.

Before I found Vets Helping Vets, I almost lost my family. I had fallen into heavy drinking and was hooked on pain medication. I quit and went to rehab. I've had maybe three glasses of wine in the last twenty years. I still take pains pills, only now, I don't take more than I'm supposed to.

I started coming to Vets Helping Vets four years ago. I held off on the Monday Night meetings for quite a while, I didn't feel like I would fit in. That changed when I started attending. Vets Helping Vets has given me a whole new life. I had to retire at 40 years of age due to my back. I had missed a lot of time at work because of it. When I did retire, I went downhill fast. I buttoned up at home, I didn't get out. I didn't go anywhere; I didn't feel comfortable anywhere. I went to church with people that didn't even know I was in Vietnam. I just didn't bring it up.

Mike Pruitt invited me a couple of times, but I didn't want to come. I didn't want to dig all that stuff up again. One day I met Mike at Sam's, and he invited me again. I walked up front, and Chuck Watt invited me. I went over to Walmart and ran into Billy Conrad. Within an hour, three men from Vets Helping Vets had invited me to join them. The next Wednesday, I was there. This group has gotten me out of the house helping people, working the yard crews. This group has gotten me involved again. I don't hesitate now to pick up a phone and call people. I keep up with many of our vets. This group has given me something to do. This group has given me purpose again. I keep going, despite my own physical issues, because I love it. Vets Helping Vets has given me a new lease on life. This group saved my life.

Rudy Ruediger

I am Elijah John Ruediger. I served in the United States Army with the 82nd Airborne Division. Most people call me Rudy. I picked that nickname up in Basic Training because the Drill Sergeant kept asking me if I was related to the Notre Dame football player. He kept asking me that constantly, so I got to the point where I just no longer fought it. You have a nickname that people will give you and then you have one that you absolutely hate. Another nickname given to me was "Broad Shoulders," because I used to work out a lot, and I looked like an airport porter.

When I enlisted, I was living on a farm in Washington State. My family owned about 1800 acres around our house. After 9-11, things on the farm, and for just about everyone my age, changed. I started talking to a recruiter but had to wait because I wasn't even seventeen yet. I wouldn't turn seventeen until the next month, so I had to go through the whole process of having my parents sign for me to be able to enlist. I eventually left home after I graduated high school in 2003.

I must look at my childhood and my relationship with my parents in retrospect. Before my military service, and then afterwards, because they are two very different things. Before I enlisted, I was raised in a very religious farming family. Nazarene actually. Every time the church was open, we were in it. I can't think of a time when we weren't doing something that didn't involve the church. Looking back, I am somewhat perturbed by how cloistered it was. It's hard to understand the world and be Amish at the same time. I started to understand the world better after I joined the Army. Just because you have one person's viewpoint, or one community's viewpoint, doesn't make it entirely correct. What Iraq and Afghanistan did to my faith is a whole separate issue.

I do have an older sister, but we seldom talk. She has a very left leaning viewpoint, and it causes strife in our relationship. She currently lives in Oregon, and I feel that her views were shaped by her time in San Francisco. She married about three weeks before I left for basic to a man who was then attending seminary. Her husband is a minister in the Methodist faith.

There were several veterans in our community growing up - WWII vets and such. A couple of guys had flown with the AVG in Burma, and another had been a Pathfinder. I found that interesting. I always hung out with my granddad's friends and loved to hear their stories. From them I got a pretty good understanding of the military. I was in high school when Stephen Ambrose came out with his book, "Band of Brother's." The Airborne Infantry in that work is what got me headed in that direction. If I had read "Six Silent Men" prior to joining the Army, my choice would likely have been different.

Getting off the plane in Atlanta, on my way to Ft. Benning for Basic, was a culture shock for me to say the least. Besides people's accents, my hometown had only six-hundred people. And we might have a handful of minorities at any given time. I grew up with a lot of blatant bigotry. My grandfather was especially bad at that. I had to push myself to overcome what I had been taught growing up. I will always be grateful to the Army for helping push me beyond that.

For me, Basic Training was more of a mental exercise than it was physically challenging. I had prepared myself physically because I knew that I had an Airborne contract with the Army. I was doing full practices for sports at school, then running six miles afterwards to prepare for the military just to get myself into shape. I was expecting the Army training to be a real "ball buster." The training was ok, but I guess I had over trained before I got there. For
the mental aspect, remember, I grew up in a very religious setting.

The Army was teaching me to kill. It was initially difficult for me to come to grips with that. I was taught that life was precious and valuable. Looking back now, I see that it is not really a hard thing to do after all. I just had to wrap my head around that. I got over that by realizing that not letting down my buddy was more important. Being part of the collective group was more important than my own personal misgivings on the concept.

We had several Drill Sergeants in Basic that were a lot of fun. I used to mess with them sometimes. We had one Drill Sergeant that taught us how to hunt turkeys on the mortar range. I was an 11 Charlie, Mortarman. I didn't want to be, but anyone who came into the infantry that could do math, was sent to the Mortar training. So, we're out on the range and the Drill Instructor tells us to take the blank firing adapters off our rifles and give him a section of cleaning rod. He begins to show us how to shoot turkeys with a cleaning rod. He even told us how, at one of his previous units, they would take the new guys, wrap them up in a sleeping bag, put peanut butter on them, then shoot the racoons off their chests.

For me, adapting to the military was a simple choice, either "All in or All Out." I had to work around my personal misgivings based on my religious upbringing. Let's look at it this way, the military gives lip service to religion, but it is not based upon religion. That was the most awkward point that I had to work on early in my military career - how to balance my faith and my chosen profession. I know which one I chose more. The guys I was with kept me alive more than anything else.

From Basic Training and Jump School at Ft. Benning, I went directly to Ft. Bragg 1/325th Airborne Infantry Battalion. I got lucky my first few days there. My unit was still deployed when I arrived. I had missed the last flight out for replacements by a couple of weeks. I was a little pissed about that because as an infantryman, you want to prove yourself. Everybody's itching to get a crack at it. However, I got stuck on the rear detachment detail, painting, and cleaning all sorts of things. "Look at me, I'm helping Uncle Sam win the war by spreading paint!" As a nineteen-year-old kid, you can imagine my frustrations with that.

The first thing I heard when the unit got back was, "Oh look, we've got a cherry!" I knew it was going to be a long road from there. The harassment was going to start. It is what it is. But what I learned was I had to prove that I wasn't afraid of anything, and that there wasn't anything that I wouldn't do for the platoon. Once you proved yourself with the guys, you were in. We used to have weekly scuffles with the Scouts in the hallway. They would gather out there to recite the Ranger Creed, and we never missed an opportunity to start some shit with them. Most of the guys are standing there waiting to use the old bay type showers. The throwdown starts, and you have guys flying and running all over the place naked. If you could prove that you weren't afraid to run in to the middle of that and take on the biggest guy, you quickly earned their respect.

Between my arrival at the unit and my first combat deployment, I was involved in a lot of stuff…we did a lot of stuff. We were being refitted and re-equipped after their first rotation into Iraq. In May of that year, we were doing EIB (Expert Infantry Badge) training, preparing for that course. I received my EIB as a private. I also did the EMTB course and received a Medic badge for that. I also had eye surgery done during that time so I would not have to wear glasses anymore.

After the unit had finished all the refitting and training, my first deployment was to Afghanistan. When Phantom Fury kicked off in Fallujah, we were the Division Readiness Brigade. We got a call to assist at one point, then they called us off and sent in the Marines instead. We were a bit disappointed because we were all itching to get into the fight. I had even had a notebook while in high school that I had scrolled across the top, "Baghdad or Bust." Not knowing that later, I would get more of Baghdad in my life than I could handle. I was still just wanting to get into it.

At the time we deployed, Ft. Bragg had been in the process of trying to mitigate the cost of sending troops to the JRTC (Joint Readiness Training Center) at Ft. Irwin, California. Instead of JRTC, we had a poorly planned training exercise at Ft. Bragg prior to the deployment. I saw what a disaster this turned out to be, so I had

some reservations as to how things would be handled once
we got on the ground in Afghanistan, or if the information we were being given was even accurate. Some of the things we were being told, prior to the deployment, proved to be quite asinine and didn't have any relevance to what was to be found on the ground. There were things like "Don't drink and don't have sex with the locals."

I'm a big fan of Lawrence of Arabia, so I went over there with this intention of gaining a better understanding of the lifestyle and culture of the country. I spent a lot of time hanging out with the interpreters we were assigned, playing cards, watching Turkish belly dancing on TV and getting to know who they are as people. I enjoyed the culture. It was a learning and eye-opening experience for me. The Pashtun culture resonated very well with me, because, it has a very old soul, I guess you can say. They respect fighters. It's about respect. Their stance is that we've been Afghani for ten years and Muslim for five hundred. We've been Pashtun for five thousand. Their tribal sense of self is who they are to the very core. I can respect that. It's just people living out in the middle of nowhere, and they just want to be left alone. They don't care about Kabul, the government, or the Taliban. They just want to be left alone. They want to live their lives as they see fit. I can relate to that because I grew up in a small town. We didn't like our government, the government in Olympia, because they just ran roughshod over us. How can you argue with their logic? They have two donkeys and a tractor in the entire village. They don't give a *** about Kabul.

We started our deployment in Galan, along Highway One. We built our own FOB (Forward Operating Base) on a base left over from the opium wars with the British. The place was really falling apart and dilapidated. We managed to get a stream incorporated into
the camp, and it had a waterfall. That waterfall became our shower. We washed our clothes in the stream and had one of our troops, who originated from Ethiopia, make fun of the way we washed our clothes. He would tell us, "You white boys don't know anything about doing laundry!"

It was a Spartan existence for us. We slept on the hoods of our vehicles or inside of them for about the first month, until we managed to steal some tents and other needed supplies. To this day, I still miss that. I miss the hardships we had to go through as a team to make it work.

We had a small engagement one night that wasn't anything much, but it amazed me as to how much I had struggled with the idea of killing someone up to that point. I found that I didn't have those same feelings anymore. Considering how big a deal that concept was to me just a year and a half prior, it became no big deal. The big shift for me came in 2006. We had lost a couple of interpreters at one point. The Taliban were double stacking land mines in the wadis. They were designed to blow up into passing vehicles.

Our Humvees had what we called the "Suicide Seat" in the back. We had armor plates in the back compartment of the vehicle, but they were not very well secured. If you hit one of these mines, it would blast upward into the armor plate and send the plate whirling around inside the troop compartment. It took one guy's head clean off. Prior to leaving the FOB (Forward Operating Base) on a mission, we'd flip a coin to see who got that seat this trip.

In some ways, I don't want to say 'contempt,' but it seemed that worrying about living didn't seem to matter as much. You're almost like, "It is what it is." The reality of death was real, and each deployment proved to be a progression of that.

Combat, up until 2006 was exhilarating. Sometimes it was mechanical. It's hard to explain to people. I refer to it as the "Apex of Human Existence." I would even put it onto the same parallel as sex because you are never more alive than when someone is trying to kill you. You hear the rounds as they snap by your head, and you know they are trying to kill you, but you are trying to get them first. There isn't anything that compares to that. Sometimes I must reign in that feeling. I was kind of surprised by it in general and how I adapted to the situation. There are somethings in your life that you can work on to improve, but other things just evolve as you go along.

We had casualties in our unit, and one that stands out involved my roommate, Benny Franklin. He was from Travelers Rest, South Carolina. David's dad was in the 82nd back in the eighties and was part of the movie, "Red Dawn." The parachute scenes were conducted by the 82nd, dressed as Russian soldiers. We had gone out on a mission and were headed back to the trucks. One of our FO's (Forward Observers), also named Franklin, stepped on a mine as he reached the door of the truck. It blew his leg off. He bled out. We couldn't secure his artery to stop the blood flow. The powers that be made a huge mistake though. They informed the wrong Franklin family that their son had been killed. They informed the family of my roommate. He had not been killed. The other Franklin had been. What a mess that was.

We had other casualties as well, Sergeant White being one, but one that hit me the hardest was when we lost one of our interpreters. He was one of the guys that I had spent a good deal of time with, playing cards and such. I was also learning Pashto from him. He got killed by the suicide seat as well. His death affected me in two ways. First, he was a great guy. Second, there was a palpable change in how the interpreters interacted with us after that. You noticed how things were off from how they had been previously.

You got the feeling that it wasn't just the loss of one of their own. I ended up buying a goat for his service, as a gesture. It was something in the way they reacted to us, something had changed after his loss. Their attitude changed in what I would call a bad
way. It was a lack of trust I felt. It could have been anyone sitting in that seat that had gotten killed. But I knew that was something we had to work on because they were our lifeline. We couldn't speak the language. They filled such a void for us. These interpreters had worked with other units in the past and were experienced. I think there are several reasons why this level of trust was eroded.

Every combat deployment was different. I don't think any are ever the same. Iraq and Afghanistan are vastly different countries as are the people. The evolution of combat changes from one engagement to another. We are always evolving in our methods of taking enemy lives. War is all about finding new ways to kill the most people in the shortest amount of time. With war you will have innovation and counter-innovation.

My combat experiences varied over the deployments. I felt the year 2006, was the most purpose filled deployment. We were hunting down and eliminating people who had it coming. That was what I joined for, and it was the best deployment I had. That deployment changed me because half of my platoon ended up being wounded. One of my good friends got killed right beside me. It was then that I hit another threshold in my progression with my personal beliefs. I recall one operation where we set up outside a Conex facility. They were making VBIED's (Vehicle Born Improvised Explosive Devices) in that facility. Our platoon had set up outside when they began dropping mortars on us. I remember they were just walking the mortars all around us, and it was stripping the leaves off all the trees around us. You could hear the pieces of shrapnel whizzing by our heads. I look over at my buddy, Merck, and he's got this big, silly grin on his face. He was just lying there laughing at it all.

Going from that to ten days later when he was killed, oddly enough, by a mortar round. That still sticks with me. At that moment we were pressed to the ground, laughing at the mortar rounds, feeling like nothing could touch us. Then a few days later, he's gone. I'm still working through all that.

I was awarded a few awards. I got an Army Commendation Medal for some of the fire missions I called in. I am just one of those guys that is not going to sit on the sideline while my team is out on the field. At one point our platoon was at a base, and I volunteered to go out with a team. I was carrying the satellite radio that I had learned to operate. I wasn't going to just sit around in the base camp and do nothing. Being stuck, after I was injured, not being able to be in the fight, really upset me. Being the Rear Duty NCO and dealing with dirtbags all day, every day, caused me great issues. "Why was I stuck doing this when I still had guys from my platoon out there in the fight every day?"

Getting back to the awards, I have a Purple Heart, several Army Achievement Medals, Jump Wings, German Jump Wings, Salvadorean Jump Wings. These last wings I cannot find. The actual medal itself is hard to come by for some reason. All I have for these is the certificate.

My injuries were sustained when I was hit by an 82mm mortar. We were inside a small tin building where we had established a Command Post, and I had set up the Satellite radio. I had gotten hit earlier in the day when the enemy fired a 60mm mortar at us. I found out later that this facility had been used as a mortar training facility prior to the war.

I was sitting at a desk we had found, with my feet up on the desk, taking a nap, and a mortar round landed right beside the tin building we were in. I woke up to the sound of the blast, flying through the air, and being pummeled with glass. That was the first time I was blown up that day. I didn't notice anything physically wrong with me as I went to check on the other men, until someone told me I was bleeding out of my arm. My Platoon Leader later asked if I wanted a Purple Heart for that and I told him, "No! If I get a Purple Heart, I want it to be for something worthwhile."

That was a bad choice of words because a couple of hours later, they put an 82mm round right through the roof of the building I was in. The round landed about a meter from me and threw me across the room. When I came to, the building was on fire. I couldn't get over to my buddy, Merck. This event is when he was killed, and that's still hard for me. He had been sitting at the radio beside me. It was my radio, but he had taken over for me so I could eat and catch a little rest.

There were three of us around that desk. We were all blown

in different directions. I could hear Brian, another buddy, screaming. He was on fire. There wasn't anything anyone could do about the situation in that moment. I ended up hopping on my one good leg out the side of the building through a hole that had been opened up because of the blast. Another buddy, who had been positioned on an adjacent building with a sniper team, ran up to me and asked about the others. I told him I could not get them out, and he took off into the building. That was the last time I ever saw him. He was killed the next day.

Several other guys and I were laid out on the ground. The doctors and medics were working on us. Our platoon got hit hard that day. It wasn't just us that got hit there in that building. They mortared the entire area that we were in. All this incoming mortar fire was taking place as they were working on us. Thankfully, a lot of the rounds they were sending our way were not going off because they had evidently gotten caught up in the rate of fire and failed to pull the pins on them. They would land and not explode.

I came home in 2006 pretty drugged up because of my injuries. I have a picture of General Mulholland pinning on my Purple Heart in Balad. There was a lot of uncertainty during that time. I had lost some toes and had a loss of feeling in my left leg. There were a lot of questions as to what my future would be. I sure as hell couldn't skateboard anymore. Some buddies from my platoon used to go around downtown Fayetteville, North Carolina, to ride skateboards, but that ship had sailed when I lost my toes.

There's a couple of things that stick out regarding Vets Helping Vets of Anderson: Jesse, and also, the Combat Veterans' group that meets on Monday nights. There are veterans of various conflicts in that room. We've not all seen the same forms of combat.

However, some things about combat do not change, like how you react. The first thing I greatly appreciate about that group is the acceptance, from all levels of Veterans. War and soldiers don't really change much, but techniques do. There are certain aspects of combat that will always remain the same. One of the things that has been brought home to me by being part of that group.

On top of that, I find comfort in the vast level of experience in dealing with the issues found within this group. I've had guys from the group talk with me about their own struggles with alcohol and pills. I had a horrible time with pills after my injuries because the Army and the Veterans Administration just kept pumping me full of that crap. These conversations helped me a lot because they have been dealing with that a lot longer that I have. That gives me hope. Sometimes all you need is hope.

Don Saxon

During the winter of 1968, I enlisted in the United States Marine Corps reporting for training to Parris Island. While on leave from basic training in the summer of 1968, I married my high school sweetheart, Judy, whom I first met in the eighth grade. Thirty days after our wedding, I was on my way to Vietnam.

I served with Company B, First Battalion, Seventh Marines, First Marine Division in the Quang Nam Province of Vietnam based on what was called "Hill 10." To prevent rocket attacks on Danang, these Marines were responsible for patrolling the surrounding area both day and night. While on one of the night patrols, my squad was attacked three times. During the third ambush, three of our patrol members sustained injuries. The Navy Corpsman was shot in the arm. A grenade was thrown between the tail-end man and me causing both of us to sustain injuries. The two of us were unconscious for a period of time and were unable to remain with the squad while they established a position in order to return fire. Being unable to reach the two of us because of heavy enemy fire, the remaining squad members engaged the enemy. They were constantly calling out to let us know they were coming to attend to us and to take us to their position. We were separated from our squad for quite some time.

After we were reunited with our squad, the corpsman (with his arm bandaged) attended to our wounds. My arm, shoulder, legs, and hip were injured by shrapnel from the grenade. The other Marine received massive wounds to both of his legs. Our squad leader used the radio to call for a medivac chopper to take us to Danang for treatment. The corpsman refused to leave. He was determined to remain with the squad in case other Marines were injured during their efforts to return to the hill.

When the chopper arrived, the crew attempted two landings despite heavy enemy fire. After the second attempt, the chopper pilot radioed our squad leader asking how many were to be evacuated. The squad leader replied three need to be medevacked but one, the corpsman, refused to leave. Our squad leader informed the pilot that he needed to get the two marines out of this situation. The pilot responded to get them ready because he was setting the chopper down this time. Under heavy fire, squad members loaded us into the chopper. We were flown to Danang. I spent three days in Danang before being transported to 106 General Hospital in Yokohama, Japan, for two weeks. Finally, I was flown to Charleston Naval Hospital and remained there for 9 months while undergoing several surgeries and receiving physical therapy.

I was awarded the Purple Heart, Marine Corps Achievement Medal with the Combat "V." It is impossible to fully express my gratitude and appreciation for the bravery and dedication of my fellow Marines, Navy Corpsmen, and helicopter pilots and crews. They often faced extremely dangerous and difficult situations. Helicopter pilots and crews literally placed themselves in harm's way to remove injured marines from potentially deadly situations. To this day whenever a helicopter passes overhead, I hear the sound of those blades in the air, and I vividly remember the pilots and crew members who risked everything to bring us to safety.

Using the GI Bill, I attended Tri-County Technical College earning an associate degree in engineering graphics and design. Then, I attended Clemson University and earned a bachelor's degree in industrial engineering and a master's degree in administration and Supervision. I was very fortunate to spend thirty-six years in public education in Anderson County: nine years in the classroom, eight years as assistant principal, fourteen years as a principal, and five years at the District Office as Director of Student Services.

In 2014, fourteen military veterans began meeting together weekly. It means a lot to me that I am one of the "Original 14." Our group has grown to approximately a hundred vets attending every week. The friendship and patriotism of these men and women is outstanding.

I encourage today's youth to realize how fortunate they are to live in the United States and the efforts so many put forth give us the freedoms we experience every day. Remember our history and give back to your community and to your country. Having been an educator for many years, I know firsthand the great potential this new generation possesses. My prayer is that the United States continues to be a world leader and I believe that the youth of today will be the heroes of tomorrow.

Robert Lee Scroggs

My name is Robert Lee Scroggs. I have a couple of nicknames that have been used in my lifetime that have stuck with me. The first is "Bud." I got that nickname from my uncle. The other nickname I have is" Snoopy." This nickname came from my mother, because she was fond of saying that I was always "snooping" around in places and things that I ought not be sticking my nose in.

I decided to enlist in the military, because I had gotten my draft notice in the mail. I had other family members that had served in the military, in all different branches. I wanted to be different. I didn't want to get drafted and placed into something that I knew I wouldn't like. So, I made the decision to enlist in the Marine Corps. Immediately, I was told by family members that I wouldn't make it. I wasn't cut out to be a Marine. For me, joining the Marines was the best decision I could have made. The Marine Corps completely changed me. They helped me. At the time I enlisted, I was a wild one. I had gotten into drinking, all sorts of other things and needed the discipline and structure that the Marine Corps provided.

Most everyone has heard that one thing the military does to you in basic training is to tear you down and then build you back up. That's exactly what happened to me, and that is just what I needed at that point in my life. If that had not been the case with me, I don't imagine I would be sitting here today.

I was twenty-one when I enlisted in the Marines. I was a bit older than most recruits at the time, and I didn't graduate high school. I quit in the tenth grade. I just left high school and kinds did my own thing for years. I had dead end jobs and moved around a lot, not accomplishing much of anything. At the time, my life had no real focus. I'd spend a little time here and there and always ended up back where I started.

At the time I enlisted, I was living at 29 River St. in Pelzer, South Carolina. My wife and I had just gotten married, and we found us a little place to live. That was difficult for us because I still had no real direction and discipline in my life, but my family also had a history in the military. I was at the age that I knew a draft notice was soon coming. I didn't want to be drafted, so I figured the best way to beat that and to get into a position that I wanted, was for me to enlist. Which I did.

Up until this point, I had never really considered the military despite all the involvement of the US in Vietnam during this time. I wouldn't want to go through all that again, but I am glad that I did. I had seen all the scenes of death and stories about the war on the news, but for some reason, it never hit home for me until I started considering the possibility of me getting drafted.

Marine Corps basic training for me was relatively uneventful. I can remember the day I left home for basic training. I had a friend who was in the Army, and he tried his best to convince me to join with him. We actually rode the same bus back to Ft. Jackson in Columbia, SC. He had been home on leave, and I was reporting for swearing in and then shipment to Parris Island. I told him that I couldn't join the Army because I had already committed to the Marines, and I was going to see it through.

I remember arriving at Parris Island very well. The bus I was on was crammed full of new recruits. There were men filling the seats and even sitting in the aisle floor. We were all tired and had no idea of what to expect. It was about 3 o'clock in the morning when we pulled up in front of the reception station at Parris Island. The next thing I remember was this big, muscular, black Drill Instructor opened the door of the bus and casually walked into the front of the bus. He looked down the line of men seated in front of him and spoke in a calm, collected manner. He said, "My name is Staff Sergeant Such and Such, (I don't recall his actual name), and on behalf of Uncle Sam, the United States Government, and the Marine Corps, I want to welcome you to Parris Island."

The drill instructor then turns and looks at all the men before him, looks out the window at the assembly area outside the bus where all the yellow footprints were painted on the concrete, and starts screaming at the top of his voice to get the **** off his bus. We were given three seconds to clear the bus with all our belongings and be lined up with our feet on the painted footprints. In our hurry to get off the bus, the drill instructor was pushed out of the way and almost trampled.

That was my welcome to the US Marine Corps Training Depot at Parris Island, SC. Basic training was difficult for me at first, at least the physical aspect of it. Up to this point, remember, I had been doing my own thing back home and getting in shape physically was not one of my top priorities. Towards the end of the first training cycle, my physical stamina had improved, and I received far less attention from the drill instructors.

In basic training, you didn't want to be personally known by a drill instructor. You did not want to stand out as a possible problem child. For that matter, you didn't even want to draw attention to yourself by smiling at a drill instructor. Stuff like that could end up being hazardous to your health and well-being.

Basic training was all about the business of making your ready for Vietnam. I mean, most of us knew we were going to end up there at some future point. We didn't engage in much outside of training, cleaning the barracks and equipment, and learning all we needed to learn. Playing pranks and such was not something many considered. I think for each of us in that class of Marines, our minds were in other places.

One thing from basic that I do remember was the day we were practicing for graduation out on the parade deck. We were marching back and forth, doing our thing and along comes a group of female Marines. Well naturally, for men who had had no interaction with a female in weeks, we turned our eyes to catch a glimpse of the as we marched past. That was a huge mistake. I think the drill instructors did this on purpose. All I did was cut my eyes towards the ladies. I never turned my head. I just kept marching forward, but my eyes were what got me into trouble. Before I knew it, a drill instructor was in my face, screaming at me for looking at

ladies. He took off his drill instructor hat and drilled me right between the eyes with it. That got my attention quickly. It knocked me backwards. But he had proven his point, attention to even the smallest of details was critical.

Apart from that, I didn't really have issues adapting to military life. In fact, the discipline and structure were exactly what I needed at that point in my life. I took up the military life fairly quickly. It proved to be a lifestyle change that was beneficial to me in many ways.

When I first arrived in Vietnam, I was assigned to an H&S Company. It was more of a reception station in country until you went through orientation, and they sent you out to your field unit. I flew into Da Nang. The reception station was at the south end of the runway there. There was a little area at the end of this runway which was known as the "Dog Patch." There were several small hooches there, and our area was just up the hill from this. On the third day I was there, we had a cargo plane full of equipment to get shot down near the end of the runway. It was carrying a cargo of Kbar knives and .45 pistols. I ended up walking guard duty around the wreckage one night from 2:00 – 4:00 am. I was out near a little cemetery. There were little Buddha and other statues all over the place. To be honest, I was scared out there.

After about three months in Da Nang, I was finally sent to my unit up the Dong Ha River. We occupied a little beach area that afforded very little room in which to maneuver trucks in. I was a truck driver responsible for hauling fuel. While I didn't see combat like many other Marines in country, we were still required to run patrols around our small base area. I remember one day we had a Recon Marine assigned to our unit. He managed to gather some men who would conduct patrols around the area in order to keep us safe and prepared. Up until this point, everything in the camp had been going fairly well. No major enemy issues, nor contact. Just small things. Then one day we started receiving mortar fire.

There was a spotter out there somewhere because they were just walking the rounds right across our compound. One of those mortar rounds fell directly onto one of the tent stakes inside the compound. A friend of mine was killed as a result. The Recon Marine died later after having been shot by one of the Vietnamese soldiers during an ambush patrol. These deaths were hard to take because they had become friends to me. We knew each other. It was a sad loss and one that I carry and remember to this day.

Most of the combat that I saw came as a result of either being attacked as mentioned above or in small skirmishes we had while out on local security patrols. I was never injured in any of these actions and was not awarded any citations because of them. We did take causalities in our unit apart from those previously mentioned. Each of these casualties hit home whether they resulted in death or not. We learned that we were not invincible. This is war and men die.

When my time came to leave Vietnam. I didn't want to leave. I didn't want to leave my friends. I had bonded with those men, and they had become my family. I felt like I was deserting them and leaving them behind.

Unlike many soldiers and military personnel back in those days, when I arrived stateside, I didn't experience a lot of disrespect that others did. Yes, people spit at us, but never on me. Words and comments were made towards us, but in all, my return was uneventful except for one incident at the airport. A buddy and I was traveling with came across a lady with her kids in the airport. We found out that they were Canadian and traveling back home themselves. She was very polite and interested in our story. She went out of her way to thank us for our service along with her kids. That meant a lot to us given the fact of how others were treated when they arrived home.

I will add this though, over the past few years, with all the war efforts in Afghanistan and Iraq, I resented the treatment we received in comparison to what young men are getting today when they arrive home. Call it jealousy if you will, but it angered me. Why were we treated so poorly and yet this new group of soldiers was being treated as heroes? Thoughts kept crossing my mind about the men we had lost or the men who were injured in ways that changed the course of their lives forever. Where is the justice in that? So yes, I was angry. I remembered the lifelong relationships that we had forged over there, the trials we had shared. How was our story any different than what men are dealing with today?

But thankfully, through Vets Helping Vets – Anderson, I have seen the issue with this. We all served in different places and at different times. Each one of us, regardless of when or where we served, we answered the call our country issued to us. My pain is no greater nor less than those who serve today. We are brothers because of our individual and collective sacrifices. I have learned that I am not the only one who has paid a price.

When I first left the military, I fell back into some of the same old routines I had prior to the Marine Corps. I became lazy. I didn't work much and again my wife and I lived with my mom. My wife had a hard time understanding me and my experiences. In fact, as news came in later years about military actions around the world, my wife would often comment that if I had stayed in the Marine Corps, I would likely have been involved in those actions as well.

I missed the comradery. I missed the loyalty men have towards one another when placed in difficult circumstances. I missed the teamwork and deep relationships. I missed my brothers in arms. I still do to this very day. Civilians and non-military personnel simply do not understand this type of relationship. I miss that.

If I could send a message to the leadership of Vets Helping Vets – Anderson it would be this…keep up the good work. Keep your trust in God, and in one another. Have faith in one another as a brotherhood. We understand each other as no one else does.

As for the generations of today, I would say this: I wish they would consider bringing back the draft or some form of compulsory service. Too many young people today have had everything handed to them and they know nothing about sacrifice. They do not understand patriotism and honor. They know very little about serving the needs of others above their own desires. Stop thinking that the world owes you everything. It doesn't. Instead, I wish young people today would be taught more about giving to their country and stop trying to take more from it. These kids, and many parents today, need to learn to take care of themselves and work hard for what they want. Earn it, don't expect it to be handed to you. Pay the price yourself and quit relying on others to hand it to you.

Carl Sharperson

My name is Carl Henrick Sharperson, Jr. I was called Sweet Meat by several of my United States Naval Academy football teammates because of the sweet way that I caught passes. I was a wide receiver on the Navy Academy football team. I entered the US Naval Academy in June 1972 as a plebe/freshman after attending a year of prep school at the Marine Military Academy in Harlingen Texas.

I graduated from high school in Spotsylvania, Virginia, which is where I was living at the time. My dad was a WWII Montfort Marine which was the segregated Marine Corps before integration of the USMC. I had planned to service select US Navy Aviation and then changed my mind to US Marine Corps Aviation the night before. I knew that I wanted to fly helicopters because of my introduction to aviation after my sophomore year in Pensacola.

I was recruited to play football at the US Naval Academy, and I did not know what the Naval Academy was, and it was only 90 miles up the road. Primarily there were not a lot of people who looked like me attending the US Naval Academy (USNA).

Plebe year or the first/freshman year at USNA was like an enlisted boot camp. Very tough physically and mentally. We were expected to memorize a lot of data about the military and be able to regurgitate it at any time when an upper class is yelling in your face. There were two months before the rest of the brigade came back for the fall. During the academic year, I had to balance academics, sports, and military obligations.

I did two six-month Mediterranean cruises/deployments with MAG 26, HMM 264 and one three-month Caribbean Cruise/deployment with HMM 263 during the Cold War in the late 1970's. We cruised on the USS Guam LPH 9Amphibious Assault ship that carried eighteen helicopters and over 1,700 United States Marines. I was a CH 46 pilot, and I had auxiliary duties in Logistics and Operations while in the squadron. After flight school I transitioned into flying the CH 46 or Frog. When asked what I did for "good luck," I reply, "I prayed a lot!"

We traveled to a lot of different ports in the Mediterranean, Indian Ocean, the Caribbean, including places like Spain, Kenya, Italy, Egypt, Greece, Portugal, France, Turkey, and Tunisia. There is nothing like watching the rising or setting sun out in the middle of the ocean. The deployments were long, and it was an opportunity to build some strong relationships with fellow squadron mates.

In 1981, I transitioned out of the military, submitting my paperwork six months before I wanted to get out. On my last day, I took some time to visit my parents in Virginia. Then I went on to Albany, Georgia to work for Procter & Gamble (P&G). P & G had a large paper plant in Albany where I took a position as a team manager in the startup of the LUVs diapers department.

I immersed myself into my new role in the new company. I also sought out and learned from some other managers in the company who were veterans. Some advice to others transitioning out of the military: As you look for a place to work or a new employer, make sure your new boss's and new company's values align with your values. Otherwise, you may bounce around because of the games that people play in the work force.

The Military gave me a great foundation in leadership and the ability to solve problems. I learned I could juggle many balls in chaos and still stay focused. My hope is to give back some of the wisdom and knowledge that I have gathered over my lifetime to others who are willing to listen. In 2017, I published a book titled "*Sharp Ability: Overcome Adversity to Lead with Authenticity.*"

I developed habits in the Marines that I implemented into my civilian life such as getting up early and sticking to a routine daily. These two have served me well in all my endeavors and down many walks of life. I served my country with honor and was willing to defend it. These two choices led to the success I have achieved in my life.

Joining Vets Helping Vets taught me a lot about the needed comradery that veterans crave on weekly basis, no matter who they are or how old they are. I am thankful for my wife, Jackie, and our son and daughter. With the love and support of my family and the Lord, I want to finish the race of life strong.

Gary Shumaker

Gary E. Schumaker is my name. My nickname is "Shu" just short for my last name. I enlisted in February 1966 with a six-month delay program, barely avoiding the draft. My county records office had already sent my paperwork to Baltimore Maryland, and I was still in my last year of college.

I was attending a two-year private business college in Winchester, Virginia, and commuting from home on the week-ends, staying in a private rental during the week. I chose the Air Force since they had a six-month delay program. Thus, I went active in July 1966. The Air Force would help me get a job related to the college education I received. I also wanted to avoid the draft that was still active at the time, since I did not want to be on the front lines in Vietnam carrying an M16.

We arrived after dark in Lackland AFB, Texas via plane from the Baltimore Induction Center. From the bus, a scroungy lot unloaded with yelling and foul language and were sent to KP (kitchen police). Basic was very interesting and at times quite taxing on the physical body. However, I must admit I was disappointed with the obstacle course training. I guess I had watched too many John Wayne movies.

I managed to make it through basic training and was able to take, and apparently pass, the by-pass test in accounting. This then meant that I went to "casual" status, which meant living six-weeks or so in one of the old WWII barracks. During this period, I was assigned a couple of duties. One was cutting grass with a hand clipper, and the next duty was being a "gopher" for a NCO group office on base, running errands, making coffee, emptying waste baskets, etc. They did allow me to access the regular chow hall for the on-base enlisted folks.

Once during basic a short fight broke out between two of the boot camp guys, resulting in a black eye for each one. Their explanation to our TI (Training Instructor) was that they had simply run into a door when someone was starting to open the door. The TI accepted their excuse, but I am very sure he knew better. Another incident involved a TI during casual status coming into the barracks around 3 AM, blowing a whistle, and yelling "Gas alert". As we came back to the barracks, we discovered the TI was intoxicated. Story was, he was reassigned the next day.

Adapting to military life meant losing all your hair during the first hair-cut, only becoming a number, learning to do what you were told and to do "it" now. Living in a new routine of activities, day in and day out, with never a period of non-activity (most of the time anyway). Most of the pranks we played through the military years involved misinformation and substitutions. One time it involved setting up a buddy with a group blind date. The trick was to find the ugliest girl, then wait for the guy's reaction when they were introduced.

From 1966 through 1968, I was assigned to Lockbourne Airforce Base, Ohio. For fun, three or four of us would sign out camping gear (tent, stove, lights, etc.) and go camping and fishing in some of the nearby State Park's lakes. I volunteered for Germany and Vietnam. Low and behold I find my way to Da Nang, Vietnam.

The major differences between the assignment of Germany and of Vietnam other than location was the first one's training was more like a normal job. Vietnam was like being in a different world with different climate, culture, language, and food. The sounds were always very loud. Our barracks were right beside our flight line; planes taking off, landing day and night. Running to the bomb shelter when hearing the siren. On-base explosions was a definite new experience.

I served at Da Nang Air Base from January 1969 until January 1970 with the 366th Combat Support Group. I arrived and left during the Vietnamese season for Tet. Tet also means to eat. They celebrate the lunar new year with a festival. My Job title was "Inventory Specialist" in our finance group on base. I used various key-punch related machines, sorter, etc., to input and retrieve all the clothing stock fund and convert Pleiku activity over to their own on-base personnel. After getting special approval for an inventory "write-off" of $60,000 from Saigon HQ due to theft and black market activity - that is.

What I remember most is watching the AC-47 "Spooky" gunship at night firing on the ground locations and seeing the continuous red lines of fire from the plane to the ground. We could see and hear our military engaging the enemy with groundfire and watch the flares being sent up in the air as well. I also remember the time our bomb dump (bomb storage area) was set off and watching and hearing explosions for the following three days. It was amazing to see the compression (shock) wave move through the air after each 500 pounds exploded. It looked like a white rainbow coming toward you, and when directly overhead, you would hear the "BOOM!"

One day we flew up and landed in a local Montagnard village on a Huey chopper, with me sitting in the gunner's seat in full military garb. The village, not being very large, had their own perimeter guard with AK-47's, and a lot of the children were wearing various USA pieces for uniforms, from boots to jungle shirts and hats. Several of the smallest children were wearing no clothes at all. I discovered while there that most of the village people actually had no "houses" but rather used small grass woven huts about three feet off the ground. They were only large enough for one or two people.

I took one or two-day trips to Cam Ranh Bay. A couple of us would from time-to-time hitch a ride to the China Sea South Beach area designated for our military. Hitching a ride on some military vehicle was our full-time transportation to wherever we might be going around Da Nang. While in Vietnam, my highlights were the R & R (rest and relaxation) trip to Taipei Taiwan, Republic of China for a week, as well as a week's time off to see a buddy on the southern island of Japan. My stay in Japan included being hosted by a local family in their home. Unbelievable experience for all kinds of reasons.

I did not actively engage in combat while at Da Nang. However, on regular occasions we did "dodge" rockets in frequent attacks from the air during the summer months. The enemy was aiming for the planes on our flight lines. After the military built large concrete reinforced shelters for each plane to park under, they started aiming at our barracks and office areas. Fortunately, I never was hit by shrapnel (I thank God) but did have dirt thrown all over me during a rocket explosion. The only medals I was awarded were the normal Good Conduct Medal and various other Service Awards.

My good luck charm in Vietnam was a simple peace sign on a leather strap around my neck. One day while on outside work detail, a passing Colonel spotted my peace sign and backed up, got out of his jeep, and chastised me for wearing it. However, I put it back on a short time later, and I wore it for the rest of my tour. My real charm was my faith in God!

Coming home to California from Vietnam late January 1970 and being honorably discharged from military service in February, I was met with all the war protest, a sheer disgrace for our country. We were warned prior to our return not to wear our uniform while flying or in public. Otherwise, you could expect to have something thrown at you, get spat on, or cursed at. No thanks or welcome home events.

The biggest challenge I faced now, "OK, now what am I going to do?" I returned to my parent's home and a very small hometown in the eastern panhandle of West Virginia. It was a real joy to see them both, and for a while I did much of nothing. Then I set out to go about getting everything set up to start back to college in Jacksonville, Florida. I had never been there before. Between the time of arriving back home and heading south for more college, my aunt introduced me to a young lady she knew. Three months later she became my fiancée and six months later my wife. Ruth and I have now been married for fifty years.

My advice for others exiting the military: go home and visit family and friends, go spend some time at places that have some special memory for you. Spend time enjoying your favorite hobby. If you have children, make it a point to spend some extra time with them, to re-bond and just have fun again. If you are a Christian, be sure to regularly attend services somewhere.

The time spent in the military helped me to simply "grow up" as a man. The military taught me the meaning of cooperation. Taught me that I could accomplish things I never would have otherwise attempted. It made the idea of single life, more meaningful, and not to take tomorrow for granted. It made me think more about appreciating the things I have instead of worrying about things I do not have. I miss the comradery we shared, but not the foul language and time spent apart from family and friends for extended time

I learned that there is a mighty BIG world of people out there and all around me. I learned to treat others like I want to be treated, even when they don't act or do the things, I believe they should, or could be doing. A good habit I formed in the military allows me to always be on time. I learned I am responsible for my own actions at all times. One negative I picked up was not being tolerant enough when others do or say simply stupid things.

My hopes for the future of our nation are that we will be able to elect men and women with a Christian view of our country and the world, and to replace today's politicians that are trying to lead our country into Socialism. We as a nation need to see this turned around. We need to get back to the basics that helped create the United States of America with states' rights, citizens' rights, and less of the big government of today.

The word that has gained meaning for me after serving is Patriotism. We just need to be really thankful that we are, in fact, citizens of the United States of America. What today's citizens need to understand about the military is the true history of our country since its beginning, what the word patriotism means, and that it is desperately needed today more than ever.

It is hard to communicate what being in a war zone was really like. I wanted my children to know about the good things and times for me serving in the US Air Force. The lessons I gleaned. I have only shared a small detail about the bad. What a true honor it was for me to be able to serve our country.

In Vets Helping Vets, I can be a part of a group of men and women who have "been there and done that" when it comes to the military. It also has proven that being an outspoken patriot and Christian is a good thing. I am able to feel some of that long time missing comradery, a good feeling. It is a real blessing to find out about and be a part of such a group. God bless America!

Tommy Spence

I am Tommy Lavell Spence. I did have a couple of classmates that referred to me as "Tommy Hilfiger "back in the day. I guess it was because I was just more a redneck than anything growing up. I enlisted in 1987, August 1987. I enlisted into the Navy. I had two uncles growing up that were in the Navy, and I liked their uniforms. The first time I saw them in their full-dress uniforms was at my dad's funeral.

I was born in Anderson, South Carolina. I grew up and went to school in Anderson, but during the summer, I would go to Monticello, Mississippi, to stay with my grandmother. My mother worked, so during the summer my grandmother was kind of like a baby-sitter, but I really enjoyed my time with my grandmother. My parents had divorced earlier but it didn't really affect me, because I was too young to understand what it all meant. I have a younger brother and sister and one older sister. We all got along fairly well, but we, like any other siblings, had our occasional spits and spats. I remember one time when we had a double seater go-cart, my older sister was driving and threw me out and accidentally ran me over. She got a whupping from our grandmother, and I stood by laughing. Then Grandmother whupped me for laughing.

My relationship with my mom was good, she just worked sixteen-hour days a lot, and we didn't get to see each other as much as I would have liked. Two of my siblings have also served, one recently retired from the Navy and the other is serving in the Army National Guard. They both live here locally, one in Anderson and the other in Greenwood, South Carolina. My younger sister lives in Fredericksburg, Maryland. I grew up and graduated from Crescent High School here in Anderson.

As for other family military history, my dad was a paratrooper and field medic. Two uncles were in the Navy, Chief Petty Officers when they both retired. One is my dad's brother, and the other is my dad's sister's husband. There are none from my mom's side of the family that I am aware of.

When I was growing up, I used to like watching Western movies, war movies and such. With my family history with the military, I guess I just liked what I saw in the movies. That's what sparked my interest in the military.

During Desert Storm, I was going to reenlist, but they could not get the paperwork done for me to have both shore and sea duty. So, once I ended my tour with the Navy, I transferred over to the Army.

Navy boot camp was at "Great Mistakes" Illinois. It was wintertime. Therefore, the name "Great Mistakes" was appropriate. It rained all the time and was cold. We had to walk around marching everywhere we went singing, "Anchors Away."

Basic Training was a new experience for me. The first day, we got there on the bus at 2:00am in the morning, go through a bunch of paperwork until about 4:30 – 5:00, then they let you get in bed. They wake you up at 5:30am and then it started. I remember one guy jumped up out of the bed when they started slamming that trash can around, and he ran straight out the door in his underwear, headed for the fence. They had to tackle him to bring him back. He was going to go AWOL.

Nothing in Basic Training gave me real problems. I was easy for me. A bunch of pushups, sit-ups, and such, but I played football and other sports in high school, so it was really no big deal. I was good on the physical part of Basic Training. Even the classroom work came easy to me.

I enlisted to be an Aviation Bosons Mate, Heavy Equipment, that's catapult and rescue gear on an aircraft carrier. I wanted that job. I picked that job because of the movie "Top Gun." You see that green shirt under the nose of that jet, duck walking to hook up the catapult, and I decided that's what I want to do. I was the guy on the flight deck, in the green vest, hooking the planes to the catapult. That's one of the most dangerous jobs in the world. It has a life expectancy of two seconds.

My first assignment after Basic Training was the USS Forrestal, CV-59, stationed out of Mayport, Florida. This was a very historic ship, and I was part of the last crew to man it. When I first arrived onboard the ship, I had to get used to moving around on the ship. Moving from point A to point B. Each deck has a number, then each deck has a bulkhead number, then there's port and starboard. You had to pretty much learn how to navigate inside the ship. If I was going to the mess hall, I had to learn that I needed to go down three flights, go aft so many bulkheads, then go down again. You had to learn to navigate the ship. On the walls, they had maps to help those who couldn't figure it out.

When I first arrived ship side, my thought was, "This is a pretty big boat." This was my new home. A boat with five-thousand other people onboard. There's no way you can know them all, but you can remember faces. An example of that came after I left the military. I drove an eighteen-wheeler for twenty years and was in Oklahoma one time. I had stopped to get something to eat, while standing in line, I turned around and this face just hit me. I knew him from somewhere. I turned around him and asked if he had been on the Forrestal. He said yes, from 1987 – 1991. I said, "Hello shipmate." I couldn't remember his name, but I did remember his face. We had a good conversation.

The flight hours were the most difficult thing for me to adapt to. You'd work thirty minutes on and thirty minutes off, twenty-four seven. You'd have thirty minutes of launch, then a break, then thirty minutes of recovering the planes you had launched earlier. They would land, refuel and then it's time to launch again. It was a repetitive cycle. During that thirty-minute break, we would rest and eat box lunches because you couldn't leave the flight deck area. Apart from that, there was nothing particularly difficult for me to adapt to in military life. During my time on the ship, we went to the North Atlantic, below the Equator, through the Suez Canal, Persian Gulf, Indian Ocean, and the Mediterranean.

As for my job, one must know that the catapult operates on steam and hydraulics. The steam is like a huge shotgun. It has two pistons in the barrel. You have the hook, which pulls down the nose of the aircraft. There is another device that holds the plane back until the time that they hit the button that shoots the steam through which launches the bird down the ship and into the air. The first time I ever launched a bird was interesting. You get under the plane, and it seems like it takes forever, but you must be aware of what type of bird you're under. The type of bird you're working with determines the exit path you re to take to avoid being sucked up into the plane's engines.

Every single bird we launched, we had to check to ensure we had a good hook, at which point they went full throttle. We had to check the entire area around us, remember what type of bird we were under, then run out. Once out of the plane's path, you had to get down, give the thumbs up. While all this was going on, the additional safety checkers were doing their checks as well. The launch officer would then receive the all clear, give his hand signals, touch the deck, and then point in the direction of the launch. The catapult shooter would look both ways down the deck of the carrier, give the all clear to launch, then push the button to launch the aircraft. There were a lot of things going on at the same time, and each one had to be done perfectly. My first time doing that was really eye opening. I was amazed at how it all worked together.

Night launches were similar but very different at the same time. At night, we used various colored flashlights with various types of cones on the end of them. The different shaped cones and colors indicated different people and responsibilities. Aircraft handlers were yellow, catapult was green, and shooters were red.

I served in the Navy during Desert Storm in 1991. While I didn't see direct ground combat, I did see the planes leaving with bombs, then returning to the carrier with no bombs and full of holes from the anti-aircraft fire they had to deal with. Seeing those things told me we were in combat. Even though we are not on the ground, we constantly had to consider that the bird may crash on the deck, and everyone on the flight deck would then become part of the firefighting crew.

While on the Forrestal we did have accidents on the ship. There was one aircraft that jumped track while in launch, meaning it came loose from the catapult. The plane ended up in the catwalk. Both pilots ejected. We were looking for the pilots in the water for a good thirty minutes when we finally heard one of them hollering. We looked up and found him hanging from the tower of the ship. The other was hanging off the antennas that are off the side of the ship that point down towards the water. Neither had ended up in the water.

The pilots were recovered, and the plane was repositioned with an onboard crane and repaired. We didn't lose that plane, and we didn't lose any in the Persian Gulf. What the Forrestal launched; the Forrestal recovered.

Some of my most memorable times in the Navy came while visiting foreign ports. I made it a point to eat the local food and see as many of the sites as I could. The best lasagna I ever had was in Italy. In Haifa, Israel, I tried the leg of lamb. That was good.

I left the Navy after Desert Storm, in 1991, and joined the National Guard. That transition took about 30 days for the paperwork to get processed. I entered the Guard with the MOS of 16S, Stinger Missiles. I chose that because after all those years in the Navy of hooking birds to the catapult, and having them occasionally tap you on the helmet, I chose Stinger Missiles so I could get even with them. I could then dish some of that back to the bird pilots. Not to American aircraft, but to those from our enemies.

I didn't have to go back through Basic Training, but I did have to go to school to learn the MOS itself. I had to learn about the weapons system. I also attended Nuclear, Biological and Chemical Warfare School. I attended that school to become the NBC Officer in the unit. I entered the Army National Guard as an E-4. My first Army unit was the 2/263rd Air Defense Artillery in Anderson, South

Carolina. My job there was crew chief of the weapons system. This was a two-man team, the platform was a HUMVEE with six stinger missiles in the system. You have a shooter and a crew chief. The crew chief was responsible for maintaining radio communications and giving the go ahead for the shooter to engage hostile aircraft.

I should have completed the last eight years to complete my twenty, but it had started to get on my nerves. I found that there was more politics in the National Guard than there was on Active Duty. After I finished my National Guard commitment, I felt it was time to move on. While in the Guard my unit never deployed to a combat zone. However, we did deploy across the state in support of hurricane relief efforts.

Looking at my time in the Navy and the Army National Guard, I realize that I gained a great deal of patience in the process. I learned not to let the stupid things in life get on my nerves.

As for awards, I have a Meritorious Unit Citation, Battle E for exercises completed with other countries. I have the Southeast Asia Ribbon, the Liberation of Kuwait Ribbon, and some Commendation Ribbons from South Carolina National Guard for hurricane relief efforts. I also have a Sea Service Ribbon with four stars representing the four deployments I did while in the Navy. I have the Marksmanship Badges from the Army National Guard.

When I reflect on my time in the Navy during combat flight operations, when I came home from those deployments, I felt a sense of relief. When it first started, I was somewhat scared, worried about what might happen. Then when it's all over with, you think, "Well, we've done our job." I didn't really think about it too much. I just put it in the past.

Petty Officer Williams is a man that I remember fondly from my time in the service. We went to boot camp together, a school together, and wound up on the same ship together, in the same work area. Fifteen years after leaving the Navy, I'm pulling out of the Port

Authority in Jacksonville, Florida. Reaching the gate to leave, I hear the guard asking for my paperwork. I hear his voice and I say, "Petty Officer Williams." Needless to say, I asked him what time he got off work. He said, "Four o'clock." So, I told him that I would be over at a nearby truck stop. "Come by and see me when you get off and we'll do something." He showed up, and we had a good time together that evening.

Onboard the ship, we didn't really have a lot of time for pranks and other such activities. We were too tired. When not on duty, you had to rest, take care of your gear, and assigned areas. I was assigned to the Admirals Passageway. On the ship, it was pretty much 24/7. The only down time we really enjoyed was when we hit the next port.

Shore leave was typically three days. One day was devoted to drinking. Day two was devoted to eating the local foods. Day three was for sightseeing. I've seen the Coliseum in Rome and Michelangelo's paintings in the Cathedral. The first port I ever hit was Naples, Italy. The first thing I saw once leaving the ship was a guy with a huge tub of iced down beer for two dollars. We each grabbed about three of them, then made our way into town to the local bars and clubs.

I finally left the military for good in 1999. When I walked out the door of the military for the final time, I felt good. A couple of years later I asked myself why I hadn't done the remaining eight years. A week later, I was over that question.

By the time I made my choice to leave, it had become too political. Even our training had become politically driven. Training would be cancelled because we had to get the facility ready for some social function going on within the local area.

My time in the military gave me a stronger sense of responsibility. Be on time. Be ready to work. The military taught me that I could accomplish just about anything if I put my mind to it. It taught me that I could learn to do things I'd never done before and do them well. It taught me to pay attention to detail.

One of my biggest hopes for the future is to live a long life. I have several health issues that concern me. My hopes for this country are that it will once again return to doing the best we each can for the benefit of everyone involved. We need to get back to people doing the right thing at the right time. I hope that at some point we can get past all the preferences afforded to certain groups, just because one falls into that group. To me, that is degrading. I feel this sort of grouping only adds to the hatred and conflict this country experiences today.

My wish for civilians is that they would learn just what it takes to serve. What service members must go through. The sacrifices they make. The hours that are required of them. Service members are constantly under pressure to perform. Their jobs are dangerous.

I miss the travel to foreign countries, meeting new people, seeing their culture. I miss the level of camaraderie found only in the military. There's nothing like it. We've been there and done that, right alongside each other. That is something civilians could learn.

Camaraderie is the ability to understand what another has been through, based upon your own experiences and being of the mind to reach out and help them if so needed. Many civilians don't understand the depths a veteran will reach to come to the aid of another veteran. If civilians learned to do the same the same, it would be different country we live in. Camaraderie exists because of the shared experiences of a group of people.

Serving in the military was something I always wanted to do. So, I went and did it. If there is something in life you want to do, do it. I am a member of Vets Helping Vets – Anderson. They have helped me regain that camaraderie I long for. It gives me an outlet to help other veterans. It has given me a deeper respect for men that served on the ground in combat operations. I have a lot or respect for Vietnam veterans, for what they did and how they were treated when they got home. I understand better, the hurt they have had to deal with over the years. They were treated poorly, no doubt about it.

Vets Helping Vets gets me out of the house. It helps me make new friends. Vets Helping Vets came through for me in times when I didn't know where to turn. I feel obligated to do the same. I go to Vets Helping Vets to help pay forward and be able to help another vet who may come our way.

Jesse Taylor

My name is Jesse Taylor and I served as a Combat Infantryman during the Vietnam War. I grew up in Waycross, Georgia. I had a fairly normal childhood. We all played baseball, football and competed in track. As young boys, my friends and I all hunted and fished or played in the park all day. I had a good upbringing. Our family relationships were good for the most part.

I did have issues with my dad though. He drank heavily and had terrible mood swings and often took it out on us kids. At the time I didn't understand what was wrong with him. During WWII, he served as a gunner on a B24 bomber. It was only after my time in the Army, that I began to understand the types of things that he dealt with.

For as long as I can remember, I had always wanted to be a soldier. My family has a strong history with the military. I have an uncle that served in the Battle of the Bulge in WWII, my dad, as mentioned earlier, served in the Army Air Corps on B24 Bombers. All my uncles served as well, so it just seemed like a natural fit for me.

Prior to my enlistment, I was working for the State of Georgia as part of a survey team. That was hard work. I spent most of my days, walking and working my way through rough terrain, cutting paths to get the surveys completed. Little did I know, this would be something I would also be doing in the very near future, with totally different objectives.

I enlisted straight into the Airborne in July 1964. I attended basic training at Ft. Gordon, Ga., and followed that with Jump School at Ft. Benning, Ga. From there, I was assigned to the 2nd Battalion, 508th Parachute Infantry, 82nd Airborne Division. I thought the uniforms were cool, with the trousers bloused into the boots, and the spit shine on the boots. I wanted to look good like those guys did. I am surprised today to see that they do not carry that tradition forward. I recently visited Ft. Bragg and none of the airborne soldiers had their boots bloused. What the hell is all that about?

For me, basic training was not that difficult at all. There were the racial tensions of the day among black and whites, but in the end, we were all serving for the same purpose. I had grown up in Georgia and had never really been around Black people much, but the Army proved different. There were men of all colors, races, and nationalities. We made it work. We knew what lay before us and what was ultimately at stake.

Adapting to the military was also easy for me. I had the mindset going in that this is the place where I wanted to be. It was my own choice. Being a soldier was what I wanted to be. I wanted to be the best at even the smallest things. I worked hard to make sure that happened. I spent a total of ten years in the Army, leaving the ranks in March of 1974.

When I arrived in Vietnam on July 5th, 1967, I was assigned to the 1st Brigade, 1/327th Infantry. This came after having served in the Dominican Republic in 1964 with the 82nd Airborne Division. The Dominican Republic had its own share of hot and heavy enemy contact at times. A presidential takeover was under way, and we were there maintaining order and peace.

While in Vietnam, my job was Combat Infantryman. I served several different roles while in country, but my primary role was Team Leader/Squad Leader. I was involved in minor skirmishes from the outset in Vietnam, but that increased as time wore on.

There are a few engagements that stand out vividly in my mind. My company, Cutthroat 1/327th Airborne landed on a mountain top late in the afternoon. We immediately set a defensive location for the evening, listening posts for ambush. At sunrise, my platoon took point down the mountain, mostly very tall elephant grass. Approximately 3/4 of the way down I came to a small area where I could observe the valley below. I observed an NVA soldier squatting down beside a spider hole. He was watching up a very wide trail. Beside him was a bank about 4-5 ft high with bamboo running down the rice paddy. The cart trail was very wide, and it ran straight toward the NVA soldier.

I called for Lt. Kanine, to come forward and we watched several minutes. I asked Lt. Kanine what we should do. He said, "Take him out." I fired and took him out. We sat still for almost 15 minutes. I told Lt. Kanine that McCabe and I would go forward, and if everything was clear, we would signal for the rest of the company to come down. We moved down to the bottom, to the edge of the trail. Once there, we listened for several minutes. Once we got on the trail we ran as fast as we could with our rucksacks on our backs. We were carrying over 100lbs of gear apiece. Once we arrived at the location where the enemy lay, I searched the enemy soldier. I found nothing of importance, so I asked McCabe to call over for the company to come down. The rest of the company was on the trail and halfway across when all hell broke out. The NVA had bunkers up the embankment and hidden in the bamboo. I was down in the tall grass, and I could look above my head and see the barrel of a RPD machine gun placing fire on the company on the trail. Five of our soldiers were shot down in an instant and our people started returning fire.

McCabe and I hit the ground. Our company thought we had been hit when we fell down and they started placing fire on top of our position. From my position, I could look up and see the barrel of the RPD. So, I started to crawl behind the NVA position. I crawled up to the NVA position, where I saw three NVA soldiers in the bunker. Further on down the bank I observed two more fighting positions. I climbed up to the edge of the berm and threw a Willie Pete into the bunker. The flash killed the three NVA soldiers. McCabe joined me and together we moved down behind the bunkers and killed three more NVA.

My company was pouring out hellfire into the bamboo thickets. I could observe farther on down the bank where it appeared to be a squad of NVA retreat into the mountain jungle. God was truly with us that day, I can't to this day understand why the enemy let McCabe and me live.

Another incident involved an ambush patrol as well. Our

squad was in this ambush position along a trail. All was quiet and we were simply waiting for an enemy force to come along. It was in an area where enemy concentrations were heavy, so it proved to be a very dangerous area to be in. After some period of time, we spotted a young boy and a dog walking along the trail toward us. He was walking in the direction of a hooch further down the trail. Suddenly, the dog stops and starts barking. He had sensed our presence. The boy stopped as well. We could tell that he knew something was hidden in the grass off the trail.

We did not engage the young boy. Instead, he moved along down the trail to the hooch in the distance. From our current ambush position, we could see the hooch. The young boy arrived, and some older men and women began what appeared to be a very animated discussion with him. We all sensed that he was relaying to them, what he had just experienced, and we needed to learn more. It was decided that we needed to get closer to the hooch to determine what our situation was. McCabe and I, one of my squad members, proceeded to move into a better position. We moved parallel to the trail while keeping our cover and concealment and eventually arrived on the backside of the hooch.

What happened next is something I will never forget. It was determined that these people were in fact enemies, and we were now in grave danger. I moved from my position towards the man the young boy was talking to. Having pulled my knife from its sheath, I cut his throat. I damned near cut his head entirely off. But we needed to maintain as much silence as we could in order not to alert any additional enemy troops that may be nearby. McCabe killed another man with a mallet that lay near the hooch. We called in the rest of the squad, did our search for anything of intelligence value and got the hell out of Dodge.

Probably the most difficult engagements we encountered were in the A Shau Valley. That was days upon days of killing. Killing for both sides. It was constant, non-stop fighting. Men died all around us, yet we kept moving forward. The soldiers we encountered in the A Shau Valley were different. They were well trained and disciplined. It was bloodbath. Clean and simple. The terrain was the worst I have ever seen. Two steps forward, slide back three. All while trying to maintain your rate of covering fire and keep yourself from becoming a casualty. Yet men fell everywhere. It seemed at times that there was nothing you could do to stop or slow down the tide of men falling. It was not only the fear of small arms fire, but we also had artillery, mortars and aircraft flying constantly overhead, dropping heavy munitions which often added to the casualty total. It was hell. Hell on earth.

I recall another situation during this same time frame. We came across some cave openings, and we needed to investigate, to see what may be in those caves. Once we had established security, we entered the cave and what I found was astonishing…cases and cases of new rifles and other weapons and explosives. There were cases of medical supplies and surgical kits. Practically everything an enemy force would need, stacked right there in front of us.

Yet, one thing stood out very clearly. In another stack of supplies, we found that these crates had been stenciled on the outside. What I saw really pissed me off. Stenciled on the sides of these boxes was, "The University of California at Berkley." Our own people were supplying our enemy with materials. Materials that were being used against men like me and others who were dying on the battlefield, yet they chose to support the very men trying to kill us. I will never forget that image. It still burns inside of me today.

Losing men is never taken lightly. It affected me in different ways. One loss I remember clearly involved a fellow soldier named Janes. We were at a small firebase and had been running patrols from there. One day we had received orders to pack up our stuff and move out. That same day, the firebase had received a resupply of hot chow that included ice cream in mermite cans. Well as you can imagine, the ice cream was pretty much like a sloppy milkshake by the time it reached us. Nonetheless, it was a treat. It was something unexpected and sweet. The men wanted all they could get.

Janes came back to me, asking if the men could go back and get more of the ice cream. It seems they had some left over. Once again, I told Janes, "No, now get your men and your shit together and be ready to move out." Janes was obviously pissed off and walked away. Not two minutes later, we hear a large explosion and look in that direction. It was just outside the wire and my first thought was, "Shit, where's Janes?" Come to find out, Janes was the reason behind the explosion. He had picked up a claymore mine for some reason and it had gone off. It took his head off completely. I then found myself walking around the area picking up small fragments of bone, hair, and other items.

That is a memory that one cannot easily erase from their mind. Here I was, picking up the remnants of a man I had just spoken with moments before. How do you process something like that? What do you do? You're at war. You could be the next casualty. You must put it behind you as best you can. Men are counting on your leadership and strength. In your attempts to put it behind you, you don't realize that you are merely putting it in a box that you will carry for the rest of your life. We had over 300 KIA's from our company in Vietnam over an 18-month period. I have rubbings of 17 names from the Vietnam Memorial Wall in Washington, DC. I spent eight months in the A Shau Valley.

I've seen war, and it's not pretty. My last days in Vietnam were filled with daily contact with the enemy. Coming home from Vietnam was an experience for me. Over there, we all heard of the treatment of men who were returning. Some were called murderers, baby killers and worse. Some were spit on and yet others had things like feces thrown at and on them. I was determined. That shit was not gonna fly with me. I was going to wear my uniform, and the first SOB that had something to say was going to be in for one hell of a payday. Turns out, that didn't happen to me. I have been fortunate. Today I remain in contact with a group of men I served with. We talk almost weekly. Vets Helping Vets – Anderson has been good for me.

There is one thing about coming home that still troubles me today. It involves my mom. You see, when I came home, I was angry and didn't want to talk about any of it. I began drinking heavily and got into some trouble. My mom had taken all my award citations and other things and had them framed and on display in the house. One night I came in and it was just more than I could handle. In my rage, I threw all those things to the ground and destroyed them. I then, simply walked away and went to bed. The next morning, the mess had all been cleaned up and my mom never said a word about it. She never brought any of that up again.

Years later, after my mom passed, my sister and I were going through things left in her house. My sister was working in one of the closets and came across a box. She called out for me to come to where she was working. She said, "I have something you need to see." She handed me that box. What I found inside caused me great emotion. My mom had cleaned up all the mess from my night of rage, but she had done more than just that. Inside the box were all the things she had kept and framed…those things that I had destroyed years earlier. My mom had put all the pieces back together and taped all the citations and certificates back together.

All I could do was stand there and cry as I peered into that box. That was my mom. She did it out of love for the son she knew had been changed because of his service in Vietnam. Looking back, I have always believed, and still do to this day, in the fact that there is a God. Sadly though, I lost my "religion" over there. I carried guilt for years and still do to some extent today. With all I've seen and been a part of, why am I the one still alive today and not others? I should be dead. But I'm not, yet others I served with are. Why are they not here instead of me?

I was awarded numerous awards and citations during my time in the Army. They include the Silver Star, two Bronze Star Medals, and two with V device for Valor. I was awarded the Combat Infantrymen's Badge twice. In addition to those, I was awarded the Air Medal, two Overseas Bars, National Defense Service Medal, Armed Forces Expeditionary Medal for the Dominican Republic, Vietnam Service Medal, Vietnam Combat Medal w/Device, two Army Commendation Medals w/V device, the Army Senior Parachutist Badge and two Army Commendation Medals w/V device.

I feel for the soldiers returning today. They, like me, served their country with pride. The enemies we faced were good soldiers, well trained and fought for what they believed in. What most don't understand today, is the simple fact that when the war is officially labeled as "over," the fight still rages on today for those men and women returning. They bring home with them things that are difficult to discuss, and a great many of them do not have a place like Vets Helping Vets – Anderson to share these experiences with. My hope is that these brave men and women of today will find such a place and begin the healing process for their lives.

Leroy Whitmire

Born March 12, 1948, I am Melvin Leroy Whitmire. I am currently 73 years old. I grew up here in Anderson, within a thousand yards of the house in which we are now sitting. I have been here since 1953. When this property became available, my daddy bought the first lot. He offered space for any of the kids that wanted to build on it; I was the only one who took him up on it, so I guess I'm stuck here. I have more than enough here, we built a swimming pool, cut trees, and graded and planted grass. It's home to me.

I went to school here as well. I attended Concord Elementary, grades 1-6; McCants Junior High, Hannah High School, then McDuffie High, grade 11-12. I did not attend college; I took some college prep classes but never attended college full time. I graduated in May 1966, got married in January 1967, then off to the Army in August of 1967.

I was told when I entered the Army, to join the Army Security Agency, we'll get you to where you want to go. This was a four-year commitment instead of the regular three because you got your choice of duty assignment. Well, that choice of duty seemed to have been forgotten. I took what was handed to me and it went pretty well.

I was the fourth of five children. I have three brothers and a sister, who is the youngest. My oldest brother is ten years older than me, so we didn't interact a whole lot just because of the age difference. My next older brother would just as soon knock you down as to look at you. My three older brothers have passed on, and it's just me and my sister now. My middle brother, Roger, was the one who would always get you into trouble. He did things to each one of us that as we grew older, we always kidded him about it. We all got along well. No major family quarrels or anything.

I got along great with my parents, especially my mom. She was a jewel. She would take care of you, run interference for you if things got too tough for you. She was a hard worker; she worked in a textile plant at Abney Mills. She would go to work, work hard, then come home to cook, work the garden, and put up vegetables. She did all that right here on these five acres of property. My mom was a sweetheart. I wouldn't take anything for her and wish I still had her here with me.

Dad also worked in the mill. He was a loom fixer. He worked where mama worked but at different times. He worked foundry steel, also. His main goal was to have a garden in the summertime and have us to hoe it out and keep the weeds out of it. He did all the planting and selling. He'd go get apples in the fall. We'd take the pickup truck and go to Hendersonville, NC, load it with apples and come back and sit on the side of the road and sell them. He enjoyed meeting people. Apples and canned goods were his way of doing that. He made ends meet pretty good.

When Mama and Daddy got up in age, me, my middle brother, and my sister, got them together and had them sit down. We need to talk to you. We need to talk about all the places where you have your money hid. Daddy said he didn't have any money hid. "Yea you do," we told him. So, he'd go back in the house and come back with three or four thousand dollars and throw it on the table. "Alright, Mama, you've got money hid too!" She claimed she didn't, but Daddy knew better. She would get up, wander around the house and then she would come back with three or four thousand dollars. We did that about five or six times and ended up with about twenty-five thousand dollars in cash. They had it hidden all over the house. We laughed about it.

Daddy developed dementia, and we had to stop him from driving. He had a wreck at the intersection just down the road. He turned in front of a lady. The first thing he said when I got there to him was, "She could have missed me!" Me and my middle brother went to him one evening and told him we were gonna have to take his keys. You're just not able to drive anymore. Daddy stood up from the chair and looked us both in the eyes and stated, "There ain't no SOB gonna take my keys!" We ended up just taking the rotor button off the distributor so the car wouldn't start.

We had a few things like that as they were getting older that we had to deal with. Mama even fell one time and broke her hip trying to help Daddy put his shoes on. We finally had to put them into a nursing home. We were able to get them into the same nursing home and in the same room.

I enlisted in the military, but my daddy had a good friend on the draft board who told him that my number was up. Even though I was recently married, I was still a 1A draft prospect. I decided that I would just go ahead and join. My wife and I talked about it and decided that would probably be the best thing. I went ahead and joined because I thought I would have more of a choice in where I ended up. I thought!

I joined the Army in August of 1967 and went to Basic Training at Fort Jackson, South Carolina. During Basic, I took some tests to determine what I was best suited to do. They told me it was my choice, yet I never had a choice in the matter. It worked out good though. I was sent to Fort Lee, Virginia, for my advanced training. I trained in office machinery repair. I had a fairly easy job. We mainly worked on typewriters. We converted them to "mils" which was simply a heavier duty type on them. They were used by the 72B's who were intercepting code. They would sit behind the machines with their headsets and radios and type out the messages that were being transmitted. I had a Top Secret clearance so I could go into these secure areas to work on the machines where the teletype operations were taking place. After I completed the training, I was awarded the MOS of 41J20.

I received orders, but no one knew what they were. They sent me back to Fort Jackson, and they told me that I was going to Panama. The folks at Fort Jackson had never seen any orders like the ones I had received. They kept me for three or four days, then came back to me and told me that I was not going to Panama. Instead, I was going to Ethiopia. I asked the lady, "Where in the hell is Ethiopia?" She said, "Africa." She was sure. I was going to Ethiopia.

About three days later, they packed me up and shipped me out. We flew from New York, to Athens, Greece where we spent the night, and I was able to walk in the Mediterranean Sea. The next day, we flew from Athens to Cairo, Egypt. You talk about security; the Ethiopian forces were loaded and ready. The military walked down the aisle of the plane looking, checking everybody out. We were told not to travel in uniform, so none of us had on uniforms. We didn't want any confrontations if we could help it. We left Cairo and went to Addis Ababa. That's where I served, on a small plateau, 7500 feet in elevation. It was a nice place, called Kagnew Station.

Going back to Basic Training, it wasn't too bad for me. I was a skinny, little fella. I didn't have the issues that the bigger guys did, having to sweat the fat off. I didn't have much fat to sweat off. We didn't really pull many pranks on one another in Basic. We were pretty straightforward. We didn't do anything that would get us into trouble. I have tried to recall some of the men that I went to Basic with and I just can't remember. Nothing really sticks out about any of the guys that were there. It's been a long time ago. I do remember some of the folks I met in Ethiopia.

When I first got to Africa, I thought it was cool. Cool temperature wise that is. At 7500 feet in elevation, it was cool. Africa was different to me. Many people simply don't understand just what a third world country is. The kind of poverty that is there. These people begged for food or anything that you could give them. You would see them carrying a bundle of sticks on their heads to have a fire to cook on. They would have a camel or donkey loaded down with different items that they begged off or stole. Most of the people were pretty good. It was a different situation.

I spent eighteen months there in Africa. My wife was able to come over after I had been there about three months. She had a little trouble getting there. She landed in Athens, Greece. They told her there that she could not go on because she did not have a Visa. We had been told before she left, not to get a Visa, because then she would have to go back out of the country. She was finally able to get into the Embassy where she was told that the only way, she could go was to buy a round trip ticket. That was about $350, and back in 1968, that was a lot of money. The reason I think they did that was because they simply wanted the American currency.

Adapting to life in Africa was not all that hard. You had things that you had to do and take care of. For us, everything was within walking distance. It was a small compound. All the needed facilities on base were easy to walk to. We had about all you could possibly need, PX, chow hall, clubs, chapel, etc. We had all the basic stuff. However, water was limited as you can expect in Africa. My first son was born in Ethiopia in August 1967. My wife had been there for nine months. We lived off the base and the housing there is a bit different. They use a lot of marble and granite products to build with - floors, walls, and such. We had to go onto the post to get drinking water. We couldn't drink the water off the base because of the hepatitis fear. We had to take shots to prevent that as well. You had to warm that medicine up in your hands before the shot or else you would really feel it.

I tried to extend my time in Ethiopia. I liked it. I had good duty; I had a car we'd drive around. I wanted to stay there but in the Army's wisdom, they sent me to Fort Devens, Massachusetts. They sent a guy from Fort Devens to Ethiopia. We crossed paths; I wanted to stay in Africa, and he wanted to stay at Fort Devens. That's part of the Army's "Choice of Duty Station" agreement.

I did serve in Vietnam, but I was again, in a secure compound. I never actually saw any ground combat personally. Our support group was the 101st Airborne. We were in Phou Bai, and they were in Hue just a short distance away. I had left Africa and went to Fort Devens, Massachusetts. I was there about three months and made E-5. That was 1970. At Fort Devens, my job there was more office machines because we didn't do any intercept work from there.

On my way to Vietnam, we flew out of California in a big stretch, DC-9. You look down the aisle and it looks like it's three football fields long. The plane was loaded down with guys headed to Vietnam, along with all their gear. Every seat and space were taken. When the airplane got to the end of the runway, the pilot revved the engines, and we started down the runway; you could hear the tires of the plane crossing the cracks in the runway. You look out the windows and see signs indicating the end of the runway was approaching. All of a sudden, the pilot throws on the brakes and starts the reverse thrusting of the engines. It couldn't possibly be that we were stopping to pick up more passengers, all the seats were full. He taxis back around to the end of the runaway. We knew what was wrong - he didn't have enough runway. When he wound it up that time, we thought he was going to wring the wings off it. We finally got off the ground right at the end of the runway. That ended up being the smoothest flight I've ever been on.

We landed in Juno, Alaska. We flew from there to Saigon. My first impression of Vietnam was this is a hell hole. When he headed in for the landing, we were told that we had fifteen minutes before we would be landing. The pilot had not even begun to bleed off altitude. I thought there was no way we would be on the ground in that amount of time. All of a sudden, he began a steep dive down, out of the clouds. All you could see around the runway were the holes in the ground caused by artillery and mortars. I understood then why he took this approach. It didn't look like a very friendly place to me. The pilot spiraled that plane in, and we landed and spent the night there.

The next day, we flew to Phou Bai, by way of Da Nang. I didn't care much for the C-130's and Chinooks. They rattle too much. It was just a different situation there. The North Vietnamese looked just like the South Vietnamese. You couldn't tell one from another. You always had to be careful of where you were and whom you were with.

My duties in Vietnam were very similar to my duties in Ethiopia. I was at a radio intercept station, and I maintained all the equipment there. While I didn't know fully why we were doing intercept work in Ethiopia, I did understand the need in Vietnam. Not only did we intercept enemy traffic, but we also assisted with downed pilots. That was a pretty good job there because I felt like we were really helping people.

I never saw open combat in Vietnam, never fired a shot and never had a shot fired at me that I am aware of. Our compound was mortared a couple of times though, and some men were killed each time. Not much you can do about a mortar round coming in.

I went to Vietnam in July 1970 and left in July 1971. I received an early thirty day out of the service. After Vietnam, my enlistment was up, and I left the Army from there. I felt relieved upon leaving the Army. I would not have to worry about my wife and child. I wouldn't have to worry about moving all the time. Going back to my time at Fort Devens, my wife had come there to live with me. As a Private, I was making about $95 dollars a month, maybe $105. It was hard to make a $200 dollar a month trailer payment. My wife had to work so we could make ends meet. But we were together. We made it. We shared responsibilities. It taught us many lessons on conserving and working together for a common purpose. My wife was with me at every location except Vietnam.

Linda and Tim Snyder are a couple from my military years that I remember fondly. They were in Ethiopia with us. Their son was also born over there. There was also Linda and Luke Lamb. I remember them. Ken Love, I remember him. They were good friends. I made one friend from Vietnam that I contacted later, Bergen Mosteller. He was our antenna guy. He worked on all the antennas at the site. I told him one day, that I wanted to take some pictures from the top of one of those antennas. I asked him if he could get me up there? He replied, "Oh yea." He showed me how to put on the safety harness and how to climb. It was a 180 foot tower.

I started climbing the tower and he followed me. Every time he'd climb higher, the antenna would shake. He was a pretty big guy. My thoughts were that the antenna was going to fall. It didn't though, and I was able to watch a Cobra gunship work out on target practice from that antenna. He wasn't far from where the antenna was.

I remember in Ethiopia, for fun we used to race each other down to the ocean. The road we ran was one switch back after another. We'd race our cars back and forth down this road. We had a good time. I had good duty. Those were good days. Even in Vietnam I had good duty and good times. I spent some time in Da Nang, just to say I had been there.

The military taught me respect and self-discipline, not to expect everything to just be given to you. The Army taught me a lot about life, especially when seeing people in third world countries. We do not know just how fortunate we are. It's a blessing to be a part of this country, to be a citizen of the United States of America. With all its faults and all its troubles, I wouldn't want to live anywhere else. I learned from the Army, that if you set your mind on goals, you can accomplish anything. Set your mind on it, worked toward it, and you should be able to accomplish anything.

The Army gave me direction on how to live my life. The military can give you good, basic morals. I wasn't one to drink or carry on like some others, but I learned that the military could be good or bad for an individual. It was all a matter of choice. Depends on what you make of it.

I miss the chow line from the military. That was always a treat, especially in Vietnam where you had to go through fifteen cartons of milk to find one that was not spoiled. I miss the green eggs. Really, I don't miss it. It is just funny. Even in Ethiopia we had problems with the chow line.

I miss the camaraderie. We had a bunch of guys that were just decent guys. They'd watch your back. I made some good friends. Some of the folks we met, we remain in contact with them as often as we can. These are people you likely wouldn't have met normally. It was a good time in my life.

I like Vets Helping Vets because it's a group of guys that know where you've been, what you had to go through, regardless of what you did, we all signed on the dotted line. I respect what this group and its leaders have gone through, and I feel like they respect me in return. Even though I was not personally involved in combat situations, I was there helping those that were. It takes us all. I did my job over there to the best of my ability. That's what other men in this group did, and many are here to tell about it. There are over fifty-eight thousand men who did not make it back. It's bittersweet in a way.

I would say to generations coming up today, that if they are not willing to give to this country, to fight for this country, then get out of this country. The military is necessary, and you should not look down on the people who do serve and have served. Without the military, this country wouldn't be what it is today. Many in my own family served, and I respect the men and women of the military. There is a lot of sacrifice involved in serving. That's a big deal. I am happy with my service. I am glad I went. It gave me a different perspective on the world.

Jim Whiteside

Hello. My name is Jim Whiteside. I was born in November 1945 in Washington, DC. My mother, Lola, grew up in Washington, DC. My dad, Jim, grew up in Bamberg, South Carolina. He was a Gunner's Mate on the USS Gantner, a Fletcher class Destroyer Escort, and spent most of his World War II service on escort duty for fleets sailing between New York City and Belfast, North Ireland. The fleets were taking D-Day troops and supplies over for staging. The German U-boats thought that was a bad idea and the fleets had to be sunk. Then the Fletchers came onto the scene and the U-boat threat gradually sunk. My mother's dad was a Spanish American war marine, and photos of her parent's home show the gold star for her brother who died in World War II.

I am the oldest of four children. We all grew up in the Silver Springs/Wheaton, Maryland area just outside of Washington, DC. I attended Catholic schools from kindergarten thru high school. I got a morning paper route when I was 13 and held it thru high school graduation, using my route money to help pay my Catholic high school tuition. My dad worked as a film salesman for Columbia Pictures. After 18 years as a salesman, he was promoted to Branch Manager of Columbia Pictures in Los Angeles. So, the family packed up in June of 1963 and followed their dreams to California. I stayed back because I was to attend the University of Maryland for the fall 1963 semester. In January 1964, about a month past my 19th birthday, I headed out for California on a solo cross-country trek. It was like a rite of passage – a car to me, a handful of maps, no interstate highways, and no schedule.

After about two months of California sun and surf, my dad began to put on the heat for me to find a job. I eventually got a job as a machine shop utility man at the Rocketdyne division of North American Aviation. I had no special skills, but I had the same surname as the clerk at their employment office. A little nepotism never hurts. I worked in a department that fabricated the rocket thrust chambers for the Saturn V moon rocket's first, second and third stages. I was promoted to lathe operator a few months later and was one of five people machining the thrust chambers for their fuel injection manifolds, turbo pump mounts, and gimbal arms for about two years. I was also attending junior college at night, and cruising in my 1965 Corvette. Life was good.

Then the good life came to a grinding halt in October of 1966 when I received my draft notice. On the morning of November 9, 1966, I reported to the Los Angeles Induction Center. Late that afternoon, I was on a Greyhound bus with forty-five other recruits heading for the Fort Ord California Welcome Center. The sun was coming up just as we reached the reception center. After an almost sleepless night with some Hawaiian recruits endlessly singing. "Tiny Bubbles," I was done, yet full of anticipation. Three Drill Sergeants fired up the morning air. We instantly forgot about the bus ride and any questions we may have had. There was quiet mass confusion. Sergeants yelling to get off their bus and line up. I had been used to the strict discipline of my high school, so the Drill Sergeant's yelling wasn't anything new.

My reception station experience included a battery of tests. Before the first test, the reception staff tried to encourage all the draftees to enlist. As a reward, we could choose our MOS. But it would cost me because another year would be added to my two-year draft requirement. They used the threat of a southeast Asia deployment if we did not enlist. I reminded them that the enlistment choice did not guarantee duty stations. I said, "I'll take my chances with the draft." We took more tests over the following days. After one test, a reception staffer came to me and said that I qualified for OCS (Officer Candidate School). I could enjoy all the privileges of an officer's life if I added a couple years to my service time. Again, I said, "I'll take my chances with the draft."

As I look back on my army service, I am proud of the way I stood up and took my chances. Things had a way of turning out for me. Deep down I was thinking I've got talent, I was smart surviving my high school with its demanding academics and discipline, I worked in a machine shop, I help build rockets, and I built hot rods for the streets of California. I know I could do something useful in this army, just aim me in a direction.

Basic Training at Fort Ord on Monterey Bay on the Pacific Ocean started off somewhat easy at first. Meningitis was going through Fort Ord at the time. Medical personnel required Drill Sergeants to give us eight full hours of sleep every night. We slept with the windows open, got an extra ration of blankets, and quarantined to our platoon. Much like the pandemic of COVID 19, we could not mix with other platoons for any reason including training or mess hall. They marked our uniforms and if we were ever caught with anyone from another platoon, we were in trouble.

We stayed at Fort Ord another eight weeks for Advanced Training, and I received a MOS 36K Field Wireman. Not a challenging job to climb telephone poles, string wire, and make a telephone system work. By the end of eight weeks, my patience worn thin, I'm in chow line at one of those WWII chow halls, and someone stepped in front of me. I didn't like it, so I hauled off and decked him. He stood up and came after me. When I regained consciousness, I was in the hospital with broken bones in my head. A good thing about this was some medical leave, the bad thing was I got separated from my class. When I got back from some medical leave, I was a loner waiting for my orders to come in. My orders came for 182nd Aviation Company at Fort Benning Georgia.

This was my first time I rode on a jet airplane. I flew from San Francisco to Atlanta, Georgia, to catch a little DC3 to Columbus, Georgia. I got to the company and signed in. This began what seemed like a long imprisonment to me. I wanting to do something great – to be part of something bigger than me. I was a non-essential field lineman with experience in building rockets and hot rods, and now stationed at Lawson Field with helicopter crew chiefs and mechanics. Their sergeants said I couldn't help and told me to stay back in the commo shop. It felt like I am being wasted. As an E-3, it seemed I forever on KP (kitchen police) or guard duty. Company morale was zero. Most everyone was either on their way to Vietnam or had just got back from Vietnam and just wanted to go home.

The Warrant Officers were a cool bunch of guys. They just wanted to fly. Warrants were not caught up in military pomp. I often watched the Airborne load up, take off from Lawson Field, and jump. Seemed like as soon as the last parachute got below the tree line, the medivac helicopters would go out and get the guys with the broken bones. John Wayne and his film crew came to Fort Benning to film "The Green Berets" They used our Hueys in every scenes that included Hueys. I always liked the final movie scene. John Wayne was talking to a small kid on the Lawson runway with an ocean in the background. All I remember on the other side of the Lawson runway was a line of trees on the banks of the Chattahoochee River. Ah, the illusions of Hollywood.

As an E-4, I was selected for CBR (Chemical Biological Radiological) warfare school. I graduated top of the class filled with E-6s and E-7s. I was proud. On graduation day, I went across the stage first, the lowest ranking student with all the career E-6 and 7's watching in what I hoped was disbelief. I got through the gas chamber a second time and get mustard gas on my arm so I could watch it blister up. Then it was back to peeling potatoes with no recognition.

Spring of 1967, I got orders for Vietnam. As with most guys in my situation, my mom got very upset. My dad was in WWII in the North Atlantic on a destroyer escort chasing U-boats and her brother was killed in WWII, her dad was in the Spanish American War and my brother was in the US Navy in the Tonkin Gulf. She had enough of war, so she says you can get a deferment until your brother gets home. I said, "OK Mom," and went down to personnel and filled out the form. Months later, I got a reply saying my story checked out, my brother John was on the Kitty Hawk in the Tonkin Gulf and my orders were delayed until my brother was home. More KP and guard duty. There were so few E-4's in the company, that we all got clipped for KP or guard duty every time we turned around.

In 1968, I selected to attend the Third Army NCO Academy, Class 6-B-68, at Fort Benning. This was a turning point for me. I learned there was a lot to the Army that I did not know, and it was about leadership. I excelled in leading our group. According to a letter I sent Mom, I ranked number one in the class until I blew the map course. I didn't finish first, but I held it for five or six weeks. Our graduation was March 25, 1968. I was promoted to Sergeant E-5 about a month later. My KP and guard duty days were over.

My discharge day finally came, November 8th, 1968. All I had to show for it was the National Defense and Good Conduct ribbons and three Sergeant stripes. My short timer's calendar in my locker had come down to zero. I had checked off the last one and played all the jokes; "How short are you? I'm so short I could sit on a dime and dangle my feet." The discharge process was in a large building and there must have been two or three hundred of us. The discharge process went in alphabetical order, so I was one of the last to be discharged that day. I needed to stay because they owed me for travel pay from Columbus, Georgia, to Los Angeles, California. Typical, I thought. I remember giving serious thought to just getting up, leaving, and thumbing back to Wisconsin.

Andy Kasarda, a friend of mine, and I left Benning together in his Chevelle SS, and drove all night up to his home in Akron, Ohio. Kasarda was a door gunner / crew chief. He was shot down a few times in Vietnam. Andy was a good guy and drove a 1966 396 Chevelle SS 396. We cruised and had a good time during those last couple of months in the Army. After a few days with Andy at his home, I caught a plane and went up to Oshkosh, Wisconsin where my future wife, Connie, lived. I stayed in Wisconsin about a month before Connie and I drove out to California.

I met Connie in January 1965, right after she a moved to California. She was living with her aunt who was our next-door neighbor. She was the girl next door! We wrote each other letters and I would call and reverse the charges. Connie would pay for those calls. Telephone calls to home consisted of standing in line waiting for the phone booth and waiting for the guy in front of you to get off the phone. It seemed like I would just get connected and somebody would start banging on the door to get me off the phone.

Early in 1969, I went back to Rocketdyne. They were getting ready for Apollo missions 12 and 13. I wanted to go back because I loved that job. I ran a lathe that could swing a 10-foot diameter. The thrust chamber was huge and had a walkway on it. I went back to see Terry, my supervisor because I knew they had to offer a job back to me. My supervisor said, "Jim, if I were you, I'd go to school." He explained that the Apollo project was about over for them, and the parts were in storage now waiting for vehicle assembly. He could hire me then, but I would probably be laid off in a short time.

I went back home and thought about something he said that stuck in my mind. He told me you'll never have another chance to start your life over again as you do right now. I was always monkeying with cars and at that time I was doing something to the family car. I went over to my toolbox I left behind at home for the Army to get a tool, sifting through the thoughts in my head about what he had said. I made the decision then to go to back to school

I entered a junior college in Glendale, California, using my GI Bill benefits. I completed a pre-engineering program and at graduation, selected as the Outstanding Science Student. Connie and I had married in July of 1970 and were living in an apartment in Glendale. UCLA's College of Engineering accepted my application for the quarter beginning in September 1970. Unfortunately, in January of 1971, there was the big earthquake in California. Our apartment started shaking, light switches jolted up and down, lights flashing, and everything moving around. This was the most.

terrifying thing I had ever been through; we ran out of the building. The earthquake was bad enough, but the aftershocks were worse. They are like having your finger in an electric socket, knowing that at any time someone is going to flip the switch, but you don't know when you are going to light up. By the way, the second most terrifying event for me was a nighttime exercise during the NCO Academy. The class had just gotten off the bus somewhere on Fort Benning property in pitch darkness. We were getting briefed on the exercise's situation and the exercise's goal when a few staged artillery blasts went off around us. The school cadre just watched while we all tried to gather our wits and create a plan. It was only the second most terrifying because I knew it was a test and not the real thing like the earthquake.

Connie quit her job at the bank, and I quit college. We called her brother in Wisconsin, packed everything we did not need right away in a moving van and the rest in our car. We were lucky to get moving van space because everyone seemed to be packing up and leaving the earthquake prone state of California. On the second day, we drove through the high desert in a sandstorm. I could smell sand in the car and the car radio said the interstate we were traveling was closed to all traffic. We made it to Winslow, Arizona and stopped for the night. Next morning, we woke up to snow on the ground. We headed out and stopped outside Albuquerque, New Mexico, at a diner. We sat with an older couple.

Just outside of Amarillo Texas, after making our way through heavy snow, I realized we were nearly out of gas, and we needed some rest. We took an exit advertising gas stations and motel rooms I start down the exit ramp and saw the bottom of the ramp closed due to cars jammed in the snow. The semi behind us had us trapped with no way to turn around. We look ahead and the Cadillac in front of us belonged to the couple we met earlier at the diner. They offer us, the young married couple driving an old Mercury Comet, to sit with them in their warm car until the National Guard rescued us. We shared a room with the older couple for three days. There were not enough rooms available for all the stranded motorists. When we left there, we drove on extreme icy roads. Call us young and stupid. In Dubuque, Iowa, the Mississippi River was overflowing and running down the streets. It was one catastrophe after another from Los Angeles to Omro, Wisconsin.

I worked for a year on Connie's father's farm to get my Wisconsin residency to keep from paying out-of-state tuition. After the year, I enrolled in the University of Wisconsin. Connie worked full-time and I worked part-time as a janitor while I attended the University. We never took out a loan for college expenses nor borrowed from our folks. We worked together and I graduated with honors with a degree in Mechanical Engineering.

My first engineering job gave me the opportunity to put my engineering book learning into practice. I worked at Wisconsin Power & Light at one of their power plants. After a year of plant experience, I moved over to powerplant construction as part of the management teams for 500 to 1000 Mega Watt coal fired power plants. This required a lot of moving around, and with a wife and little baby, I needed to settle down.

I decided I needed engineering system design experience. I took a job with a consulting firm that designed heating, cooling, and ventilation systems for large commercial buildings. Health insurance became more important to my family, and I was building a reputation as an engineer in Madison, Wisconsin. I took a job as an engineering supervisor for American Family Insurance Company. I worked there for 18 years and when I left, I was Director of Facilities for a Fortune 500 company. I lead a group of 127 people responsible for the appearance and availability of nearly 2 million square feet of facility, including the corporate data center. I ended up playing more corporate politics than engineering. All I wanted to do was work for myself as an engineer.

At fifty-five, I finally reached a career point where I felt secure enough to go out on my own. I started my own engineering firm, Whiteside Facility Engineering and did well building my own clientele. I was able to work with design engineers, contractors and building owners, providing them many engineering and facility management services they needed but could not easily find.

The most positive thing about my military service was the NCO (Noncommissioned Officer) Academy at Fort Benning, Georgia. Someone saw that I had potential beyond KP and guard duty. The leadership and teamwork skills I learned there served me throughout my career.

I am glad to be part of Vets Helping Vets. I like the mission of Vets Helping Vets. I feel I have something to offer and something to give and it is appreciated.

Jay Wright

Game Changer - Bang! I leaped to a standing position from dozing on Dad's couch. Before my eyes, Jack Ruby had just shot Lee Harvey Oswald live on national TV! I was still bummed over the assassination of President Kennedy two days earlier. Until that moment, the only shootings I'd seen were actors in movies or faceless soldiers on the evening news. That was real – and very scary. I picked up my mail from the coffee table, and there it was. . . the Selective Service letter I'd been dreading telling me to report in thirty days for active duty. One week later I became dog tag 770-41-01, my identity for the next two years of active duty and on weekends for another two.

I'm Jay Wright. I was raised by a single mom in a small mill town in northwest Georgia, fifty miles due west of Atlanta. I'm talking REAL small: a city limits of one square mile from the center of town, where two railroads and two US highways all crossed at the same spot. A town of 3,000 – and, to this day, still only 3,000. My high school years were spent dreading Ms. Stith's Literature classes, what to do if I ever got past first base with a girl and signing up for selective service when I turned 18. What if I got drafted into the military and ended up in a foxhole with a real gun and bullets and mortars flying all around me? I was, frankly, afraid of guns.

Eight of my friends all got that same Selective Service letter that week. Things were really heating up in Vietnam. Reports of casualties, M.I.A.s, and defections to Canada began to contain names of people we knew. All nine of us worried about finding ourselves in combat within weeks. Two joined the National Guard, the other seven of us joined a Naval Air Force program at the Naval Air Station (N.A.S.) in Marietta, Georgia. That program required two years of active duty and two years of weekend drills.

These events and the people I encountered in the next four years would prove to be the biggest game changers in my life. Following an abbreviated boot camp and some weekend training locally, our group of seven arrived in Charleston, South Carolina for reassignment in January 1965. We soon learned that the recruiter had lied to us about several things.

First of all, reassignment took two weeks, not "a day or so." My days were 4:30 a.m. until about 7 p.m. or whenever the mess hall passed final inspection that day. I would collapse onto my bunk after all those hours of sweeping, swabbing, stacking, unstacking, and doing whatever the fat, lifer cooks ordered us to do.

It was a learning experience. I learned to be a little skeptical of everything reported. And I learned that I could work sixteen hours a day at the most menial tasks. With no breaks. Under the direction of world-class bozos. Also, I was able to triple the number of four-letter words in my vocabulary.

The second big lie was that the seven of us would be able to serve together. Not! We were reassigned to seven different naval bases. Two buddies served on carriers in the South China Sea. I was assigned to VP-7, an anti-submarine warfare patrol squadron at N.A.S. Jax in Jacksonville, Florida. I went from somewhat skeptical to VERY skeptical.

I checked into VP-7 shortly before midnight. The petty officer on duty welcomed me as he looked over my orders. He asked if I could type. Very skeptical, I answered "no." He smiled and said, "Too bad, I hoped to save you from three months of mess cooking, starting (looking at his watch) in about three hours. We need someone in Ops who can type, but we're loaded with Kiddie Cruiser dropouts who've never seen a typewriter. And no one wants the job because it's working with pilots who think they walk on water. "

My mind flashed back to my worst course in high school: typing. "I'm not fast but I learned on a Royal just like the one on your desk."

He asked me to type my name, rank, and serial number. I struggled but managed it. He smiled. "Up to you, mate. What'll it be? I go off duty in five minutes."

Though I dreamed about Royal keyboards, I got at least five more hours sleep that night. The next morning, I ended up working with the most patriotic, respectful, intelligent group of guys I've ever known – some pilots and flight crew members.

Soon, the squadron deployed to N.A.S. Sigonella in Sicily, a million miles from nowhere. Our base was surrounded by poverty-stricken farmers and an orange orchard about the size of my hometown. The orchard was full of armed patrols who would shoot to kill anyone stealing fruit. Beyond that orchard stood Mt. Etna, the tallest volcano in Europe - 11,000 feet high and 97 miles in circumference. It erupted often.

Many nights were also punctuated by shots from the orchard's patrols just over the wall from our barracks. We all kept night sticks close by, but having a real gun began to make a lot of sense.

Seeing an active volcano and rifle-carrying orchard patrols every day for months on end convinced me that we can control much of our safety but not everything. Seeing third-world poverty taught me that even a mill town where most folks can rent a decent home, have a little garden, and own a vehicle, offers blessings and hope.

Most importantly, living and working closely with courageous, ambitious, patriots taught me that freedom isn't free and that real leaders aren't defined by title or rank. Leadership means constant education, speaking up, and stepping up to do your part when needed – even when weapons are involved.

A Tribute

Vets Helping Vets
by Jay Wright

In different lands we stood our watch
to keep America first, topnotch

Some days mundane; some days insane,
in desert sun; in pouring rain

Some days trapped – solitude and fears
some of us carry those scars for years

Scars remain: seeing good buddies fall
flag-draped coffins – those who gave all

I saw too much, but returned home a man
by proudly serving my dear homeland.

***

Vets Helping Vets, each one deserving
a brief, sincere "Thank you for serving"

Made in the USA
Middletown, DE
15 May 2024

54250098R10170